AMAZO

THOUGHT-PROVOKING TREATMENT OF THE MEANING CARRIED WITHIN PAST LIFE DETAILS.

By Wolfspecter (Western NY, USA)

Reincarnation: Past Lives and the Akashic Record (Kindle Edition)
This is Wetzel's second book of case studies describing past lifetimes which I have read. As with the earlier book—Akashic Records: Case Studies of Past Lives—she goes into great detail, both about the context which she is shown and the individuals and interactions. Wetzel's treatment of this subject matter is unique in the genre. She approaches each lifetime as if it were an urgent message to her client. Not only must the message be clearly communicated but the client must willingly take responsibility for absorbing it with full intention to "grok" its rich meaning in both the past and current lifetimes. There are many writers who approach reincarnation and the stuff of past lives as an entertainment, or a hunt for historical celebrities. Wetzel's readings remind me of clinical therapy interviews, in which the client is telling the stories and, with the guidance from the therapist, putting together all the pieces, stepping back emotionally to gain the objectivity that will free him or her from endlessly repeating the past and yet never getting the point.

I am significantly impressed by her rare ability to peer into past archives of individual lives, which she accesses much like watching streaming video with not only all five physical senses fully enabled but also emotional receptivity— empathy. She is not just narrating the action for her clients. She is trying to help them gain new insight. Wetzel seems to emphasize forgiveness as a common theme. Not so much forgiving others but forgiving oneself. She explains how a client's focus on shame, guilt, inadequacy, envy, betrayal, greed, self-importance—any of a host of all too human emotional reactions—obfuscates the simple lesson to be learned in a lifetime. She talks about the difference between forgiving and forgetting, and how failure to forgive turns a set of actions and a group of other souls into a never-ending carousel ride inside a hall of mirrors. As the Eagles sang in the late 1970s: "You can check-out any time you like, But you can never leave!" Checking out is not learning the point, not "getting" it. The client must see another way to view the situation, reframe it, have a different reaction and opinion that will lead to RELEASE.

Wetzel's interpretation of past lifetimes is from the perspective of love and compassion, for self and for others. Each of us is capable of being our own worst critic, our cruelest jailor. That is a true waste of life. Wetzel mentions that she frequently receives feedback from readers who report a sense of healing themselves, as they relate to her stories about the past lifetimes of strangers. I can readily understand how this is the case. I recommend anyone with an interest in reincarnation read both of Wetzel's books describing her case studies for clients. Read them not as vignettes but place yourself in each story, as one of the primary actors or even a close observer. You will get far more than just entertainment value out of it.

Clearly, in an easy to understand voice, Lois speaks with integrity and compassion.

By Alice Horton

Reincarnation: Past Lives and the Akashic Record (Kindle Edition)
Lois speaks to this subject so clearly in a voice that is easy to understand. She knows her stuff, and our stuff, on this topic of Reincarnation, Past Lives, and the Akashic Record. Her integrity and compassion flows page after page, as she helps the reader grasp this sometimes difficult to understand subject, and reassurance that all is right with the world.

I thoroughly loved this book! Very healing on a deep, profound level.

By Mary Drake

Reincarnation: Past Lives and the Akashic Record (Kindle Edition)
I thoroughly loved this book! All of the stories were fascinating. I really appreciated the beginning of the book which explained the process and purpose of a past life reading and why souls incarnate. The explanation was cohesive and rational. It helped me integrate and process the depth of significance from all of the past life readings. I felt a kindred connection with those in the stories. I found that I related in some ways to so many. Not necessarily the events, but to the commonality of human emotion and experience. The innate truths and realizations were thought-provoking and spontaneously triggered responses in me. The book evoked healing in a profound and meaningful way. This book is a must read for those on a journey for healing and a greater understanding of their own lives.

Reincarnation

Past Lives and the Akashic Record

Lois J. Wetzel, MFA

Hot Pink Lotus

Reincarnation:
Past Lives and the Akashic Record

ISBN 978-09832002-7-7

Published by:
Hot Pink Lotus
http://HotPinkLotus.com
lois@hotpinklotus.com

Printed in the USA

"The Universe is under no obligation to make sense to you."

NEIL DEGRASSE TYSON,

AMERICAN ASTROPHYSICIST

Acknowledgments

Those brave people who gave me permission to include their past life readings in my book are appreciated more than they can imagine. This is quite intimate material, and sharing it with the world took courage. That said, I did change everyone's names and identifying information, just as I did with my first book on this subject: *Akashic Records: Case Studies of Past Lives*. Of course, I do this to protect the privacy of all concerned.

I want to express my gratitude to my editor, Lora Premo, for the excellent job she did with this book, and for her understanding of my need to preserve the integrity of the channeled material. Channeled work contains very different syntax from either the spoken word or the written word. My request was that she maintain the integrity of the material while at the same time making it readable. It was quite the tightrope to walk, and she did it.

Finally, I appreciate you, the reader and Spiritual Seeker, and I honor you on your sacred path toward the Light.

May your journey be blessed!
Lois J. Wetzel, MFA

Contents

A Note from the Editor

It's been my pleasure to assist the author, Lois J. Wetzel, in bringing this, her second book on her remarkable Akashic Readings, to fruition. It is an unusual work on an unusual topic, and it may be worth noting some of the differences between this, a largely channeled work, and the writings of someone who is directly transcribing their thoughts on paper with the full freedom to rewrite a sentence as often as necessary to get it right.

In order to read the Akashic Records for a client, Lois goes into a trance and begins speaking aloud what she is seeing, hearing and intuiting, or knowing. A variety of atypical senses are brought to bear in "reading" the information she is given. Lois is a conscious channel, meaning she is fully awake and aware of what is happening. Just as you do when you are speaking aloud, she hesitates, she backtracks, she corrects herself, and so on—all the usual stops and starts of any spoken conversation. To add even more complexity, Lois is forced to actively create a spoken transcription while she reads the records, as she is verbally translating myriad images, thoughts and feelings into understandable speech.

Preserving the integrity of what is said is very important to Lois, especially since some people report being healed of their own physical or emotional pain as a result of reading what was told to others. To make the text version as accessible as possible, while keeping the original meanings intact, a great deal of effort has gone into trying to smooth out the syntax—correcting the grammar, adding punctuation and capitalization, deleting unnecessary repetitions, and so on. All of these changes notwithstanding, the transcribed portions do not read the way a novel would. The wording more closely resembles the closed captioning on the television at the gym which, as most of us know, is fairly rough-edged. Transcriptions of the spoken word are almost nothing like the regular written word, and we ask the reader's forbearance in understanding this.

It is also important to note that these readings were performed over the course of several years, during which time Lois occasionally altered her methods; for example, at some point she completely stopped doing readings in person in favor of remote readings. These small changes are reflected in minor inconsistencies in the way the readings are presented. Although obvious to the attentive reader, these differences in methodology in no way affect the accuracy of the information. In addition, Lois prefers that all her writings, spoken or not, be completely accessible to her readers. She therefore, purposefully and with deliberation, uses colloquial expressions that may seem informal or ungrammatical to some.

As editor, I frequently found myself so fascinated by what I read that I forgot to keep my proofing glasses on, losing track of my role for minutes at a time because I was so riveted by the content. I particularly enjoyed discovering several validations of Lois' non-corporeal sources. One example can be found in a past life said to be taking place early in WWII; Lois "sees" the subject teaching a class at a traditional British university dressed in what appears to be antique garb, including robes. Lois comments that perhaps the subject in her earlier incarnation enjoyed dressing up in historic costumes as part of the teaching process; I, on the other hand, was quite sure she was seeing the normal garb of an Oxbridge don, almost certainly still the standard at that time. Lois clearly had no idea that was ever done, and yet the image seemed completely normal to me. Similar revelations will no doubt occur to others.

Finally, I was surprised to find myself unexpectedly releasing, or healing, one of my own issues while reading Lois' response to someone with similar current-life circumstances. What Lois is doing here is very profound; she is probing largely unexplored areas of human consciousness and therefore, almost nothing should surprise any of us. It is to be hoped that you will also experience learning, wonderment, healing, excitement, a sense of recognition, and the sure knowingness that you, too, have accessed the mystical in the past, had you only known it then, and you need only open your heart to do so again and again.

—Lora A. Premo
Colorado Springs, 7 June 2014

Introduction

This is my second book of case studies about past life readings. I refer to these as case studies because I collect this data similar to the way in which cultural anthropologists collect data—through both my observations and the self-reports of the subjects. My intent in writing this book is, first, to explain a few things which readers of the earlier book seemed to trip over that seemed obvious to me, but apparently were not obvious to everyone. Second, I will elaborate on some things I did explain, since greater detail was evidently required. Finally, I want to share even more of the physical, emotional, and spiritual healing experiences that my clients have had over the years, healings that happened from learning about their past lives.

Within a year of writing my first case studies book, I received hundreds of emails from complete strangers all over the globe, thanking me for writing the book. Quite a few reported that they felt they were actually healed by reading it; such is the universality of the human/spiritual condition. These people did not know each other, yet they were reporting the same thing. I was both surprised and delighted. My goals in writing the book were to teach a wider audience and to spread the word about this form of healing; naturally, I was thrilled that the book itself had a healing effect.

How can people be healed by learning about the past lives of others? I suspect in the same way that persons in group therapy are often healed by witnessing others within the group work through issues similar to theirs. Seeing one's own issues outside of oneself makes those issues easier to recognize and process because of the added safety of distance. In art therapy, arranging small toys in "sand tray" work is one method used to project issues outside the Self so they can be dealt with safely. Puppet play is another way, as well as theatre play, drawing or painting. Often in our dreams, we will see the issues represented as various elements that are actually symbolic of pieces of ourselves. When we see them symbolically, we can more easily deal with them. Otherwise, we might not ever be able to face the pain or fear of dealing with them, due to the sensitivity we feel around those issues. The perception of safety comes by seeing our issues projected onto a puppet, on toys in the sand tray, as dream symbols, or in the past lives of another person who has issues similar to ours. Since I already understood that concept, it perhaps should not have come as a surprise to me that my book functioned in this way. Yet it did; it was a complete revelation.

I wrote that book, and now this one, because I know that we are all immortal, spiritual beings having a physical experience, and we reincarnate repeatedly to learn specific lessons for the purpose of our Soul's evolution. My understanding is that this goes on until we have completed our evolution and no longer have any need to reincarnate. Those who have evolved to this state are called Master Souls. Once we reach this point, we are then allowed the option of moving on to other levels of development in the spirit world, and my understanding is that most of us do. This seems the appropriate place to mention that if another person has not finished a karmic issue that originally had to do with us, they cannot hold us back. When we move on to another level, they simply find someone else with whom to work through that issue.

Not all immediately move on to the next level, however. It is said that some of us continue to reincarnate as a service to the rest, teaching and healing others until everyone has reached their spiritual goals. Other

Master Souls may also come back a few more times for a variety of reasons of their own.

Until we attain mastery, we continue on in the reincarnation cycle. Some Souls choose to do their learning in Spirit form—meaning not in a body—some reincarnate frequently, and some do both. Often there are similarities in our faces from lifetime to lifetime, even though we may choose to be of different races or sexes for the purposes of learning. For all of us who do incarnate, there are emotional, spiritual or even physical issues that are carried over from lifetime to lifetime until we get the related karma balanced, the issues healed, and finally learn our lessons. This is the Earth School, after all, the fast track to spiritual growth and evolution. The Immortal Soul comes here over and over, in the guise of one person after another, wearing a different body like a suit of clothing, to live a partially pre-scripted life for the purposes of learning and growth. Yet free will allows us ample choices within the various lifetimes, and this determines how quickly a Soul progresses. In other words, our choices absolutely do matter. Our lessons are set up by our own Souls prior to incarnating each time. This is done with help from our Teachers and Guides. Our lessons are orchestrated in the hopes of learning them at certain periods in each lifetime, and other Souls agree to show up and do pre-agreed-upon things to help us learn them at those times. This is how the Earth School works, stated simply.

Please note that due to the ever-changing nature of the internet, some links in this book may not work. If you are interested in the subject and the link does not work, try searching key phrases to locate the information.

1
Overview

"You do not have a soul. You are a soul. You have a body."

~ George MacDonald

To assist with the evolutionary experience of the Immortal Soul, I have been fulfilling one of my own life missions by using my ability to open the Akashic Records on behalf of others and narrating what I see. I do this so that these Souls may heal unresolved issues from past lives. Within the pages of this book are many of my clients' stories. I have found that the vast majority of my clients experience mild to profound healings after hearing about their forgotten experiences from prior lifetimes—though not everyone. A small percentage of clients are highly resistant, or just not particularly introspective. In the latter cases, changes may occur in their lives as a result of the past life knowledge, but they do not connect the changes to the new information.

The purpose of this book is not to prove to anyone that past lives are real. In the first place, the very definition of what constitutes proof will vary from person to person. Besides, I expect the people who read my book to already believe in past lives—otherwise, why buy a book about case studies? To date, no one has actually proven empirically that reincarnation is real—and not for want of trying. However, in my opinion they have come quite close. For example, Ian Stevenson, MD, spent forty years travelling the earth, researching children who reported remembering past lives. He carefully followed up to learn if the persons they reported they were in prior lives ever existed, even contacting the prior incarnation's families, if he could find them, to learn how accurate the children's memories of their prior lifetimes were. This is as close as anyone with a Western mindset has come to proving the veracity of reincarnation, as far as I know. Of course, that all hinges upon what you will accept as proof. If you are interested in this material, I recommend you read *Life Before Life: A Scientific Investigation of Children's Memories of Previous Lives,* by Jim Tucker and Ian Stevenson. I found this book to be particularly compelling. Jim Tucker has also used facial recognition software to compare the faces of the children with their faces from the prior lifetime. The results are stunning in some cases.

Other books that might be seen as a type of proof of the existence of past lives would include, in my opinion, *The Search for Grace,* by Bruce Goldstein, and *Many Lives, Many Masters,* by Brian Weiss. All of these authors are scientists. Goldstein's and Weiss' books are derived from information about past lives that came from adult clients who were hypnotically regressed. These are therefore past life regressions—and not past life readings.

What I do is called a past life reading. The client does not view the past lives. I view the past lives and narrate them on behalf of the client. One advantage to that method is that the client does not have to re-live the experiences. Just knowing about past trauma starts the healing process, and many, though certainly not all, of the past lives will involve some trauma—otherwise the issue probably would not be unresolved. Some of the past lives tell of heroic deeds or forgotten accomplishments and abilities, as well.

I am doing all of these readings remotely at this point in time. Early in the morning, while the client is asleep, I look at a photograph of her/him in which the eyes are clearly visible and open. Next I close my eyes, go into a trance and, while in that state, I narrate the past lives that I am shown for the client, recording digitally what I am "seeing, feeling, hearing" while in trance. Then I send the recording to the client via email so that he/she can listen repeatedly and integrate the past lives fully. No one will "get" everything all at once. The connections come in but gradually, for otherwise the experience would be entirely too overwhelming. I call this process "integrating" the past lives. Bits and pieces of correlation to the current lifetime, or an understanding of what some past life meant, will come in slowly over a period of months.

This seems like the place to mention that, in addition to incarnating as humans, while we no longer incarnate as animals with group souls like lions, tigers and bears, we may occasionally have lifetimes as cetaceans (whales, porpoises and dolphins) since these are sentient beings: evolved spiritual beings with individual Souls as we have. Other animals may evolve to the point that they can begin to come in as humans, but we humans no longer come back as animals with group souls—with the rare exception of that Master Soul who wants to come back "just one more time" to experience Earth as a family dog, for example.

Some Souls may even incarnate as fairies or other extra-dimensional beings, or they might spend a few lifetimes as Spirit Guides to others. This is what I have learned from the Guardians of the Akashic Records. I did not see this because I wanted to see it. In fact, I was annoyed to see humans having other lifetimes as fairies and dolphins because it did not fit with my worldview. However, I faithfully reported what I saw and stridently attempted not to censor my visions. I still do.

This time around, I incarnated with an ability to go into trance and access the Akashic Records. The realization of my inborn ability to do this work was triggered by a very vivid dream I had in my mid-thirties, in which the Archangel Gabriel appeared and reminded me of this important life mission. In that dream, He symbolically handed me a leather-encased copy of the Akashic Records. A detailed description of this dream is in my first book, *Akashic Records: Case Studies of Past Lives.*

When I go into trance and immerse myself in the client's past lives, I actually experience each life as though I were a participant. For this reason, there is a limit to how many readings I can do in a given period, so as not to exhaust myself. Doing this kind of work takes what I call "psycho-spiritual energy." Even though I may be sitting perfectly still, I am still using a massive amount of energy. Said another way, this is hard work, physically, emotionally and spiritually. As a matter of fact, the greatest trance channel of the twentieth century, Edgar Cayce, died before his time because he did too many readings too close together and destroyed his health, despite the fact that while channeling, he was told to slow down and do fewer readings.

In a 2013 radio interview I did on my BlogTalk Radio Show with Michael Hathaway—author of several metaphysically themed books, many of them in the *Everything* books series, and a past life hypnotic-regression expert himself—I learned something important. Michael has done many past life regressions, and he has learned a lot about the process. I learned that the way I do this work is by moving back and forth between actually experiencing the past life and stepping outside it and viewing the bigger picture, while listening to the Guides and the Guardians of the Records. Michael says most people can either do one or the other; only a few do both. In other words, I alternate between seeing the past life from two different perspectives—back and forth, immersed in the lifetime and then outside of it. For that reason, there are verb-tense changes in the transcriptions of the past lives that can be annoying to some. If that kind of thing bothers you, please try to set it aside so you can benefit from the content offered herein.

Another strange and interesting thing about past life work is that, after the readings that I have chosen to transcribe come back to me and I begin crafting the spacey, trance-state spoken words into the written word, I involuntarily go back into a light trance. For that reason, I see and understand even more than I initially did while performing the reading. I feel sure that had Edgar Cayce written books himself, he, too, might have seen further details as he wrote. But he did not write books.

About three years after I wrote *Akashic Records,* I was living for a few months in a little cabin nestled among 100-foot-tall pine trees on the shores of Lake Hamilton in Arkansas, healing from overwork and exhausted adrenal glands. One morning I wandered into a used metaphysical bookstore in nearby Hot Springs. There I picked up a yellowed copy of a book about Cayce's past life readings and read it for the first time. I was shocked by how similar his way of doing this work was to mine. Yet I had only listened to my guidance and done the readings exactly as I was instructed by the Guides. I had thought I was the only one, aside from my students, who had ever done readings in this manner.

For over twenty years I had assiduously avoided reading about anyone else's past life readings so as not to be influenced. I had, however, read a few books on past life regressions, as well as Michael Newton's books on Life between Lives® Hypnotherapy sessions, since I was not doing either of those myself. I had avoided reading about others' past life readings because I knew from my academic background in fine arts how easy it is to be inadvertently influenced by the work of others. I wanted my work to remain pure, uninfluenced, and true to Guidance. I feel I have successfully managed to do that.

A rather large part of the proof, to me at least, of the truth of the past lives I narrate lies in the reactions of my clients to what I have seen. This often involves material specifically referring to things about them or their lives I could not possibly have known. A more important signpost for me is the visceral, emotional client reactions to a lifetime I have seen. It is this spontaneous, instinctual validation that most convinces me that what I am seeing is for real—and I need that validation. I am still harboring a certain degree of skepticism.

2
Overlapping and Parallel Lifetimes

"Because a fact seems strange to you, you conclude that it is not one... All science, however, commences by being strange. Science is successive. It goes from one wonder to another. It mounts by a ladder. The science of today would seem extravagant to the science of a former time. Ptolemy would believe Newton mad."

~ Victor Hugo

To address some commonly held misconceptions that seem to have confused some readers, I want to explain about parallel and overlapping lifetimes as I understand them at this time. From the viewpoint of the Soul, which exists outside of time and space, everything is happening at once—all our lifetimes are simultaneous. There is no linear time. Just because a person assumes it is not possible to have more than one lifetime going at the same time does not mean that any Soul, hers or anyone else's, is limited by that person's lack of understanding. It should be no stretch at all to think that the lives of two different personalities could overlap each other by twenty years or even more—and by this I mean two persons with the same Soul. Why on earth not, since everything is simultaneous anyway and time is merely an illusion? So what if they overlapped by twenty or more years? The Soul (or Oversoul as some call it) is far more powerful and unlimited than most of us can even begin to imagine. The more experienced Souls have no trouble at all multi-tasking like that. As Albert Einstein has implied in his theory of relativity, linear time is just an illusion we have because we are on a spinning planet. It actually does not exist at all.

What I have realized is that the illusion of linear time just makes things more convenient here at the Earth School, so we can see "cause and effect." This helps us grow as we learn from the choices we make, so that in seeing our results, we can make better choices in the future—an important part of our spiritual evolution. The understanding that all our lifetimes are simultaneous also helps make it easier to understand how the healing of an issue in one lifetime can affect all the others. Our individual lifetimes are all interconnected, no matter when in linear time they appear to have happened.

Another concept that most people would rather not consider is that of parallel lifetimes. I am going to talk about that briefly. This is how I understand parallel lives presently: every time I make a major life decision, there is a fork in my life path. When I make the decision, I split into dual versions of myself in space-time. One version of me takes one path, and another takes the other. For example, the version of me that did not get a divorce in 1988 died of cancer of the breast and uterus, which simultaneously appeared in 1993. I would have lived to be only fifty-five years of age had I remained in that marriage. I know this because my Guides have told me. I had to get out of that relationship to do my spiritual work. My spiritual work would never have happened within that highly unsupportive environment. The ex-husband had successfully stopped me from doing what

I was supposed to be doing with my life many times before in prior lives, which I learned only after I had left him. Although his personality is not conscious of this, at the Soul level one of his pre-agreed-upon jobs in this lifetime was to offer resistance once again so that I was forced to really stretch myself and be fiercely brave. I needed to finally learn that lesson. The lesson was doing what I came here to do no matter what—no matter how harsh the consequences of doing my mission. When it became clear that I would have to leave him to do this, I was terrified. He did make it difficult. But I finally did it—not as quickly as I now wish I had, but I did it. I dug down deep, felt the fear, and did it anyway. If I had not felt fear, the action would not have been courageous at all. Courage is not the absence of fear. Courage is feeling the fear and doing it anyway. And do not kid yourself, either, when the fork comes and you need to make a decision—*not making a decision is also a decision. You have just made the decision by default. Not deciding is like not showing up for a soccer game you are scheduled to play. When you do not show up, you are deciding to lose that game.*

There was a decision to be made, a fork in the road, and this time I took the more difficult one. It has made an enormous difference. In this parallel lifetime, the one I am in right now—the one I am writing from within—I had a lump in my breast and a large polyp displaying high density dysplasia located on my uterine cervix which appeared simultaneously in early 1993. But because this version of me had left the marriage and chosen to walk my spiritual path, neither of these turned out to be malignant. I had them surgically removed within a couple of weeks of each other, took pain pills for a while, and kept on living. As a result, I not only get to do this amazing work in the world, I got to attend both my sons' weddings and welcome my first grandchild into the world. And who knows what else awaits me!

This is just one example of a fork and the results of the two decisions. There have been others. We all have them—several in each lifetime. Each time that occurs, my understanding is that a parallel lifetime is created. The timeline splits, or replicates itself like a cell dividing. The Universe is big enough to handle all of these parallel timelines. It is infinite. Since they are far more fully aware than our personalities, the Oversouls, Higher Selves, and the Guides do not have a problem with this business of overlapping or parallel lives. Parallel and overlapping lifetimes will maximize the Soul's growth experiences, since we are learning from multiple experiences of life and multiple choices all at once. It is rather like taking several classes at the same time, rather than just one per semester.

There are different understandings of parallel lives, and one of them states that there are many versions of Cleopatra or George Washington in different versions of Earth, and that different Souls inhabit each different version of each of us. I do not resonate with this explanation, but I offer it here because there are many who believe this is why several people may claim to be Napoleon or Saint Teresa. I believe they share the same Monad, which is a ball of light like the Higher Self and Oversoul, only more elevated, from which many Oversouls are descended, just as Higher Selves come from the Oversouls. Because these Souls are all related via the Monad, they are spiritually connected to these well-known personalities and can access their memories as though they were their own.

A fascinating example of parallels that I will share with you is going to require that you just read it and either accept or not accept what this man told me happened to him. I believe it, but you must use your own discrimination. I have a former energy medicine client who is now a friend, Todd, who has had three near-death experiences in his sixty-five years on the planet. The first one, when he was twenty-seven years of age, happened as he was driving over a very long bridge in Louisiana. He went into the Light and was told many things, one of them being that he was not finished with this lifetime and needed to go back to accomplish certain things. Right after he left the Light and headed back toward his body, Todd became aware of five parallel lifetimes, or five versions of himself. All had been involved in the same type of horrific car accident he'd just had, and two versions of the accidents were far worse than the others. In the worst two accidents, Todd had died permanently. Yet he and two other surviving versions were returning to their bodies simultaneously. He noticed that his own version of the body was seriously damaged, so he decided to slip over into one of the less-damaged versions. He almost made it, but at the last second was jerked back over into his original body.

Todd spent a year convalescing in the hospital. I recount this just to let you know that some people have actually seen their parallels. Prior to that experience almost forty years ago, Todd, at that time a professional scuba diver who worked mostly around oil rigs located in the sea, had never heard of nor considered the notion of parallel selves or parallel lives.

Now the following part of Todd's experience is rather hard to accept, but I know him and believe him. Feel free to just let it go if you do not. It this is too much to accept, it is okay. Do not worry if you cannot accept everything I write here. Just let what you cannot accept be like a twig in the river. If you don't like that twig, let it float past you. If you stay on the river, you may find that you end up with a collection of nice new twigs you do like, but please don't feel you have to collect them all. They are just concepts, after all. You certainly do not have to accept each of them to accept some of them. So, here goes...one time just after that near-death experience I mentioned, Todd was daydreaming and found himself briefly inside the consciousness of one of the other Todds whom he had seen while returning to his body after the car wreck. When this occurred, our Todd was walking through an airport carrying a bag. The other Todd was walking through a sunny meadow carpeted with flowers. Our Todd could not see the inside of the airport for a minute or two, only the field of flowers, as if he were actually there in the meadow.

Todd snapped back to attention when a man walking toward him in the airport gasped loudly. Apparently while being immersed inside the field-of-flowers-Todd's consciousness, our Todd had walked straight through a concrete pillar supporting the roof of the airport. The bags he was carrying went through the pillar with him, too. At first, Todd glanced at the shocked-looking man who was staring at him, smiled, and kept on walking. Only when he looked back at the man did he realize that he had walked through the three-foot-wide cement pillar. He quickly decided that it would not be a good idea to hang around and try to explain what had happened. How could he explain? What would he say?

The quantum physicists do say this kind of thing is possible, if we could only figure out how to do it. Todd has never done this since. It was just a fluke. But many other people who have had NDEs also report extremely strange occurrences afterward.

Quantum physics and its mechanics actually allow for all the things I have mentioned, including reincarnation, parallel realities and walking through solid objects, but most people are completely unaware of the scientific advances in understanding of the past hundred years. The consciousness of the average person in Western civilization is gridlocked at the level of understanding held by the scientific community of a hundred years past. In addition, most people, even scientists, still believe that empiricism is the only way to prove if something is real or true.

For those who do not know, scientific empiricism goes something like this. You measure and observe something, posit a theory or hypothesis about it, create an instrument or plan to test the hypothesis, conduct the test, collect the data from the test, and then statistically analyze that data so you can draw a conclusion from that data which is then assumed to be true. If it is good research, some other scientist can do the same exact thing you did and get the same results. This works well for certain things but, in actuality, this is a limited approach. Many things are real, we know they are real, and yet they cannot be empirically tested, proven and, most especially, they cannot be replicated. The most obvious example would be the existence of love, or the appearance of a "ghost." For some of us, this also includes the existence of the Soul and the Creator—at least for now. My intuitive sense is we will soon discover another way of proving reality beyond empiricism. For the time being, however, we must trust in our experiences. And why would we not trust our own experience? Reality is true, whether the scientific community currently accepts it as true yet or not.

Albert Einstein once said imagination is more important than knowledge. I believe the reason he said this was because he was fully aware that knowledge—scientific or otherwise—is constantly being updated. We learn more all the time. Scientific knowledge is not static. Imagination helps us grow the body of knowledge. Scientists without an active imagination could never try new experiments. They would just replicate the experiments of others, and human knowledge and progress would come to a standstill. But that is not a problem for us right now. In fact, at this point in time, knowledge is increasing at a faster rate than ever before in our known history. It is truly impossible to keep up with it all. The best way to cope with that level of uncertainty is to remain wildly open-minded. Consider everything while exercising discrimination.

3
Our Ancient History is Wrong!

"What is real is real, whether the scientific community accepts it yet or not."

~ Lois J Wetzel

In the long course of doing past life readings from the Akashic Records, I have seen quite a number of lifetimes that occurred prior to recorded history. Often I am told that what I am seeing happened 100,000 or 250,000 years ago, or more. When I have asked the Guardians of the Akashic Records how long humans have been on this planet, they have said over 500,000 years. At first, I was both stunned and puzzled by this answer. I wondered if I were hearing the Guardians correctly.

Lately I have been getting confirmation of the truth of this, which was rather a relief. Why? Because I had seen hundreds of lifetimes that I was told were far prior to our recorded history. In fact, a couple of years ago I spontaneously recalled a past life of my own where dinosaurs lived at the same time as humans, and we most definitely were not hairy cave-men. We were civilized people with transport vehicles with wheels and engines, and we had freestanding houses backed up to the sides of cliffs; lovely houses that we had built. Now, I had always been taught this was incorrect—that humans never lived alongside these gigantic beasts. But then, in a vivid, visceral vision, I saw one of them in the equivalent of a rear view mirror while driving a transport vehicle carrying several other occupants—all of whom were children. This was a very traumatic lifetime. I remembered this lifetime myself, all alone, and was sick, literally crying and throwing up, for three days. That is how the memory of this lifetime affected me, because it was effectively a spontaneous regression. I knew it was real by my physical and emotional reactions. Yet it was confusing, because in school as I was growing up we were taught that dinosaurs were extinct long before humans had evolved from monkeys. I now know that this is not true. Our beliefs about ancient history are wrong.

Fortunately, external confirmation has recently come to my attention that dinosaurs clearly existed at the same time as humans. There are anomalous proofs of strange things out there, stunning things which get no attention in the press. Many are on the shelves of museums or parked in basements where no one can see them. Why? Massive change in our understanding of history threatens commonly-held beliefs about our past, narratives that have been built over hundreds of years and upon which rest the reputations of a lot of college professors, museum curators, and the like, whose doctorates and books are based on the assumption these old narratives are accurate. Here are some examples of confirmation of the co-existence of humans and dinosaurs that have come to my attention recently.

Starting in 1944, tens of thousands of dinosaur sculptures were dug up in a region of Mexico called Acambaro, discovered in July of that year by a German hardware merchant while he was riding his horse at the foot of a mountain called El Toro. He noticed some partially exposed hewn stones and a ceramic object half buried in the dirt. Soon he hired farmers, who dug up perfect stone-carved and ceramic-fired replicas of dinosaurs, over thirty thousand of them. Humans had clearly made them, and there is no explanation for how they could have accurately created these images of supposedly extinct reptiles, other than that they had actually seen them. Some of the dinosaurs were quite rare, and almost completely unknown to the public at that time. Other varieties were totally unknown by scientists until recently. Since no one knew of the existence of some of these dinosaurs at all, it would have been impossible to hoax these sculptures. To learn more about this, follow this link:

http://discoverynews.us/DISCOVERY%20MUSEUM/DinosaurWorld/DinoFigurines/Dinosaur_Figurines_of_Mexico_3.htm

By way of further evidence of dinosaurs living alongside humans, there are numerous, massive sheets of rock all around the planet with interesting fossilized footprints preserved on the surface—i.e., rock which was once mud. Dinosaurs stepped on the mud, thereby partially overlapping the human footprints, which of course means that the humans had been walking there when the mud was wet and a dinosaur came along shortly afterward—while the mud was still wet. At other times, vice versa occurred, with the humans following the dinosaur. Here is a link to photos of these rocks:

http://www.bing.com/images/search?q=human+footprint+inside+dinosaur+footprint&id=01E5934F62C07DD88EFAED7B976BE2CBDD4A6DD0&FORM=IQFRBA

More evidence of the extreme antiquity of modern humans came to light in February of 2014, with reports of the discovery of very ancient human footprints. They were preserved in layers of sand and silt for hundreds of thousands of years before being exposed by the recent tides.

Located at Happisburgh, England, these footprints were examined and dated by a team of archaeologists from London's Natural History Museum, the University of London, Queen Mary University, and the British Museum. The footprints were dated between 800,000 and 1,000,000 years old. Once they were uncovered, the prints were recorded using highly sensitive digital photographs to create three-dimensional images that showed the arches of the feet and even toes. Sadly, once exposed, these footprints, which had been covered and preserved for a million years, were washed away by the tide after only two weeks. (Massive tides associated with storms hit England in February 2014, including hurricane-force winds, torrential rains, flooding and seventy-five-foot-high waves.)

Dr. Simon Lewis from Queen Mary University said that even though they knew the sediments were old, they had to be sure the footprints were ancient and had not been created recently. As proof, he stated that there were no known erosional processes that could create the pattern in which they were found. Plus, the sediments were far too compacted for the footprints to have been created recently. Also taken into account in dating the footprints were evidence of associated animals now extinct, and the geological position of the footprints relative to the glacial deposits which comprise the nearby cliffs under which the prints were found.

My own personal questioning of the history of human origins began in the early 1980s when I realized, while sitting on a bench in the ancient Egyptian art section of the Metropolitan Museum of Art in Manhattan, that I could hear and feel some kind of mechanism constantly emitting a steady frequency. This bench faced a large barrier made of glass in the Egyptian art section which, as I recall, was located in the basement at that time. Oddly, however, no one else around me could hear or feel it. But I could; I was sure of that. Back then I was an agnostic, so the notion did not for a moment cross my radar that it might be any kind of spiritual sound or frequency. It had to be a machine of some kind, I felt certain, and I still believe that this was what it was.

I attributed my ability to hear the frequency to the fact that I had musical training as a child, and that I come from a long line of musicians. Perhaps I am more sensitive than most—at any rate, I heard it, and others did not. Whatever the sound was, it made me feel peaceful and quite happy. I did not want to leave. The person I was travelling with was not interested in remaining there, so I had to leave sooner than I wanted to go. I dreamed all night of ways to get behind that glass and discover what was emitting those frequencies. Of course, I could not really do that, but I profoundly longed to connect with the source of that tone. Ever since then, I have been certain that there were once, long ago, technologies about which we today simply have no clue, technologies which were far more enduring and powerful than any we currently have.

Over the ensuing years, I have learned that there are hundreds, perhaps thousands, of similar oddities. Take, for example, the coins with markings in scripts or languages we cannot read or attribute to any civilization at all which were dug up many years ago in various locations all over the world. Some of these were found in North America as a farmer was digging a well for water—recovered from hundreds of feet down. Machines have also been found with complicated gears lying near shipwrecks on the floor of the sea, machines that are over 400,000 years old. Do an internet search and you will find more. Recently a machine with gears was found embedded in a mass of 300,000,000-year-old coal in Russia—which means that the machine was created over 300,000,000 years ago. This is one of those links which will not work for long, so I suggest you google this information. Someone is trying to hide this bit of knowledge from the public, it would seem.

As I mentioned earlier, these kinds of things are often placed on museum shelves in basements or storage areas and marked as anomalous, meaning, "we don't know what this is, so to heck with it—just shelve it." Such objects do not fit into the current paradigm of how long mankind has been on this swirling ball of minerals called Earth, and so are ignored. However, I know in my gut that they tell a story. Hopefully that story is about to be reclaimed by humanity, and when that happens, we will begin to awaken from a deep slumber. We will begin to realize who we really are. And that will be a magnificent day. Another stunning confirmation of how ancient our human civilizations are on Earth is fround at the world's largest and oldest pyramids, located in Visoko, Bosnia. The Bosnian Pyramids were discovered in 2005 b y my friend in this life, and sibling from several past lives, the brilliant, multi-disciplinary scientist Dr. Semir "Sam" Osmanagic. I have visited this, the world's largest archaeological dig twice, once in 2010 and again in 2011, and I can attest to the truth of their stunning glory. No stone aged people built these magnificent structures that still emit beams of energy from their peaks measuring at 28 KHz, the precise frequency that lowers the blood-brain barrier. Some perpetual motion machine inside nthe pyramids has been emitting that frequency right through the ice age right up until today. These beams defy known physics by growing stronger the farther from the source of the energy that they go. The measurable healing frequencies inside the Ravne Tunnels near the pyramids are also no artifact of a primitive civilization. The ancient builders' technological knowledge was clearly superior to ours, and carbon dating has recently proven these pyramids to be at a minimum 28,000 years old. Recently, multi-disciplinary scientist Dr. Paul LaViolette, PhD., author of *Earth Under Fire, Genesis of the Cosmos, Secrets of Antigravity Propulsion, A Systems View of Man, Galactic Superwaves and their Impact on the Earth* and many more, studied the Bosnian Pyramids and concluded that they are the real thing. Here is a link to his report:

http://etheric.com/bosnian-pyramid-complex-signs-technically-advanced-ice-age-civilization/

Occasionally I have telepathic conversations with "extra-dimensional beings" including Starbeings. What they tell me is that absolutely all of us are the product of genetic engineering: by that, they mean all the beings on all the planets and stars in the Universe. That is how we all evolve, under careful supervision and with assistance from those more evolved than we, but with minimal interference. We have been visited repeatedly by those from other planets and stars. We solve our own problems, but get evolutionary boosts via genetic engineering from time to time. Occasionally they will also show up and teach us—either directly or indirectly—something important, like how to make a fire or how to plant crops, if it seems that we need to know these things at that point in our evolution. They also assure me that we have been on this planet as a race of beings for over 500,000 years. We go through very long up cycles followed by very long down cycles. As I mentioned before, that is also what I see when I do Akashic Records readings. So, I believe it is important to keep an open mind and investigate the anomalies, the oddities, and those things that other people scream loudly cannot be what they obviously are, because what they are does not fit their preferred paradigm. The most ridiculous thing anyone can say is "That cannot be true because everyone knows it is not," but still, they do. Where is the scientific curiosity?

My fascination with the true history of our race, along with contact from other races of beings, is part of why I love doing Akashic Records readings. I get to see all these brilliant, curious, fascinating cultures. As an artist, I love seeing the clothing, the hairdos, the houses, furniture, earth-cruising vehicles such as cars or wagons, or things even stranger than that, like flying contraptions, seagoing vessels and other technology, plus gardens, fields and forests that humans have lived in over this enormous period of time. And the extinct animals are fascinating—there are many which have left absolutely no trace. Some are really bizarre-looking, too. Seriously, I could not make this stuff up. It is way too complicated, and far too cool, for me to make it up. I hope someday to have the time to paint some of what I have seen.

It has been a fascinating confirmation for me of what I have seen to learn of these recent "discoveries" of our ancient past.

4
Indirect Proof of Reincarnation?

"So as through a glass darkly, the age long strife I see, Where I fought in many guises, many names, but always me."

~ General George S. Patton

ALTHOUGH IT IS HIGHLY UNLIKELY that certain people will ever be convinced that reincarnation is real, it would seem that taking a stab at this subject might be helpful to some readers. Let me repeat that I do not have any real *desire* to convince anyone, but many people who pick up my books on the Akashic Records seem to want convincing. So evidently, they must be searching. I have deep compassion for all Seekers, since I am one myself.

Here are some past life stories that I personally find compelling. Maybe you will, too. Use your discrimination, though. Ultimately, each of us has to decide what he/she believes. It is possible to listen to and consider an idea without accepting it or rejecting it immediately. I like to mull things over. Oh, and I find if I am doing my "mulling" right before I fall asleep, many times I awaken with the answer I needed.

What follows are examples of cases of past life experiences that have been written about elsewhere. A few come from past life readings or regressions, though most are from dreams or the spontaneous memories of the person involved.

The Cathar Priest

A psychiatrist by the name of Arthur Guirdham was a complete skeptic about reincarnation until he treated a patient by the name of Amanda Smith, who said she remembered him from a past life as a Cathar priest. She even knew his name in the past life: Roger de Grissoles. For reasons that will soon be obvious, it did not take her long to convince him this was true. He did some research and found that there actually was a Cathar priest of that name who was murdered in 1242. Amanda had had dreams ever since she was a teenager that she had been a peasant girl in Toulouse, France, and that her family, who were Cathars, had befriended a Cathar priest by the name of Grissoles, who had been captured and died in prison. Oddly, the psychiatrist had been having similar dreams since childhood, which is why he was so easy to convince.

The thirteenth century was the period when the Cathars, a French sect of Christians, were completely wiped out by the Roman Catholic Church, having been branded as heretics. This mass genocide was part of the Inquisition in France, and the Cathar trials are on record with the Roman Catholic Church to this day.

Furthermore, it was not just the psychiatrist and his patient who had reincarnated at the same time, as it turned out. There were more women from England, near Bath, who came forward and reported that they had memories of living in the thirteenth century as Cathars. From this, Dr. Guirdham drew the conclusion that group reincarnation was possible.

Another interesting detail is that, starting at the age of thirteen, Amanda had been recording previously unknown songs from thirteenth-century France. The exact same songs, many years later, were discovered in some archives of the Languedoc area of France. She had also drawn layouts of specific buildings that it was later discovered actually existed at the time, including a church where the persecuted Cathars were held, as well as accurate drawings depicting antique French jewelry from that time period.

All of these were spontaneous memories for all persons involved. None were from past life readings or regressions. Much of the information came from the persons involved having had either dreams or flashbacks. Dr. Guirdham wrote a book on this subject called *The Cathars and Reincarnation.*

Actor Brian Blessed and the Dalai Lama

When he visited with the Dalai Lama, the actor Brian Blessed asked about his brother, who was in failing health. The Dalai Lama told him that his brother would be dying soon, but not to worry, as God would take care of him. He said that the brother would reincarnate soon as a boy in Halifax, Nova Scotia. This story is from the *Hindustan Times,* September 28, 2007. Apparently, Mr. Blessed got enough information from the Dalai Lama that he later found the boy in Nova Scotia using details the Dalai Lama gave him, and the child looked remarkably like Blessed's brother. It is said that the boy was immediately quite fond of the actor.

Singer Phil Collins and the Alamo

Apparently British singer Phil Collins was present at the Alamo, an old mission in Texas that served as a fort, right before the battle with Mexican General Santa Anna and his troops, which killed almost everyone present. The only persons spared in the battle and afterward were women and children.

As a child, Mr. Collins had been obsessed with the time period of the Alamo, beginning when he first saw the Disney series, *Davy Crockett: King of the Wild Frontier.* He began dressing like Davy Crockett, coonskin cap and all, which his grandmother made by cutting up one of her fur coats. Not too long after this, he moved on to "the hard stuff," as he put it, by watching John Wayne's film *The Alamo.*

Later, in the mid-1980s, Collins was on tour with his band, Genesis, and came across a letter written by David Crockett in a shop in Washington, D.C. This intensified his interest in this era, since it hit him at a deeper level that this was real—there were actual artifacts remaining from that time period. Much later, his third wife gave him a framed receipt of the sale of a saddle by a man who had been present at the Alamo, John William Smith, who had been sent out from the Alamo for reinforcements just before the battle with the Mexican troops began. For that reason alone, Smith survived.

The gift of the framed receipt marked the inception of his collection, and deepened his fascination with the history of the Alamo, which was where Davy Crockett had died. He became fascinated enough to visit the Alamo many times, becoming friends with the owner of the gift shop. The two of them talked often, and the shop owner actively helped Collins expand his collection of artifacts. At one point they decided that since the floor of the shop, which was inside the Alamo itself, had never been excavated, they would do that together. When they did, they unearthed many artifacts, including the personal effects of soldiers, musket balls, cannon handles, and so on.

While in San Antonio, Phil became acquainted with a lady who was a psychic. She told him that she believed him to be John William Smith, the one man who had survived because he was sent for reinforcements when the Mexican forces attacked. Mr. Smith later became mayor of San Antonio, Texas, where the Alamo is located. Mr. Collins resonated deeply with this, and remembered the intense, profound feelings he had when he first saw the receipt of Smith's sale of his saddle, which was the first piece of what is now his vast collection of Alamo artifacts.

Mr. Collins is now completely convinced that he was John William Smith.

A British Child and Her Egyptian Past Life

At the age of three, Dorothy Louise Eady fell down a flight of stairs. The year was 1907; the location was London. Her mother called the doctor, who examined her carefully and pronounced the child dead—there was neither a pulse nor any sign of breathing. He carried her to her bedroom, saying he would be back with a nurse to wash the body and prepare it for burial. When they came back in an hour, they were shocked to find her sitting up eating chocolates with her much-relieved parents. The doctor tore up the death certificate he had prepared and swore to the girl's father that she absolutely *had* been dead.

From that point on, Dorothy began repeatedly insisting that she wanted to go home and that these were not her parents. The following year, when she was four years old, her parents were dragging her along as they went through the British Museum because she seemed to get into trouble whenever they left her with someone else. They were surprised, to say the least, when, as they entered the Egyptian section, Dorothy ran around to all the statues of gods and goddesses and kissed their feet. Finally, when they entered a room in which there was a mummy in a glass case, Dorothy lay down beside it, tranquil at last. The family continued touring the gallery and, when it was time to leave, they went to fetch Dorothy. She would have none of it, and held onto the side of the glass case and said loudly, in a voice that her mother said sounded like that of an old woman, "Leave me be...*these* are my people!" Her mother, shocked, dropped her immediately. Dorothy had to be removed forcibly from the museum, kicking and screaming.

Later, her father bought her a children's encyclopedia in which one of the books had images of Ancient Egypt. She poured incessantly over these pictures with a magnifying glass. Another time, her father brought home a magazine with photos of the Temple of Seti I inside, and she became very excited, claiming that this was her home, asking why was it broken, and where was the garden? Her father became quite enraged with her, called her a liar, and told her to stop making up stories.

As one might suspect, her parents had a hard time finding a school for a girl who refused to worship anything but Egyptian gods. By the time she was ten years old, she began regularly playing hooky and going to the British Museum to visit the Egyptian galleries. There she eventually met a white-haired, distinguished-looking older gentleman who asked why she wasn't in school, and she explained that they did not teach what she really wanted to learn. When he asked what she wanted to learn, she replied with excitement that she wanted to learn to read hieroglyphs. He was so charmed by this that he agreed to teach her hieroglyphs himself, for he was Sir Wallis Budge, an extraordinarily prolific Egyptologist. This tutoring went on for quite a few years, even throughout the bombing raids during the First World War.

Eventually, Ms. Eady married an Egyptian and moved to Egypt, but by her own admission, she turned out to be not much of a wife, since her real interest was ancient Egypt and its religion. She went on to become a famous Egyptologist herself, and a highly gifted translator of hieroglyphs. Other Egyptologists remarked that she seemed to have an intuitive feel for the meanings of the more obscure texts.

From her own spontaneous memories, Dorothy recalled her past life as Bentreshyt (Harp of Joy), a teenaged priestess in the Temple of

Seti who happened to accidentally meet an attractive man in his fifties in a garden on the temple grounds. The attraction between them was powerful and instantaneous. The two had a passionate yet forbidden love affair; forbidden since, as a priestess, she was required to remain a virgin. Young and fertile as she was, Bentreshyt became pregnant, and the priests demanded to know who the father was. When she finally realized that she would have to die in order to protect him, she killed herself. Not long thereafter, the older man who had been her lover, Pharaoh Seti I, learned of her suicide and also killed himself out of deep grief. He was succeeded by his young son, Ramses.

When she first went to Abydos, after many years of working in Cairo, Dorothy had the local Egyptologists test her on her familiarity with the Temple of Seti, even though she had never been there physically in the current lifetime. She went into completely dark rooms in the temple, never having seen them before, then went to specific locations where certain things were to be found; the men testing her would then turn on their flashlights and confirm that she was spot on, proving that she knew her way around the inside of a temple she had never once entered before, and that she knew it even in the pitch darkness.

There is a carefully documented, detailed story of the life of Ms. Eady, including her ongoing contact with the Pharaoh Seti in physical form in her lifetime as Dorothy Eady, as well as careful descriptions of her long life as an Egyptologist at the Temple of Seti in Abydos, Egypt. That fascinating and detailed story can be found in the book *The Search for Omm Sety,* by Jonathan Cott, written in 1987.

A Serial Killer – Back Again

Dr. Bruce Goldberg, who was initially trained as a dentist and later obtained a Master's Degree in Counseling Psychology, is also a trained hypnotherapist. He had a client by the name of Ivy who came in wanting to work on releasing a love obsession with a man who had tried to kill her three times so far. Using hypnotherapy and past life regression with Ivy to determine the cause of the inexplicable attraction to her lover, Johnny, Dr. Goldberg discovered that in at least twenty of her forty-six past lives, she had been involved with Johnny. In each of them, he had successfully killed her. This certainly gives a new twist to the term "serial killer."

Goldberg readily admits that out of the 11,000 people he has regressed, this is by far the most dramatic case of a documented past life from a woman who could not have known the details of that lifetime by any other means than having lived the past life. The details of her prior lifetime as Grace Doze were corroborated by independent researchers. Again, these details were physically impossible for the current personality, Ivy, to have known. Knowing about her past lives with Johnny saved Ivy's current life, and her story was made into a CBS television film that educated millions about the reality of past lives.

Ivy had been living most recently in 1930s America as a woman named Grace, and in that lifetime was murdered by a prior incarnation of her lover, Johnny. While regressed, Ivy recalled many details of the murder that had never been released to the public by the police. It is a riveting story. The name of this wonderful book is *The Search for Grace.*

When I read this book several years ago, I realized something that was quite profound for me: it is quite possible that the main reason we come together with a particular person is simply so we can finally muster the strength to walk away from someone with whom we have been in similar situations in other lives—situations in which they harmed us. It is not uncommon for us as Immortal Souls to need more than one lifetime to learn any given lesson. If we are with someone so as to finally turn away from them and rescue ourselves, we must do this under our own steam. No one can do it for us. Often this is someone to whom we are strongly drawn, but who is psychologically or physically abusive, or in some cases homicidal. Strange as it sounds, one big lesson certain Souls must learn is to refuse to be a victim. Unconditional love does not require us to be the objects of abuse. We are often here with such a person to learn to put ourselves first, learn how to love them, forgive them and ourselves, and then move on.

Remember, the ultimate goal of our Souls in reincarnating over and over is to evolve and mature our Souls to the point that it becomes possible to step off the wheel of reincarnation and on to the next level of spiritual existence—whatever that is.

James the Pilot

Perhaps you have seen the YouTube videos or the TV shows, or read the book about the little boy who, when he was about four years old, began telling his father and mother that he was a former fighter pilot who served in the Pacific Theatre in WWII. On his fiftieth and final mission before returning home, his plane was shot down and he was killed. The little boy gave stunningly precise details of the aircraft, how it operated, where he was shot down—near Iwo Jima—and some of the names of his friends on the aircraft carrier the *USS Natoma Bay*.

At first, his parents were just annoyed, since they did not believe in reincarnation at all, but after a while, given their son's insistence on his past life, they decided to fact-check. This tiny boy was correct in all the smallest details of the aircraft. They not only found out the specific aircraft existed and was shot down, but that the pilot had the same first name their small son had claimed he had—Lt. James Huston. Ultimately, the parents contacted some of the survivors who would have known the prior James, and the child actually met with them at one of their reunions. He recalled aloud some things that passed between them during wartime that only the people there at the time would have known. These former military men, then in their eighties, confirmed that the boy's information was accurate. The child recognized several of them and greeted them aloud by their first and last names accurately, without ever having seen or heard of them before in this lifetime.

The family wrote a book at James' urging called *Soul Survivor.* Following is a link to a YouTube video of the family talking about this. The video was made when James Leininger was eleven years old, but on the internet there are many videos that were made when he was as young as four years of age:

http://www.youtube.com/watch?v=VnXxC-nVsJY#t=12

So does any of this prove that past lives are real? You must decide that for yourself using your own discrimination. I cannot decide that for anyone else. And I will repeat, it is neither my mission nor my desire to *prove* they are real. My only interest is to tell people who already believe in reincarnation what happened to them in the past lives that their Guides and the Guardians of the Records decide to show me. I do not get to choose those past lives, and neither does the client. And if the client already knows about a past life, it probably will not even come up. Their Guides and Higher Selves usually want them to learn about even more past lives which need resolution so they can grow as a Soul, since the past life reading is not for entertainment or for merely satisfying anyone's curiosity, though it can be both. However, that is not the reason for doing them.

And even though some clients have actually tried this, much to my amazement, let me emphasize that one cannot place an order with the Akashic Records as though purchasing a meal. "Give me one from Atlantis and three from when I was a king or a queen or a movie star." Or "Give me details on the past life in Indonesia that I found out about already." Nope. It simply does not work that way. These readings are for our further enlightenment and spiritual growth. This knowledge is a gift from Spirit, and I am a conduit. Further, I respect the nature of the gift, and I never open the records for anyone under the age of eighteen (except rarely, in the case of dire emergency), or demand to see specific lifetimes, or argue with Spirit about what I am seeing, though I often ask for clarification as to why I am being shown something. I work hard to respectfully honor the gift.

5
Forgiveness and Compassion

"Forgiveness happens inside your own head. It has nothing to do with the other person."

~ Louise Hay

REGULARLY, CLIENTS ASK ME HOW they can stop reincarnating with another particular person. Forgiveness and compassion are how we discontinue reincarnating with anyone, including an abuser. Has the person killed you repeatedly, or taken all your money again and again, kidnapped your babies and raised them as her own, enslaved you, taken credit for your creative work, stolen your ideas and patented them, or done any of a million other deeply painful things? How do you keep from incarnating with this person again? Yes indeed, I hear this question a lot. The answer is simple. To finish the karma with a person we must first forgive them, and then develop compassion for them. Once we have managed to do that, we no longer have any need to reincarnate with that person if we so choose. And sometimes to progress as Souls we have to forgive ourselves. That is another lesson many of us choose to work upon.

When we forgive ourselves—and we may need to if we have done things that haunt us, that gnaw at us with guilt—or when we forgive those whom we believe have wronged us, we heal ourselves. Thoughts, including hatred, resentment and forgiveness, as well as love, passion and peace, are things. They have energy. Forgive, and you send out waves of energy that heal you and others down to the cellular level, even down to the DNA itself. This affects not only this current lifetime, but our other lifetimes as well. Our DNA contains actual links to our past and future lives that energetically look like threads of light. When we forgive and heal ourselves, we heal our other lifetimes to a certain degree, as well as those of our progeny and our ancestors, all of whom are connected to us via our shared DNA. Whether we are forgiving ourselves or our so-called perpetrators, this healing will occur. When it occurs, we not only heal our children, but their progeny out to infinity through their DNA. We are also connected to our parents and their parents for thousands of generations in the same manner, and forgiveness in our lives affects them and countless others connected to us genetically—including cousins so distant we do not even know they exist.

So precisely what is forgiveness? Many people tell us to forgive the other person, but few say what that actually looks like. What is the process? How do we do it? I struggled with this question for many long years, seriously wanting to forgive a couple of people, and not being able to do so because I did not know how. I thought I somehow had to get over believing what they had done was wrong.

Forgiveness is not saying what the other person did was all right—not at all. Here is what forgiveness is. When we forgive we are saying, "I refuse to be held hostage in my own mind or thoughts, in my own life, in my daily experience of life, by what you did to me. I am not re-telling this story either aloud to others or inside my head and getting upset over and over by something that occurred in the past, because I know this affects me negatively down to the tiniest cell of my body. Chemicals are released inside my body when I rage about the past, and those chemicals damage me. I am taking back my power and letting go of what you did. I am moving on." That is how to forgive. That is how to heal. I am not saying it is easy, but I am saying that is how it is done.

Oddly, once we have forgiven someone, and I know this because it has happened to me, eventually all that is left is compassion. It becomes possible to see them with fresh eyes. It becomes possible to put ourselves in their shoes just long enough to understand how and why they might have done something so heinous to us, or to someone we love. It becomes possible to feel their pain just long enough to understand them. It does not require we say what they did was okay. It may never be okay. But we might be able to discover the hidden gift in what happened to us. Perhaps because of them we learned how to spot a fraud, or the importance of not betraying another person. Maybe we learned from them that love is an activity, not merely hollow words.

A person can say "I love you" until she is blue in the face, and yet these are nothing but meaningless words if she is knocking you around, talking behind your back, betraying or sabotaging you repeatedly, or doing any number of unkind things. She (or he) does not love you, although they may think they do. But empty words, even romantic ones, are not love. How the person treats you even if she never says the words is what is important. Actions truly do speak louder than words. Look at her actions. Many people do not even know how to love. It might be that their gift to you was nothing more than helping you discover forgiveness and compassion—yet wouldn't that be a gift of immense proportions?

Many do not understand the word compassion. This word, compassion, does not mean pity. Pity is actually insulting. To pity someone means that you do not recognize the immense bravery of the Soul in taking on such challenges—be it birth defects, ankylosing spondylitis, schizophrenia, having your entire family killed in a lunatic's rampage, being paralyzed in a car crash, or any number of seemingly unbearable conditions, including the ongoing tendency to harm others. Compassion means imagining yourself inside the other person's skin just long enough to feel what it would like to be them—then taking compassionate action where appropriate, and doing so without pity or emotion or judgment.

What is compassionate action? Perhaps it is telling your perpetrator that you forgive them over and over in a calm voice, even while they are telling you the incident never happened, although you know it did. Sometimes the only way a person can deal with their past wrong acts is to pretend they never happened. Their lie is their imaginary shield, but it is not about you. You know what you know, regardless of what they say.

Maybe compassionate action would simply be rounding a corner and finding yourself looking into the eyes of a child with severe burns all over her face and controlling your reaction so that you do not recoil, but instead lock eyes and smile at her—as if she had no burns.

Here is another example. When I was doing energy medicine full time, I would listen to people's stories just long enough to hear all their symptoms. I also tried not to allow them to dump their emotions on me, but this was sometimes hard to stop. If the healer is an empath who allows the clients to dump in her presence emotionally, eventually the healer may become ill. There is a difference between telling a story and emotional dumping, it should be said. If one is telling the story without emotion, it does not negatively impact the listener, but if during the telling one is angry, crying, sad, or yelling while expressing negative emotion, that is called emotional dumping. I have often compared that to relieving oneself in the swimming pool. It gets all over everyone in the pool. It is not healthy or acceptable to do that.

Compassion in that situation would be listening to the symptoms without feeling their pain, and then giving the client the very best energy medicine session I possibly could, because I could. It was not always easy, but I managed to do this even when I did not especially like the person, which fortunately was rare. Of course, sometimes I had to refer clients to others because I could not work on them...I am human, after all. Most of the time I could relieve their suffering and help them heal in body, mind and spirit, so I did. I did this from a neutral space of compassion, not from the space of teary-eyed, "boohoo, poor you," nor from "look at what a good person I am." Both stances are actually condescending.

Whatever they were going through, they chose it for a reason, prior to incarnating. I learned this before I started doing energy work, fortunately. I respected them for their courage in taking on their challenges. Some of them came to me because their Souls wanted them to advance spiritually. They experienced healing many physical things, just not everything, until they had the opportunity to achieve the level of spiritual progress which well-performed energy medicine can facilitate. The spiritual advancement was what their Higher Selves had actually desired for them, most of all. It was why they were guided to me in the first place. Of course, most experienced overnight or, at least, rapid healing, because that was what they needed. A few stopped coming too soon because they feared change, or were not yet ready. Giving each person, to the best of my ability, what they needed, what their bodies requested, was compassionate action.

Compassionate action is standing in a neutral space emotionally and giving someone what they need (assuming they have asked you to do this) and doing it because they need it and you can. It is not that you should or must do this; it is done only when you decide to do it, on a case-by-case basis. If the situation calls for it, you can also walk away—for example, to protect yourself. It is certainly acceptable to do compassionate work for a living, and taking money for your effort is not wrong. In fact, in energy medicine the sessions are stronger if there is an energy exchange, and money is one form of energy. Some people do compassionate activity as volunteer work, as well. But please hear me deeply. I am not saying that it is a good thing to give people what you think they need without getting permission. That is actually self-serving, and violates the other person's boundaries. An example is doing healing work without the person's conscious permission. That is wrong on so many levels. I talk in more detail about this in my book *EDINA: Energy Medicine from the Stars!*

To summarize: first, we forgive someone by letting go and refusing to dwell on what they did to us, deciding to move on with our lives. Next, we develop compassion for them by briefly imagining what it would be like to be them, so we can understand them. Then, we let go of them completely. If we do this successfully, we will no longer be required to reincarnate with them. This is simple to say, not as easy to do. It is a decision that we make when we are ready.

6
My Own Life Mission

"The most satisfying thing in life is to have been able to give a large part of one's self to others."

– Tielhard de Chardin

SOON I WILL TELL YOU about some of the lifetimes I have seen and how hearing about them has benefitted the client. As I mentioned earlier, after I published my first book on the subject many people reported experiencing emotional, spiritual or even physical healings simply from reading about other people's prior lifetimes.

Before I do anyone's reading, I explain why I do these readings, which take so much of my psycho-spiritual energy in order to go into the altered state of consciousness and maintain the necessary level of openness and receptivity. One reason for doing them is part of my own life mission: to help heal people's Souls so that they can more effectively continue with their quest to learn and grow as a result of coming to Earth. Someday I believe I will complete that mission, and then I will only train others, not doing the readings myself any longer.

Most of all, I do these readings to heal the clients. Many times, there is injury or damage or "scar tissue," for want of a better term, affecting Souls as a result of occurrences in other lifetimes. When we are not in the body, the Soul does not experience the effects of this damage. It is only while we are incarnated in a body that the issues bother us and, to the best of my understanding, that is the only time we can effectively heal them as well—when we are incarnated in a body. To do the healing in spirit form is far more difficult and takes much more time and effort, I am told. As I do these readings, the client is reminded of prior experiences, and the forgotten issue surfaces to conscious knowing for the client. Then the healing can begin. As with psychotherapy, the repressed issues are the ones that continue to cause problems. The integration of the lifetime and the healing that comes with that will be gradual, usually taking a few months. Over time, clients will have various realizations, or "Aha!" moments...usually while doing some mindless task like washing dishes, weeding the garden, doing home repairs or sweeping the floor. They do not pop in when a person is doing something that requires focused concentration like watching TV, reading a book, engaging in conversation, or doing math. But during those relaxed, mindless states we get into when walking in the park or watering the lawn, our analytical mind steps aside, allowing the realizations to pop in spontaneously. Sometimes they may come in via dreams or during the meditative state. Again, just knowing about the past lives will allow healing to begin.

It does help if the client will listen to the reading at least once a month for the following three or four months after the reading. By doing this they integrate the past lives more completely.

The lifetimes I see will not necessarily be in chronological sequence; the most important past life for each client to learn about at the time of the reading will show up first, then the second most important, and so on, in sequence.

Before starting the reading, I remind the client that there is no judgment in the Akashic Records. This is the Earth School; we are here to learn, to grow and evolve, but we are not here to judge or be judged. Our Guides, the Guardians of the Records, our angels—none of them judge us or anyone else. We are all here, incarnated into bodies, for the purposes of learning and growth. With the help of our Teachers and Guides, we plan certain events to occur at particular times so we can learn those lessons. Other Souls agree to show up and help us learn by doing pre-agreed-upon things. Sometimes these things do not feel good, but they are designed to help us learn and grow. Often, the other Soul has to love us a great deal to do some of the difficult things they agree to do in order to help us get our lessons. If we do not learn certain lessons, then at the end of that lifetime the Guides work with us to determine what lessons in the next lifetime would benefit us, and what events would help us to learn those lessons. We study the most recent lifetime to learn more about the choices we made and how we might have done things differently. Then, when we are hopefully rested and ready, we plan the next lifetime. But nowhere in the entire process do we get judged.

In the next chapter will be a selection of single past life readings, cherry-picked from full readings stored in the treasure troves of the readings I have done. In a later chapter, I will show what complete past life readings, containing four to six past lives for each client, look like, including the email correspondence between me and my client. I always change names and identifying information to protect everyone's privacy, both the clients and their loved ones, as well as their so-called enemies.

7
Brief Examples of Past Lives

"Souls are poured from one into another of different kinds of bodies of the world."

~ Jesus Christ, Gnostic Gospels: Pistis Sophia

In this chapter, I will be selecting just one lifetime each from five different individuals' readings to relate. Each of their full readings actually consists of four to six lifetimes. Full readings containing all the lifetimes I saw for different individuals will be reported in a later chapter. Again, I have changed everyone's names to protect their privacy.

Sons and Lovers

Most of the people I read for these days have read my first book on the subject, but I have never met them before. All I actually know is what their questions are, if they have any questions—some people do not—and what time zone they are in. I do these readings remotely for people all over the world. I connect with them by looking at a photo of them where I can see their eyes—and I look for a while into the eyes to connect with them. Then I close my eyes and go into a trance state, holding a digital recorder to preserve the reading. It still requires of me a gigantic leap of faith every time I do this. I report what I am seeing and being told, and in response I mostly receive terrific feedback. Sometimes I get no feedback at all, and only very rarely do I get any negative feedback. Some of the feedback boggles my mind. To this day people's responses to the readings can still do that—and naturally, I appreciate their words. It helps me continue to do the work.

In doing this kind of long-distance past life/life purpose reading recently for Sandy Strong, I saw a civilization that existed long ago. I had not seen this civilization before. In this lifetime, she was the mother of a small boy about two or three years of age. This was one of those civilizations which existed on Earth prior to recorded history with no traces left today—not even small artifacts—at least, not that I know about.

The people in this highly evolved civilization chose to live inside caves because they believed that it was deeply in harmony with nature to do so. In this particular home, there were gorgeous blue stones growing in the sides of the walls. The dwelling was very well built-out, too, with a shiny, smooth, wooden plank floor butted nicely to the walls. Even though the walls were irregular in shape, the wood was carefully cut so that it butted up to the uneven shape. It was exquisite craftsmanship.

More of nature's elements were incorporated into the home seamlessly. There was a naturally occurring waterfall inside the living room, which fell into a shallow pool. Aesthetically pleasing furniture, which was very comfy but quite unusual and yet natural looking, filled out the interior spaces.

The mother and son had been outside working in the garden at the time I was allowed to see. I am calling it a garden, but it was more like a wild, woodsy area, where the plants grew in languid profusion wherever they wanted to be, but the people cultivated and pruned them, and they also fertilized in a most natural way. The two of them came back in. I am watching the scene unfold as the mother begins putting the food away, cutting root crops away from the stalks, and separating the beans from their pods, washing the dirt off the roots. The mother hears the child splashing around in the water and thinks, "Oh, he is playing with toys in the shallow pond again." Then he becomes too quiet. As any good mother would say, when it gets too quiet, it is time to check on a child.

So she does go in the next room to check on him. What she sees horrifies her. Her little boy is floating face down in the pool and has drowned, even though the little pool was so shallow he could have easily stood up. She never even considered that he could drown in such a shallow pool; it was only about eight inches deep. But because she did not check on him when she first heard splashing she felt deeply guilty, and grieved intensely for years. Teetering on the brink of mental illness, she was so depressed she almost could not function for quite a long time. She blamed herself entirely for his death.

This event happened to teach her compassion, among other things. Sometimes children come in to live a short while to teach those around them something. This kind of thing is agreed upon by everyone involved before incarnating. For Sandy, there is a recurring pattern in many of her lifetimes of either being a child who dies due to not being cared for properly, or being the parent who fails to supervise adequately. One of her lessons at a Soul level has been learning the importance of watching small children "like a hawk" as they say, and taking responsibility for their fragility when young. So this experience was part of her learning that lesson. She also learned that the unimaginable can happen—things that we cannot predict at all. This Soul was learning compassion for people who make mistakes, and now has fully learned this on a Soul level. The Soul has also learned a deep sense of protection for children, more than most people ever experience, and working with children in some way is one part of her Life Purpose in this lifetime.

In that lifetime, her husbands (this was a culture which practiced polyandry) convinced her after about five years that she had a responsibility to bear more children, and they hired people to help out, rather like nannies, so she would never have to be alone with a child again—as this was her request. She then had three more children. I told Sandy I was pretty sure this little boy was reincarnated as the ex-boyfriend she had asked about earlier, Randolph, about whom I knew nothing except that he was a former boyfriend. I had known nothing about Sandy, either.

This was one of five lifetimes that came up for Sandy in this reading. What I found most fascinating was her reply the next day to her experience of hearing about this particular lifetime. Here is the pertinent part:

> *Thank you very much Lois. It was a great reading!*
>
> *I do believe the boy in the cave was Randolph—primarily because he is afraid of water and never learned to swim. However, he built by hand an exquisite, curvaceous wooden deck outside his home with an integrated pond and waterfall. This seemed entirely strange for someone so afraid of water. He also loves to garden. I even remember him telling me how deathly afraid he was of children getting near his pond.*
>
> *As for the life purpose of having/being around children—I agree! Everyone calls me "mother goose" because I'm so protective of others.*

I suggested she share that lifetime with Randolph for his healing as well. This is her reply:

I'm sure Randolph would appreciate knowledge of the life as well. We don't speak anymore because he and I got too close a few years back, and I was already married. I met Randolph at my first job out of college, and we immediately became friends even though he was seventeen years my senior. He just seemed to get everything about me, and he always seemed so interesting and intense. We spoke to each other every day for four years. It was strange, but yet compelling. No one else understood why we were so close, including me!

He is a special and gifted person. His craftsman skills are amazing and his gardens are bountiful. The cave explains so much about him and me. Even your description of the uniqueness of the wood floors, furniture, and beautiful blue stones on the walls resonated with me. I've had an affinity for stones my whole life. I would have a house full of them if I could (maybe I will!). The furnishings sounded like what I would use today—super comfortable and yet special. Creating special environments was my intent and reason for going to design school.

Knowing about this past life with him helped me immensely in understanding why I was attracted to him, and at the same time allowed me to see what it about. It was the finishing of old business we had with each other. We needed to be together because we had been separated too soon in the mother/son lifetime. It was good to love this soul again, though in a very different way. Love is love, I guess.

Thank you again for helping me to understand more of my life and purpose. If you'd like more of my revelations as they unfold, I would be happy to share them.

Love,
Sandy

This was only one of her past lives in the reading, but it was the first one I was shown and as is often true, it was the most important one to her out of the lifetimes I was shown at the time. It helped her to understand why the relationship happened, to understand more about Randolph, and it allowed her to let go more fully.

I am constantly amazed at the relevance of the past lives of total strangers that I am allowed to see and narrate. Knowing about their past lives helps my clients understand why certain things have happened to them, why they feel the way they do about children, or a particular person, or animals, or phobias. Amazingly, just knowing about these forgotten pieces of our Soul's journey allows the healing process to begin. It is such an honor to be allowed to do this part of my life mission!

Lovers Separated by Jealous Murderer, Reunited

Charlene, a lovely, physically fit woman in her early fifties, exuded that perky energy that one might naturally expect from someone who was an Iyengar yoga instructor. She had been divorced for several years and explained to me that she'd had more than one ill-fated relationship with unavailable men. But, she finally found one who was available. This most recent relationship was with a much younger man, Lars, whom she met while on a vacation to Sweden a little over a year earlier. She had gone there on vacation with her loving adult son Juarez, who is an airline pilot.

Immediately, Lars was head over heels in love with Charlene, begging her to come back to him, so Charlene scheduled a return trip a few months later. The two had a romantic, passionate love affair. They talked almost daily via the computer. Charlene became convinced that this man was the love of her life. She began to consider ways she might move to Sweden to be with him. She quietly put her house on the market to have the additional funds and freedom to move, and began to research how she might get a work permit for Sweden.

Charlene returned to see Lars every few months. But a strange twist came about with Charlene's son when he learned she was going back to Sweden the first time. His initial disapproval of the relationship turned to a blinding rage. His normally adoring attitude toward his mother suddenly shifted. He told his mother that all Lars wanted was sex. He screamed at her uncontrollably, and then refused to answer her phone calls. No one who knew him could fathom his reaction.

Yet Charlene continued to visit Lars, and when she was home they talked almost daily over the computer. About a year later while visiting him, she told Lars she was planning to move to Sweden. Everything shifted in that moment. He told her he did not feel as she did, and that she should not plan to move there. She was devastated, and when she came to see me it was because many months later, her grief was still just as raw as it was initially.

In the reading, which was done in person, I saw and narrated a total of five lifetimes. One of them immediately jumped out at Charlene with its uncanny relationship to the current life. In it, she had been a wealthy, bored, older Englishwoman in the 1700s. This woman went to Germany to visit some distant cousins, who were a much younger married couple. She moved temporarily into their home as a guest. The young couple had a sexless marriage; the wife was simply not interested. As there was a powerful attraction, Charlene began having an affair with the man, who reassured his wife that he wanted from their cousin nothing but sex. This went on for months before the wife, who felt her position was being disrespected, carefully plotted her revenge and poisoned Charlene, killing her.

Charlene and her lover had been violently separated at the peak of their passion for each other, and the man had instantly known it was at his wife's hand. As I told Charlene about this lifetime, it was clear that Lars was the husband in this German lifetime and Charlene's son, Juarez, had been the wife. I knew it and so did Charlene, even before I told her. The guilt of her having been murdered over him was profound, and this guilt made Lars fear Charlene's coming to live with, or even near him, again.

The uncanny part of this was that I had not known prior to the reading that Juarez had become disturbed when he found out Charlene and Lars were together, nor that he had sought counseling and been prescribed antidepressants. Juarez had stated to the doctor (and later to his sister) that he was so enraged he wanted to kill his mother. He was feeling just exactly as he had felt in his past life as the "wronged" wife who had killed her cousin. Since he did not know about the past life, none of this was logical to Juarez. Charlene found out about his desire to kill her from Juarez' sister, who was worried for Charlene's safety.

Immediately after the reading, Charlene felt a wave of peace come over her. By the next morning, much of her unresolved pain over Lars was significantly diminished. While the pain was about eighty percent less, Charlene knew she still loved Lars. We both suspected the relationship was not over, but the numbing, unrelenting pain was lessened, and she could function once again. This healing of the past life trauma will positively impact her relationship with both Lars and Juarez. Why? I have observed for many now that this is because unremembered events and relationships from past lives affect us until we know about them. We automatically begin to heal when we recall what was not remembered. This is how psychotherapy works with repressed childhood memories. Just remembering in a safe, non-judgmental environment allows the healing to take place. It is my job as the reader to create that space when I relate the past lives to the client. Once the client heals, the relationships with others in her life will change in response to her different state of being.

Charlene hopes that when her integration of the past life is more complete within herself, she can share the information with her son Juarez, so that he can benefit from the knowledge as well. I told her to be sure and ask him if he wanted to know about a past lifetime with her and Lars before telling him the story. We need to ask permission before telling someone about a past life—or before doing a reading of any kind. Charlene's relationship with Lars is continuing, but she is moving more slowly with him now, to give him plenty of time to heal as well from the past life trauma, and not to rush him.

Hummingbirds Speak!

Yes, they speak! Recently I did an Akashic Records reading for a young woman, Annie Chung, and in one of the five lifetimes I saw for her in the full reading, she served as a "bird whisperer" in Lemuria. Now, Lemuria predates Atlantis, for those who do not know, and sank beneath the sea hundreds of years before Atlantis did. The tops of the Lemurian mountain ranges are still above the water in the Pacific Ocean, and they include the Hawaiian Islands. It is said that the indigenous Pacific Islanders are the direct descendants of the Lemurians. This was an extremely highly evolved race of people, with a spiritual technology quite beyond anything we are aware of ever having existed.

While doing this reading, I learned that there were animal communicators for every species of wild animal back then. The reason was so that the Human Kingdom could stay in balance with each of the Animal Kingdoms. They also did not keep pets in the sense that we do today. They had relationships with wild animals, but did not restrict their movements, or imprison or cage them at all. During Lemurian times, we referred to the different kingdoms as The Wolf People, The Bird People, and so on. They were treated with the ultimate respect, and the ecological balance was of utmost importance to the people of Lemuria. If we humans did something to misuse animals or to upset the balance of life for any of these species, whether intentional or not, appropriate action would be taken. The human emissaries to the different kingdoms would communicate with their animal friends, and find out how to restore balance. The emissaries would then pass that information on to the governing body of Lemuria, which would see to it that the "wrongs" were redressed.

The ability to be an animal whisperer was inherited through the maternal line, and in that lifetime, Annie was a member of a family that had produced many, many bird whisperers. I knew nothing at all about Annie prior to doing this reading. We had never met, nor had we had any conversation at all. She was on my newsletter mailing list and decided to get a reading from me. When she asked for her reading, I requested that she send a photo of herself, and then a few weeks later I did the reading for her.

Now, some people have asked how I know that what I am seeing is real. I wonder the same thing myself from time to time. However, a startling number of times I get confirmations from the clients themselves—and usually from clients I do not know at all, like Annie. After she listened to the five past lives covered in the reading, Annie wrote me an email. Here is part of her email to me:

> *You have mentioned that I communicated with birds during Lemuria. I actually have a little friend, a hummingbird that I met a year ago while I was walking in nature. She flew right in front of my face and looked at me. I asked her name and was told that her name is Nini. I see her often when I go for a walk in that same area, and she visits me at my home a few times a week. I hear her singing and when I look outside the window from the living room, she is there. Isn't this funny? I thought I was making her name up or something.*

I was amazed and pleased that Annie made this connection so quickly. Some people are more adept at making these kinds of connections when first they hear about their past lives. Others have a harder time with it. But I have noticed that given a few months, people make more and more connections, have realizations, and are stunningly healed in many different ways by the experience of knowing about their past lives.

There was more to Annie's reading. In the Lemurian lifetime, a bird told her that she was not going to have a daughter in that lifetime because the ability was not going to be passed on through daughters any longer. She was told to build a boat and sail west to relocate her family because Lemuria was going to change completely and she needed to leave. She reported this information to the governing body, which was not happy with that report and ignored it, but she built her boat and left anyway. A few years later, Lemuria began sinking beneath the sea and most people did not survive. Annie by then had relocated her family on what was a then-tropical Australia, and they became part of the seeding of the aboriginal peoples there.

The reasons Annie needed to know about that lifetime were many. Among them was so that she would know she had an ability she could tap into: the ability to talk to animals. She also needed to know that she was a trailblazer in the past, having built the boat and taken her family to safety far away, despite the attitudes of the prevailing culture.

Share the Lifetime with My Wife?

Not too long ago, I did a past life reading for a man who has been married for over thirty years to the same woman. He had questions about his past lives and recurring patterns, just like almost everyone does. In doing the past life reading, we answered most if not all of his questions in the five lifetimes which came up for him in the reading. Something rather interesting and unexpected surfaced in one of the lifetimes I saw, and it was regarding his wife. I knew nothing at all about her, but I had seen a photo. She was very pretty, and looked quite young for a woman who had been married that long. There was a sweet, perky quality about her in the photo.

The lifetime that came up for him was one in which he had been a bit of a rogue, wandering the countryside during the era of the three musketeers, wearing clothing that looked like theirs. He was in France at the time I saw him in that prior life, and he was on his way somewhere, stopping for the night at an inn. He went for a walk out behind the inn and saw a lovely, innocent, sweet young woman milking a cow. They struck up a conversation, and he turned on his usual charm that worked so effectively with women. She was quite naive and before long, he had seduced her.

He stayed at the inn longer than planned, a couple of weeks, and had his way with her repeatedly. When he packed up to leave, she was distraught, having thought of the two of them as married. Men where she lived did not make love to a woman and then abandon her. In her innocence, she had no idea this could happen. When her father and brothers found out what was upsetting her, they did the best they could to keep him there, to get him to marry her. But it was to no avail. He was of an upper-crust family, and had no intention of limiting himself by marrying a milkmaid.

So the callous rogue did move on, and thought he would be able to forget her. But throughout the rest of his life, thoughts of her would surface from out of nowhere. He never followed up and sought her out, though. She was just another conquest of many, and he could not think why her face showed up in his mind's eye so often, or in his dreams.

She on the other hand, thought of him daily. When she soon realized she was with child, she became inconsolable, and ultimately committed suicide by hanging from a tree near where they had met. He never learned of this until after he passed from that lifetime. Part of the reason for their being together in this current lifetime was that he was supposed to marry her in the earlier one. This would have meant stepping outside the box of his normal life, but he would have been a much happier and more fulfilled person. So would she have been. They came together in this lifetime to fulfill an earlier contract.

When I sent Craig his past life reading, he sent me back this message:

> *Thank you very much for the readings. I have listened to them a couple of times now and will continue to do that over the next three months, as you suggest. There are a few things as you noted that already hit a chord with me. I am sure that over time, there will be more I will get out of this.*
>
> *I have no questions at this time, but one thing does come to mind I feel curious about. It has to do with the past life in which I was from France and while travelling I stopped at an inn. I met a woman who was in the back milking a cow, and I extended my stay as we became involved. The woman is my wife in this current lifetime. I ended up leaving her and she hanged herself. The question is this. My wife has always had a huge problem with her neck in respect that no one can touch it. She cannot wear anything around her neck, not even shirts that are high on the neck. No kissing, touching...nothing can touch her neck. I am thinking that this past life when she hanged herself could be the reason why she has this problem with her neck. Is there anything I can do in sharing this past life with her that might help her with the neck problem? Might it help relieve this feeling she has?*
>
> *Thank you again, and I look forward to future sessions.*

I was quite stunned to learn that his wife had these issues regarding her neck. I had known absolutely nothing about her except how long they'd been married and what she looked like.

Here is my reply:

> *Yes, that hanging experience probably does relate to your wife's neck issues. There may be other lifetimes contributing to the neck pain as well, but definitely this hanging business is the kind of thing that causes people problems in later lifetimes—whether hanging comes from suicide, or an execution, or is accidental.*
>
> *Often when people share past lives with someone in the family who was affected by that lifetime, it heals the family member as well to know about it. The only question is, would she be offended by the whole idea of past lives? You have to weigh everything, of course, before sharing anything with her. If she is open to the information, then definitely share; it will likely help heal the neck issues.*

It is experiences like this, hearing about unexpected healing, or seeing the unimaginable synchronicity between the readings and a stranger's reality, that help keep me going. How does it happen? I do not quite know. But I am grateful when anyone shares this kind of thing with me. I looked forward to hearing what Craig decided to do about sharing the past life with his wife.

Update: The Wife Who Hanged Herself

A few months later I heard from Craig, the man whose wife had committed suicide by hanging in a prior life. He contacted me for an intuitive phone consultation about business matters. After the reading was complete, I asked him about the neck pain his wife had, wondering if it had abated. He said that yes, he had told her about the past life, but he felt she was not really listening.

He went on to say that he had urged her to get a reading from me as well. He told me that her chiropractor, who could not get the neck pain to go away no matter what he did, had also told her that she had probably been decapitated or hanged in a past life, and that she should get some past life therapy if she truly wanted that neck to heal. The husband said sadly that her neck is still painful, and she absolutely refuses to get past life therapy, but not because she does not believe in it. She does believe in it! He was puzzled.

I replied that on some level she may know that she has experienced one or more massive traumas to her neck in many different lifetimes, considering that repetitive issues are not at all uncommon. I suggested that it might just be too much for her to confront this level of trauma at this point in her life; her fear of what she might find out was possibly too great for her at this time.

Everyone is on their own unique journey, on their own path to Enlightenment, and mine is not the same as yours or his or hers. The challenge is to allow those who are close to us the undisturbed freedom to proceed on their own path, knowing that they have a life mission and Guides of their own. It is in everyone's best interest for us to allow others the space to proceed on their path unimpeded, in their own time and in their own way. This is one very selfless way of showing others how much we love them, by honoring them with the freedom to proceed as they choose, trusting both them and the Universe.

Meltdown Over an Actor

The next past life I wish to discuss involves a strange yet overwhelming reaction a woman had in response to seeing a certain actor in a video. Here is the letter she initially sent to me:

Dear Lois,

I only have one specific question, and it pertains to someone I don't know personally but had a very intense experience connected to him, so much so that it is what pushed me to request a reading with you. I'll try to make the explanation as brief as I can. The person is an actor. [She named the actor, but I will leave that out.] He is an actor I recognize by sight but could not remember his name, what I'd seen him in or even the sound of his voice. There was no strong connection at all.

However, a few weeks ago I saw him briefly in a music video and felt an instant, intense desire and longing. Over the next few days, the feelings intensified to the point that I felt there was more than hormones going on here. I could not stop thinking about him; it was misery. I also felt an increasing nervous energy that made it almost impossible for me to sleep or to focus on anything. To keep it short, this all culminated several days later in my crying. Now I've cried uncontrollably before, but this was different. . .like a tsunami. I had no control of my body; I felt more like an observer as I heard myself wailing at the top of my lungs. It felt like these wails were being torn out of my chest, out of my heart. I woke up everyone in the house. And when it was done...I felt fine. The nervous energy was gone.

In its place, though, was a great feeling of complete love for this person. It felt unconditional, eternal. I have never been in love or anywhere close to it, so this was completely new. I also felt heartbreaking sadness—the feeling of loving someone and knowing you cannot see them, that they have to go away and you have to let them go. It was horrible. I barely ate for a week, and only got out of bed when I had to. It was like someone had died or left me.

I now somewhat have my appetite back, and this guy is not triggering such strong feelings in me anymore. But there are still these up-swellings of sadness (like now, writing this email)

I work with an energy healer, and she said that whatever happened, it had cleared out something in my heart area and allowed me to feel a type of love I could not before. I really believe that. I feel it was a positive experience but also kind of like a punch in the face—it was so intense and inexplicable. I feel like a crazy person. I would just really like to know if there is any connection between me and this actor, and if so, anything else I need to know or that needs to be healed.

Thank you for doing this reading for me (and reading all of this email!). I look forward to whatever information or advice you and the guides have for me.

Sincerely,
Amanda Zimms

Lois' Notes: My first reaction was to wonder if this woman were simply another nut case obsessing over an actor. But before I went into trance I carefully set that notion aside and focused my effort on remaining neutral so I could do an objective reading. What I saw stunned me.

Paralyzing Restraint

Out of the four lifetimes that I saw for Amanda that day, there was just one that was relevant to the actor she mentioned. It was the first past life that showed up for her, which indicated that the Guides and Guardians believed it to be most important for her to know. Here is the actual transcript of the reading:

The first thing I am seeing is that you are in some sort of boat, but it does not look like any water craft that I have ever seen before. In this life they are showing me first, I am seeing a round boat skimming along the top of the water. You are on top of what looks like a gigantic lily pond with lotuses and other water lilies. The water is just full of plants and this boat is designed to do the least amount of damage to the plants as it glides along the surface. It is much like the swamp boats they have in Louisiana that skim the water. This vehicle is shaped much like a saucer. It is a shallow, partial dome that has some sort of mechanism at the back. There is not a propeller, but the propulsion mechanism pushes air out and that causes the forward movement.

You are sitting cross-legged atop some cushions or folded blankets inside this thing that is large enough to hold five or six people. It does not have any chairs; it is just curved sheet metal and appears as though it was hammered into the curved shape by hand. It is quite lovely, and looks like a work of art, actually. It is made of copper. Interesting. It is gorgeous—like a sculpture. Sorry—I am just fascinated with this object. So anyway, you are sitting cross-legged in the bottom of this boat, and now I am seeing that there is another person in the boat with you, a child. Also there is a man operating the controls at the back, turning the air-blowing mechanism left to right like a tiller on the back of a sailboat. I am hearing that this was a culture that predated ancient Egypt and some of the people who started Egypt—I mean the ancient Egyptian culture with the Pharaohs and everything—they came from this civilization. I am being told it is not Atlantis. A lot of people came from Atlantis to start the Egyptian culture just before Atlantis sank under the water, but this was another group from elsewhere…who joined them, and that no one seems to know about. They came from (pause), oh, I see now, they came from North America. It was an Atlantean Outpost in North America, but their culture was different. They brought certain things to the mix that people from Atlantis did not bring, so that is where this water-transiting device and these people came from. I am actually seeing you in North America but it was so long ago I did not even recognize it. It is near the east coast and it was very tropical then...the southeast coast. Near where the Carolinas are now. There was a huge lake there at that time not far from the ocean, but inland, and this is what you are scooting across—this lake.

Now I see...you are on your way to a temple...you and your husband have been told that your child...Oh, this is not what I was expecting... your child has been identified by the prophets and the seers and the priests and virtually everybody at the temple as a reincarnation of a very famous religious leader. They would not have called him a priest or a monk, but devoted to the temple like that yet without the celibacy. Your child was that reincarnation, or they were pretty sure your child was he—and he was being taken to the temple so they could test him. This was because if indeed he were a reincarnation of that monk, your child would need to go live at the temple. You were just hoping and praying that he was not, because you did not want your little three-and-a-half or four-year-old child taken away from you. However, you knew that was how it was when there was a reincarnation of someone special like that. Naturally, you were crying, trying not to let your child see you cry. Finally you three arrived at the temple, which was on a little island inside of this very broad lake. The island was surrounded by lotus plants and other water lilies. This was not an extremely deep lake, but it did cover a lot of territory.

Upon arrival at the temple, you were greeted, honored and housed in a very beautiful place, much nicer than anything you lived in while these religious officials took your child to test him to see if indeed he were the person who they thought he was. You were wined and dined, and treated like royalty while this process was going on. It goes on for three days. At the end of three days you were called inside the temple.

There was a ceremony in which you discovered your child was being retained at the temple to be trained, since he was indeed the reincarnation of the famous religious leader. This small boy was your only child, and you had waited such a long time to have this baby; there was difficulty with your fertility. This was an unspeakable loss for you. Sadly, the rules required that you be very calm and collected and not get upset in front of your child, because he did not need to be any more traumatized than being separated from his parents was going to cause him anyway. This group had been doing this kind of thing—separating children from their mothers—for thousands of years, so they knew from trial and error the best way to do this.

Temple personnel had counseled that if you were going to cry, you should wait until you got home. Unfortunately, since you were an extremely emotional person who was also a very good mother, that was extremely hard for you. Struggling intensely to control your feelings, you forcefully stuffed the emotions. When the ceremony was over, you hugged your child, told him you loved him and you would come back to see him once a year as you were allowed to do. You repeated to him that it was a big honor for him to be here, and you would miss him very much, but this was where he needed to be. None of you—not you, not your husband, and certainly not your small child—had any choice in the matter. This was just the way it was done in that culture. After the ceremony you went home again in that strange looking, beautiful copper boat across the water to your home. For countless hours, you sat rigidly staring straight ahead, silently forcing yourself not to cry, and therefore never really let the tears out.

To maintain control of your life, you stuffed all your feelings for this little boy; all that pain was locked away inside. You did have two more children, and they were both girls. You were never the same after this loss of the boy, though, it was so deeply traumatizing to you. You went back once a year to see him and were very formal with him because he was a very special person. Each time you went there and saw him you were afraid that you were going to break down and sob uncontrollably, but you took a vow that you would not do that, and in that particular lifetime you would never, ever cry again.

Your precious son was about thirty years old when you saw him for the last time. After you went home you passed away from a heart attack; it was sudden and you died without ever having grieved over losing this little boy whom you had loved so deeply. This was, after all, your first child and only son. Added to that, you had known him in other lifetimes. As an adult at about thirty, he looked almost identical to the actor you mentioned. The actor is not a reincarnation of your son, but he looked almost exactly like him. In fact, they may be ancestrally related. Your son could be an ancestor of the actor, but that is beside the point. The actor was not actually the person you were involved with in that past life, but what seeing that video did for you was that it allowed you to finally grieve over losing your little boy. You just gut-sobbed, screamed, and allowed yourself to feel that pain in your heart and soul stuffed away for so long. It happened so you could finally let go of all that you had tragically been carrying from lifetime to lifetime.

The experience of seeing that video was set up as a trigger, so you could finally release all that pain and grieve the loss of the child. That is what that experience was, seeing him in that particular—there was something about that particular movie or video—that triggered the memory.

That is all you need to know about that lifetime.

A few days later I wrote to Amanda:

Dear Amanda,

I am wondering if you might allow me to write about your past lives reading in my next book. Yours was an unusual request for past life information, and I think it could benefit many others to learn about this kind of experience you had after seeing the video—to even know that this kind of thing can happen to a person. I would change your name and all identifying information, including the name of the actor.

Please let me know how you feel about this, and also please know that it is okay if you do not want me to share your story.

Luminous Blessings,
Lois J. Wetzel

She answered the same day:

Dear Lois,

I would be happy to let you include my reading in your book. When I initially wrote to you with my request, I wondered if you'd ever had a client come to you with a similar story. It was such a weird experience, and kind of embarrassing to talk about. I was afraid it would be interpreted as someone simply becoming infatuated with a celebrity and deciding, of course, they must have had a past life history together! So, I can't overstate how grateful I am that you were able to give me an answer and a reason for what I experienced.

The original incident occurred when I saw the music video with [the actor] in it happened last June, and it took me about four weeks to feel mostly back to normal. I actually could tell that the past life reading was about to happen because two days beforehand, I started to feel very anxious and the old feelings of sadness started welling up again. After listening to the reading for the first time I was pretty much a wreck for the rest of the day! I've been feeling a little better every day, but I did not expect the feelings of grief and loneliness to come on so strongly after listening to the reading. Even writing this is tough. There is something unspeakably difficult about losing someone without having the consolation of actually remembering them...remembering all the good times and experiences. When the grief passes you are supposed to still have all those good memories that keep the person alive in your heart, so to speak. It never occurred to me how horrible it would be to not have that, to just have the pain. There is this awful feeling of losing someone twice over. It's hard to describe.

As far as the video is concerned, I think there was something important about me seeing that actor in motion. Photos did not have the same effect on me. I think I needed to see his expressions, his energy, to shake something loose in my mind. I rarely watch music videos, but of course some innocuous chain of events led to me watching this particular one. What is interesting is that even though that actor is playing the part of a villain the moment he appeared on screen I felt the attraction. All I saw was his smile, and his eyes, and the laugh lines around his eyes. I actually felt a strong electric current go up my legs, through the soles of my feet, so strong it made my legs jerk. The image that stayed in my mind was of that sweet smile and those eyes, which seemed like the most beautiful eyes I'd ever seen, a rich brown that almost seemed to glow. When I went back to re-watch the video though, I realized that although he did smile, it was never that sweet smile I had fixed in my mind, and it was impossible to tell in video whether his eyes were brown or black, the lighting was too dim. Those details were so seared into my mind though, and with such a loving feeling, I couldn't understand why I would "remember" such clear details that didn't exist. It was like I was superimposing something that wasn't there. That was a big clue to me that something funny was going on

I'm actually feeling a lot better now that I've written all this. Evenings (er, I guess it's early morning now) are when the sad feelings really take over, but writing this wall of text has helped! Anyway, thank you again so much for doing the reading for me, it's given me peace of mind and is helping to release all these awful feelings. Once I get past all of that I hope I will start to see how my life is changed for the better. There is no doubt in my mind that this grief has been seriously blocking my ability to connect with others from my heart on a truly deep level. I'd never previously experienced the kind of unconditional love I felt when I started grieving for this lost son. It makes it hard to let go, because I know as the sadness goes away so will the feeling of love, and it is so much stronger than anything I've felt before. But I hope this means I will someday be able to feel it for someone else, who is actually here in this life.

Sincerely,
Amanda Zimms

This was my reply to Amanda:

Dear Amanda,

Of course, I feel certain that the immense overwhelm is because of how very long the grief has been stuck and unexpressed. I believe it is good to do the grieving loud and long. This will actually heal your DNA (where our connections to past lives are—in part). Please go to my website www.HotPinkLotus.com and then on to the newsletter page and read The Orchidium, channeled from the Hathors by Tom Kenyon. That newsletter is dated July of 2013. The Orchidium is a technique for assisting with overwhelming feelings, and drawing in more sustenance to the energy body from the cosmos—great for when we are going through a rough patch, or have low energy.

Once you finish with the integration of this past life, and the grieving is all done, you will still love your little boy, albeit in a spiritual way. By that I mean it will seem more "subconscious" than anything else. The love is eternal. He is soul family. You are right about this: the important piece is that you will be healed deeply, and all kinds of profound love possibilities will open up for you.

If writing this letter made you feel better, I highly recommend you keep a journal about your experiences with integrating all these past lives. Writing can be highly therapeutic, and you write really well.

Blessings,
Lois

The Trouble with Screaming

This is a past life of five I saw for a middle-aged woman named Bree. She had several questions, none of which addressed her tendency to speak very loudly at times, but this past life seemed be dealing with that. It also had to do with fear of striking out on her own, which she had not mentioned to me at all. About five years after the reading, Bree realized the most important thing that came from knowing about this one lifetime was not apparent at the time of the reading. It could only be seen in retrospect. I begin:

Once again, I am seeing another ancient culture of which we have no record. I cannot tell you how long ago it was, but it was long before recorded history. I see you as a woman living in a cave under...the entrance to the cave is under water. To get in and out of your home, you must swim in and out. This is some of the most gorgeous water I have ever seen. I have never seen water this color—it is bluish turquoise and as crystalline clear as anything. It is stunning, this deep small sea. The entrance to your home is in an idyllic cove surrounded by land yet connected to the sea.

The doorway or opening is about twelve feet below sea level. Everyone who lives anywhere around there resides underground in these caves—no one lives on the surface. I see that you have special swimming gear, and you slip on what looks like a mermaid tail—a tool that makes you swim faster. You pull it off when you get to the land, where you go to hunt for meat. What meat was once living in the caves has long since been hunted out. You also want plants from the surface because you need food that has absorbed all that sunlight, which you do not get inside the caves. You are a woman hunting alone with a bow and arrow. This allows you to travel light. You carry a little pouch with food in it and a water bladder beaded intricately with a sacred geometry pattern imprinting your water. I don't know why that is important, but it is. I think your people knew something about imprinting water with vibratory frequencies. The decoration is intricate and precise.

As you wander on the rocky land, you are constantly at the ready with your odd-looking bow and arrow. Something darts out from behind a rock, and you shoot it. Stringing it up, you carry it on your back. This animal is about the size of a rabbit. Suddenly, somebody jumps out from behind a big rock and starts screaming at you. He is a big person, and no one you have ever met. He is from a race of people that you have never seen before. Apparently, he feels like these animals belong to him and maybe they are even pets. It seems he had been feeding them—so they were his property, in his mind. He behaved as if you were trespassing, when in fact your family had hunted there for many generations.

This man was trying to find a new place to settle down. For some reason he had to leave his civilization, which was hundreds of miles away, and he brought his wife and two small children. They were just trying to survive. You did not back down the way he thought women were supposed to back down. In fact, you drew a bead on him—you pointed the arrow at him, and that made him even angrier. He lunged at you and, missing the projectile, he knocked you down. When you fell, you hit your head, which knocked you out. He carried you back to his camp. His wife was there, and when you woke up, she was cleaning your wounds— trying to help you. Afraid you were being held captive, you started screaming and trying to escape. This desperate man finally tied your hands and feet. You would not stop screaming, so he sewed your mouth shut because that is what they did where he came from. His wife was crying and begging him not to do it, but with a needle made from bone and with crude sinew from animals he had been collecting, he sewed your mouth shut, fearing there were others with you and they would hear you. He knew no other way to silence you.

You never stopped resisting, and kept squirming and making muffled noises. He originally intended to let you go when he was sure that there was no one else around looking for you, but he did not know how to communicate with you. Finally, he decided to pack his stuff up to leave and just keep going, deciding this was not a place to settle down because even the women were dangerous. When they were all packed and ready to go, he took a big rock and hit you on the head, then dumped you into that body of water to drown so he would not be tracked.

The point of all of this seems to be that you still have residual fears regarding striking out alone because, on that day, everything you knew was turned upside down. Your people had been hunting alone there for many generations. Women even hunted alone, as it was your custom. Everything that happened was so foreign, so alien, and such a shock. When you realized you were going to die, you thought, "I should not have been out here by myself. I cannot be alone. It is not safe." This indicates there is some residual fear of being alone or traveling alone or maybe even living completely alone. This is coming up so you can integrate it, so it will no longer affect you on any level.

<u>Lois' Notes:</u> *Bree had never mentioned being afraid to travel alone, but looking back, I noticed she never did travel alone—even though she passionately loved to travel. Additionally, Bree was a person who had long-standing trouble with excessive fever blisters all over her mouth, face, nose, and even eyes, ever since childhood. They happened frequently and were not only unsightly, but painful as well. They were mostly concentrated around her mouth. She was tortured by it and had never heard of anyone else having this kind of experience with herpes. I will say it did seem radical, even to me. She had told me about that casually, not in the context of the reading. We knew each other socially, so I had heard her speak about the fever blister problem.*

Bree reported something to me about five years after the reading. She had realized after randomly re-listening to her reading one day why she had stopped getting fever blisters. They had stopped right after that reading. However, it had never occurred to her to mention the healing to me. The only thing that now happens to her is that she will feel soreness around her lips at times, but they never become full-on blisters, they just hint at it and leave. She had told her family years ago how odd it was the blisters had just stopped happening, and she had no idea why. She did not make the connection to her past life reading until she was guided to listen to it again after five years. Then the truth of it hit her right between the eyes, so to speak. She was sure the sores were in the spots where her mouth had been sewn shut, and the other places where she got them were probably where she had been hit on her head and face with the rock, since it was all part of the same traumatic experience that day!

Now I find myself wondering how many other things heal that people do not connect to their past life readings.

8
A Series of Case Studies of Past Lives

"A conscious lifetime is a priceless treasure."

~ Lois J. Wetzel

THE FOLLOWING ARE FULL PAST life reading sessions with a series of clients. I have changed their names and identifying information to protect their privacy. These are all remote readings, so I will either include or summarize the emails they sent me before the reading that contain their questions and concerns. Then I will relate the reading, and after that I will share each client's feedback, if any, from the reading.

As the reader will see in this first series of past lives, often there is a series of lifetimes that address or relate to the same issue. We come back again and again until we learn the same lessons. Those lessons will repeat with different variations. This is why, in the realm of our past lives, a conscious lifetime is a priceless treasure. When we know what the lessons are, most of us find it easier to learn then. No more "hit and miss."

Some people asked about their life's purpose or mission, and those are given right after the past life reading, though I have recently stopped doing the two separately—they flow together naturally.

Past Life Reading

Alice Peel – June 29, 2012

This is the email Alice Peel sent when she first requested her past life reading:

> *Dear Lois,*
>
> *The main question that I'm hoping to get answered concerns my ex-husband, Mark. We had a very passionate courtship and marriage, but then he confessed to sexually abusing my oldest daughter. He was of course arrested and sent to prison. I always felt like that experience was to help give meaning to my own childhood sexual abuse, and felt like he rather sacrificed himself here to help me. That probably doesn't make sense. But, even though he's been gone thirteen years, I still feel very connected to him. To be honest, I felt more grief at losing him than I did over what he did to my daughter. I feel much guilt admitting that. So my first question is about him. What has our relationship been about, and if it's over in this lifetime. I feel that I could again live happily with him after he gets out, but that I will lose my whole family and the respect of all of society if they were to find out. Thinking on that payment is overwhelming to me.*
>
> *My second concern is about my sexuality. I used to think that I had sex with just anybody because I was abused as a child, though I never really understood that connection. But now, it's almost an addiction. I think I'm addicted to porn and*

masturbation—just wanting to feel numb, but feeling something. I don't know why I am the way I am. I hate it and it disgusts me. My sexual relationship with Mark was very satisfying for me, my only satisfying relationship like that. Again, I still have much grief over losing him.

My last question or concern is just basically that I don't feel like I've grown any in the past decade or so. Since Mark has been gone, I've raised four children alone—they were between seven years and five months of age when I became single. I'm very bitter and closed off to other people. Every night that I'm not working, I'm numb on whiskey and sleeping pills. The traumas of the sexual abuse, both as victim and as non-offending parent, have just paralyzed me and I don't want this anymore.

So those are the issues that I'm hoping to have clarified for me through this. But I do understand that I will hear what is wanted for me to hear. I appreciate your willingness to help.

If there is anything else you need from me, please don't hesitate to let me know.

Thank you again,
Alice Peel

<u>Lois' Notes:</u> *After reminding Alice why I do these readings, and that there is no judgment of anyone in the Akashic Records, I did her reading:*

Attila the Hun's Army

I am seeing you as a warrior in the army of Attila the Hun in about 400–500 CE. Part of what this army did was to conquer as much land and as many people as possible in what is now Russia, approximately, and some of the Balkan States. Attila conquered a huge amount of land

and the people living there. That took time, so there seemed to be a constant war of about twenty years' duration. This was a barbaric and brutal time, and Attila's enemies, the Romans, were brutal as well. There were many rapes by your army, and much pillage and plunder. Many of us who have been warriors in what would now be referred to as barbaric states or times in history have experienced this. You did engage in rape, and it did not seem to matter to the soldiers whether these victims were women or children. It is certainly not as though you were the only one, but you did participate in this—not everybody did this—but it appears that maybe half of them did. The soldiers who did that all have subsequently had the experience in later lives in some degree of what it is like on the receiving end of this activity. So that would be part of the explanation as to your own childhood experiences.

In this lifetime you were fierce and a great fighter. This went on for such a huge percentage of your adult life that you really did not settle down until you were a fairly old man, and by then you were really worn out. You never had children, but you did settle down with a wife who wanted protection—which was what you offered her. The man you are married to in this lifetime, Mark, was your wife in that lifetime. Even though there were no children, there was some happiness found in settling into marriage and feeling peaceful.

You lived maybe another fifteen years after the next ruler took over, and he was not quite as fierce. You were out of the army by then, and were old enough to just be allowed to leave. Upon your retirement, you began working with metal doing a variety of jobs, like sword-making and blacksmith work, which you had done as a soldier as well.

The reason you need to know about this lifetime was because of the rapes. Knowing this helps put things into perspective; it helps you to see why you might have chosen to experience sexual trauma in this lifetime. Also, this is one of the places you have known Mark before. He had been a rape victim—remember that the behavior was so pervasive that a majority of people had either raped or been raped. It was just a sign of the times, so you have a common theme in the past that you both had raped and have been rape victims. Your wife was fairly young when she was raped—perhaps about fourteen or fifteen years of age, which was considered a woman in those days, though that seems like a child to us. You did protect her in that life as you promised her you would.

That is all you need to know about that lifetime. This is a very important past life that you two had together.

The Scottish Doctor

I am seeing a lifetime in about the late 1500s in what is now Scotland. You were labeled as an invalid, meaning you had some sort of physical disability. You were female, again, and your family was hard-pressed to take care of you, so the local doctor offered to take you in. Bear in mind that a doctor did not have the same background and training that they do these days. They mostly dealt with leeches and bleeding people and using herbs.

And so this kind doctor volunteered to take care of you, and everyone in your family thought he was a very great man to take care of this woman who was such a burden. They were tired, and it was a burden taking care of you—they even had to change your diaper. What afflicted you was almost like cerebral palsy... but it was something else. I am sorry; it is not clear to me what was wrong. You could think and you could talk somewhat, but you could not get to the bathroom very well or control your bladder or bowels. Your speech was slurred; you did not have a lot of muscle control.

This doctor who volunteered to care for you was not a married man. His wife was dead and his children were grown. After his wife died, this was a pattern for him. He took in helpless persons every few years or so.

He would take somebody in and care for them until they passed away or until their family was in a position to take care of them. Again, this man is your ex-husband in this lifetime, and he routinely raped and sodomized you after he got you into his house. That was the price for taking care of you as far as he was concerned. He knew you would not tell because there was no one else to take care of you. But to all appearances this was a protective relationship. He did feed you and bathe you and so on, but at the same time he was abusive in a sadistic way, which would be quite a nasty setup for a person who was sick or disabled.

The reason you chose to incarnate as a person who was sick and needed to be taken care of was that it was intended as a lesson in learning to relax and trust people to take care of you. It was supposed to also be a lesson for your family in sacrificing to do the right thing. That right thing would have been to take care of you because you were ill. There was so much they could have learned from that situation, yet they did not because they passed the buck. They let this doctor take over even though his wife had died under mysterious circumstances. What really occurred was that she committed suicide because he was making her do things sexually that she did not want to do, and she did not see any other way out of it. He was quite sick; what he did would be illegal in most places even today.

One of the things you learned in that lifetime was what it felt like to be vulnerable, to need protection and to have to entrust your well-being to other people. In this case, you did not have any choice but to trust other people and experience what it felt like when betrayed—because one way or the other you were going to experience betrayal. Actually, I am seeing that the sexual abuse started before you moved in with him. He would insist on being alone with you to work on you and that is when he would do it...even in your own home. Your family suspected because you were making noises, and they just let it happen. No one ever voiced their concerns; they just exchanged guilty glances.

Anyway, that is what happened in that lifetime and here is the thing: when the man got tired of each victim, he would mix up a concoction of lethal herbs. It happened three different times that some woman died mysteriously in his home—besides his wife—in the course of his lifetime. After each one died he would say, "Poor thing. She finally passed." And everybody believed him because it was easier. Nobody wanted to confront the only doctor for 100 miles around.

Not only were you betrayed and abused, but it was the only sex you ever knew. You had this disability from a pretty early age; it started right around the onset of puberty. But the only sex was the sex you had with that doctor and, consequently, the combination of pleasure and pain was confusing and addictive and that is where the pattern of addiction of pleasure and pain—not tenderness, but cruelty combined with sex—that is where that pattern got deeply ingrained in you. It really imprinted the Soul. Because sex should be a sacred spiritual experience and this was confusing, to say the least. It felt a little of both for you—sacred and profane. That is all you need to know about that lifetime, so it seems clear to me that there is a pattern here that needs to be healed. In one lifetime or another you are going to need to heal this pattern by doing some deep therapy so that your Soul is finally healed and you do not continue it in subsequent lifetimes. Knowing about this will begin the healing process, but I also still am hearing you need to follow up with the healer of your choice to work on this issue.

Oh, and by the way, in that Scottish lifetime...your mother in that lifetime was your daughter in this lifetime, the daughter who was abused.

I am pausing to wait for the next lifetime to show up.

Athletic Discipline

I am seeing another lifetime and again you are a woman. I am seeing you dance ballet and, while you are not the star of the ballet, you are a very gifted dancer. This is how you make your living. This lifetime occurred in France, and it is not clear what the time period is. I am hearing that it does not matter. You just need to know that you have athletic ability, that you have artistic ability, and that you have had this very satisfying lifetime. You did not marry and you did not have children because by the time you were through dancing, it was too late to have children. You spent your later years teaching other young women and children.

What I am seeing is a beautifully lit home. You are an older woman dressed in a soft, frilly style, and you are teaching children to dance—both girls and boys. This is a very peaceful, happy lifetime. It was very productive. And so you do have tendencies to work well with children. This was an awesome type of work for you to do, because of the self-esteem that comes for a child with learning to dance or do anything artistic, express themselves, and get praise. This is what you did for them: you told them what a great job they were doing, and you gently corrected them when they made mistakes. You were not one of those teachers who belittled children, or smacked them with a ruler, or were punitive in any way. You were a good, kind, gentle teacher.

Your Guides wanted you to know about this because not all of your lives have been difficult or painful. This was a positive past life and some of your talents are exposed here like the ability to teach, to nurture children, to perform, to be really disciplined athletically. I am hearing that exercise is one of the ways your Guides may decide to help you—if indeed you decide to get some therapy to get out of addictive patterns. Exercise of some form in conjunction with therapy would be especially powerful for you because of the positive association you have had in the past with your athleticism.

Just know that you have this ability to draw upon, this ability to be highly disciplined as an athlete. The dancer's name was—I am seeing the letter "E" and then "Danielle." The last name starts with the letter "E". It is not clear what the name was. Anyway, they wanted you to know about that life because these are some of your strengths.

I am going to pause until I see the next lifetime come into view.

Slippery Slope

Now I am seeing a lifetime where you are a child of about nine or ten years of age. There are about six siblings with you, and you are one of the middle children, living in the Austrian Alps. It is not clear what the time period is, but maybe about one to two hundred years before our current time. You are all sliding down the side of a hill playing a game you call something similar to slippery slope. So when you hear the phrase slippery slope, if that makes you giggle or you think that is somehow a silly thing to be calling spiraling downward into a bad place, on some level you think that is a silly term from long ago when the term made you giggle. You each had these round metal things rather like a curved dish just big enough to sit inside, and you could not really steer it since it curved up on the sides all the way round. You were spinning and sliding all at the same time. It was a lot of fun. The people who were your children in this lifetime, they were your siblings in that lifetime, and you played beautifully together. So if you had a feeling with your children that you were in some way considerably more of equals than most people think of themselves with their own children, this is why. You may have felt like you were not really the boss, because you had that lifetime as siblings in which you were neither the baby nor the eldest, but just part of the crowd.

I am not seeing anything unpleasant occurring in that lifetime. It looks like you all grew up healthy and strong and all married except for the one who was younger than you. This was a boy, and he went off to join an army in another country, and he never came back. No one ever knew what happened to him, which was sad, but everybody else grew up, got married, had good jobs, were good citizens and, given the trauma of those first two lives, your Guides are trying to counterbalance the knowledge of them with pleasant lifetimes, because it is going to be somewhat difficult to assimilate those first two—especially the second one.

This was a close-knit family, you and your children, and actually the brother who went off to war was quite young, maybe age fourteen or fifteen. People did that back then and God, it is amazing. They either lied about their age or had their parents sign saying it was okay for them to go to war. Oh, now I see. This brother was actually your ex-husband Mark in this lifetime, but he had not yet become old enough to start acting out sexually. He was doing a good job in that lifetime, not harming anyone. Oh, yeah, here we go. They are telling me that is why he only came in briefly, so he could get a taste of what an uncontaminated life would be like. He was nice to everybody, and everybody was nice to him. He did not hurt anybody, but he died young, before he had a chance to revert to his old patterns. That was a good experience for him, because he came out of that lifetime without incurring any negative karma at all, and everybody else got a positive experience of what it was like to be with him when he was being a kind, loving person.

Cuban Sugarcane Farmer

I am seeing you as a man again, a sugarcane farmer in Cuba. You have a small sugarcane plantation, not a big one, and you worked out in the fields with your family and a few hired hands. You all cut sugarcane with a long pole that had a curved blade attached to the end. You also had a machine consisting of two large stones that rubbed together and crushed the sugarcane to squeeze the juice out.

Sadly, though, you died in the Cuban Revolution in the 1950s. A good father, husband and provider in that lifetime, you still died young—in your late thirties or early forties. It was a brave death, as you were defending your land, your family, and your right to own a business. This is viewed as a heroic, successful life.

That is all you need to know in this particular reading, and if you want another past life reading, please wait at least four months. Give yourself plenty of time to assimilate, especially those first two lifetimes, and listen to this at least once a month for those four months to help you fully integrate it all. No one ever gets it all at once. Trust me, Alice, you will not be able to get everything at once, because if you did it would be too overwhelming.

You may have some emotional releases after this reading, and I recommend apple cider vinegar baths to release the feelings safely and easily. There is no need to feel the feelings all over again; they belong to the past.

Alice sent feedback right after the reading:

Dear Lois,

Thank you so much for taking the time to do this for me. There are quite a few thoughts and comments that I'd love to share. In the first past life as a warrior/rapist—as soon as you mentioned warrior and the time period, I knew what I had done. It was hard to hear that I did that most of my adult life. I'll come back to the second life as an invalid in a bit. The life as a dancer, I'm so grateful that you shared that with me, especially that I had the discipline to be an athlete. Discipline has always been a weakness of mine. About a month ago, I began training for a half marathon this December. I started running completely from scratch. I was unable to run for a minute non-stop before this! This past month has been exciting seeing how far I've come. About the life as a sibling with my current children, that one just made me grin ear to ear. I have a very good relationship with my kids—it's been just us for so long. They appreciate me and respect me and I've always treated them with respect, too. It isn't that we're equals, I'm certainly the parent, but I can see us being equals in the past. Interesting that Mark was there with us too. I didn't really feel anything hearing the one about the Cuban revolution, but I did think it was interesting that it was so recent.

Now, the one as an invalid. Wow. As I was first listening to it, I couldn't feel any thoughts just yet. But as you were finishing that life, completely an afterthought, you said that my mother then was my daughter now—that just took my breath away, literally, and I had to shut the recording off and cry. I seriously bawled for about fifteen minutes trying to catch my breath. I'm not sure the feelings behind that reaction –it was so sudden and so deep. That she "gave" me to him back then, and in this life I "gave" her to him.

After I heard the whole thing and was contemplating it, my first thought about that particular life was that this life was almost the same thing. I wanted him to protect and care for and provide for us, and he couldn't do it. When he started leaning toward the perverted again, that's when he started abusing Emily. After two and a half years of that, he turned himself in. He wasn't caught—he just came forward and admitted it. He wanted to stop and couldn't, so this is how he stopped.

How does our Soul heal of this? Do I heal with him or am I supposed to forgive him so I don't have to come across his Soul again? Is the pull I feel toward him simply an old pattern that needs to be broken or is it real? I guess those are my questions.

I have one more question that doesn't involve the reading–perhaps you could just recommend a book? I'm curious about

Jesus–how I am supposed to incorporate his life into mine. Is there a book that you're aware of that could explain Jesus? I hope that question makes sense. Again, thanks so much for taking the time to help me with this.

Thank you,
Alice

Here is my answer to Alice:

Dear Alice,

Thank you for the beautiful feedback. I appreciate it more than you can know.

Mark is a member of your Soul family, and you will doubtless be with him again one day. But I do not see that it would be wise to be with him again in this lifetime. It would cost you entirely too much, namely the love and trust of the rest of the family, including your children. I feel sure that Emily would view that as a betrayal. However, what you do is always up to you. This is why we are given free will.

But yes, you need to forgive him, which involves not being angry with him or resentful, and deciding to move on with our lives in whatever way we choose. We forgive others for ourselves, because carrying anger and resentment harms us—not the other person. It devours us from within.

Getting help for the addictions will move you in the right direction to find someone else if you wish, a partner with whom you can enjoy the rest of this lifetime. There is never only one person in the world for us, though it seems that way sometimes. Remember, you and Mark will both be back in different guises at later times and other places. My understanding is that you will see him between lifetimes—we all have that option. Your Guides will help you both heal, and that is part of what happens in the planning stages between lifetimes—lessons are planned to help the Souls heal.

Also, just knowing about these past lives puts you on the path to healing. Once we know about and remember them, we begin to heal.

I suggest that if you feel guided to learn more about the teachings of Jesus, you search out some of the books of the Bible that were removed in the fifth century, like the Books of Thomas and of Mary Magdalene, and that you also learn about Gnosticism. These are closer to the true teachings of Jesus, in my opinion, than what is in the Bible at this time. Also, one really good way to find the right book for you is to ask your Guides for help as you surf the Internet looking for books about the life of Jesus. The author William Henry has also written several very enlightened books about Jesus and the meaning of his life.

Luminous Blessings,
Lois

<u>Lois' Notes:</u> *I felt that Alice was still down on herself for continuing to love a man most people surely would agree is a monster. If you find yourself in a similar situation, remember this: if you are down on yourself for loving someone who is abusive, just remove yourself permanently from this toxic situation. However, if after you have successfully done this, you find that you still*

love the person in spite of it all, just know this does not mean that something is wrong with you. It simply means that you are capable of unconditional love. This does not mean you should go back to her or him, or that you are star-crossed lovers who belong together. It simply means that you personally are capable of a high form of spiritual love, and since you have that ability, you have the tools to find that with another person or persons.

Past Life Reading & Life Mission Reading

AnneMarie Nelson – September 2, 2012

AnneMarie wrote me the following message about getting a second reading from me:

> *Dear Lois,*
>
> *Here are my questions:*
>
> *First, I would like to know about any life or lives with Alexander, my youngest son. Currently it's pretty smooth with him, but I've had behavioral issues with him in the past. I'm interested in past karma and want to be prepared if problems arise.*
>
> *Second, I would like to know about any additional lives with Chaz, my boyfriend, and why I have trust issues with him cheating.*
>
> *Last, I want to know where my weight (overweight) issues come from. I know I chose this body, but I want to know why.*
>
> *Thanks again!!*
> *AnneMarie*

Here is AnneMarie's Reading:

Teaching Respect

In the first lifetime I am seeing, you are married to the Soul who in this current lifetime is your son, Alexander, and back then he didn't think much of women. It was an era and culture when men didn't think much of women, period. Women were to be seen and not heard; they were second-class citizens. This is an Asian culture. Actually, he was abusive to you. He talked down to you and was horribly disrespectful to you as the mother of his children. He was more abusive a husband than most of the other males in that culture; he was just absolutely contemptuous of you—and it seems his father was like that, too. And you know, it wouldn't be the first time somebody came back as your child that used to be your parent or a loved one, your spouse or your best friend. You came back with him in this lifetime to teach him respect for women. It is that simple. And you came to specifically teach him to respect you, not to physically punish him, but to teach him how important it is to respect other people—particularly women.

This will be new for him because he hasn't had a lot of lifetimes on Earth since women's liberation came along. In fact, who has? Yet this Soul has a repeating pattern of being disrespectful and abusive, especially of women when he is a male. You are here to teach him, lovingly, that you are the boss and he had better respect your authority, and that there are consequences if he does not. There many ways to teach that… behavioral modification, for one. You are really going to have to give him some structure and teach him that you are the boss. That is primarily why you are with this particular child in this lifetime…to lovingly, yet firmly, teach him to show women respect.

Fooling Around

The next lifetime has to do with your inability to trust. Not just Chaz; there are a lot of people who will trigger your concerns about infidelity.

You were very successful—yes, you owned a newspaper on the west coast in the United States in the 1800s…I want to say in northern California. You were wealthy, had a big house and had a really bad habit of being, well, a big-time womanizer. You had many paramours and a wife who looked the other way because she didn't want to give up the money and the position—though she did not appreciate that behavior from you. While you felt guilty about it, you kept on doing it, and you didn't control your urges. This went on until you were in your late fifties and there was a potential scandal when the woman you were having an affair with became pregnant. She didn't want more children, especially by someone she wasn't married to…and you did not want this child since you were a public figure as well as married.

Someone who worked for you misunderstood you when you said, "Take care of this problem," meaning relocate her, pay her off…they misunderstood you, killed her and disposed of the body. Since she was pregnant, this killed the baby, too. You were distraught when you found out. You never quite got over it. You certainly didn't intend to have anyone killed. That episode ended your days of running around with other women.

When you came back this time as a woman, the Soul in knowing its own past mistakes made it really hard for you to be female. I would be surprised if you could trust much of anybody male. There may be a few men that don't trigger your "Men are all dogs" attitude, but in fact, they are not. They are not all dogs and it would not be just Chaz; I suspect there have been other men you really did not trust, afraid they were going to betray you. I am not telling you that he is not fooling around. He might be—that may be part of your karmic balancing—but I am not telling you that he is, either. I will say that you need to trust your instincts. Clear your head, gather your adult information, and make your decision about whether you want to be with him or not, while remembering that you are seeing everything through the lens of that past life.

Entitled Sultan

This one is coming in quickly on the heels of the last one. I think it is because the two of them are related. You are a sultan in a Bedouin…let me back up. I am not sure if these are Bedouins or not. You are wearing a turban and the trappings seem to be a North African culture. Again, I see you as a wealthy man with a lot of power and control and a large harem…lots of wives and concubines, forty to fifty kids, something like that. You have a huge number of wives, and of course a great number of women to sleep with—and you just slept with all of them. You believed this was how it ought to be, since it was socially acceptable. There was nothing wrong with it in those days. In fact, having a lot of women was a mark of being a very powerful, successful man. It was your right as a man to have numerous women and plenty of children by all these different wives. That being a part of your past makes it really difficult for you, now that you are in a situation where you are the woman and you want a monogamous relationship. This past life experience makes you feel resistant to trusting that it will ever happen, because you know from experience that this is not the nature of men. Monogamy comes naturally to women, but not to men, due to the way the two have evolved. Therefore, monogamy is a gift that men give to women. It is not anything women can reasonably demand. The woman is wise to wait until he is ready to give it. Some men can and do, and some never do.

Nomadic Army

In the next lifetime, I am seeing that you are again male and part of a nomadic army along the lines of the one of Genghis Kahn. Not Genghis Kahn's specifically, but that kind of army that moves across the countryside taking whatever they want—food, horses, money, or women. You have a sword and you use it freely. If you do not like something somebody says, you just lop off his or her head. Even at the end of that lifetime, you had only barely begun to settle down. You were an old man; you had a wife, but you were not particularly gentle with her because she was just part of the spoils of war in your mind. Because of your upbringing and prevailing culture, you never saw women as anything except property. You had been inducted into that army when you were just thirteen or fourteen years old. The fact that you lived to be an old man was something of a miracle. You settled down, but never had children. The wife was not particularly well treated.

So you have had far more lifetimes as men than as women, or at least those are the ones you are working on at this time. You came in this time as a woman so that you could experience what it is like to be on the receiving end of some of the worries that women have where men are concerned. Does he really care about me? Is he just using me? Am I just an object to possess? You may have been drawn to those kinds of men into this lifetime, men who do not treat you well, so that you can have a balancing experience in knowing how that feels. Once you have deeply learned that lesson on a Soul level, it will be time to move on to other lessons. You do not have to spend your whole lifetime learning that, but it is important for you to know that this is why you have had these experiences with men who either are being unfaithful to you or who do not reassure you sufficiently. You wanted the experience of doubting that they are being faithful because whether they are being unfaithful or not, just knowing how it feels to worry like that, not feeling safe and secure in the relationship, is part of the balancing of that karma. Knowing about this will help you speed up the lesson, of course.

Weight Issues

You wanted to know if there was a past life having to do with your weight issues. I am being told that there are several. There was one in which you starved as a woman who was in a war zone. The food supply was blocked, or was withdrawn in order to starve out the soldiers, but women and children starved, too. At the moment of death you were wishing for food, which puts an imprint on the Soul of longing for food and wanting to just eat and eat and eat and eat when next you are in a body.

Next I am seeing that there is a lifetime where you are imprisoned—again, as a woman. It is not clear precisely why you are in prison, but you are chained as you did something to displease a ruler in a very—what looks like a feudalistic environment. You were there a very long time and barely fed enough to stay alive which, again, yields the same result. When you died you were hungry…you were actually in a dungeon dying of infected rat bites, but you were hungry for a really long time, years in fact, and that imprints itself on the Soul. The desire to eat is strong because deep down, you do not want to have to ever worry about starving again, because you know that you can stay alive a whole lot longer if you have fat reserves to burn off. You have had several lifetimes like that. These starvation lives were for balancing of the "rape-pillage-plunder" lifetime mentioned earlier, because the plunder portion of that meant people were left with no food once the army moved on.

That completes the past life portion of your reading.

AnneMarie's Life Mission

In addition to those lifetimes, there is the desire on the part of the Soul for you to learn to love yourself regardless of what your body looks like; to love yourself despite what other people think about you, or what kind of childhood you had, or what kind of boyfriends or husbands you have had. You are here to learn to love yourself unconditionally. This definitely is a challenge for a lot of people, and so the plumpness, the weight issues as you call it, had to do with more than one thing. It had to do with balancing other lifetimes related to hunger, which is very common, but it also has to do with learning to love yourself and appreciate your body. That is a very important piece of what you came to Earth to do this time—to learn to love yourself unconditionally, because only then can we learn to love others unconditionally. That is one major thing we are all here to do—learn to love unconditionally. Some of us come in capable of self-love, and some of us are more successful at learning to love others in spite of the baggage they bring in with them.

You also wanted to help others learn this once you have. At some point in time, not now, maybe you need to wait until your kids are older, your Soul hopes you will start support groups for other women who have physical issues...whether it is being too heavy or too thin, people with food issues...emotional support groups of some kind. I think it is to be centered around spiritual growth and meditation. Yes, it appears that you are going to weave a lot of really unique things into a support group for women, and there will be a blog or website involved eventually.

Now this is not all going to happen overnight, this is something that is going to happen gradually, but unconditional self-love is one of the things that you wanted to come to learn this time, and then to share it with other people...this self-love in spite of...whatever the physical limitation may be. There might even be people in there who are in wheelchairs...people with birth defects...I see you helping people learn to love themselves once you learn to love yourself, because we are far more than our bodies.

To get healed and move in the direction of this work you are to do, you might want to start meditating. There is more than one type of meditation, so find out what works for you by experimenting with various types.

Another piece of your life purpose is to learn to separate the wheat from the chaff. In other words, to gradually, over time, while you are learning the self-love piece of it, be able to let go of people who are not treating you well—whether it be friends, family or boyfriends, husbands—to not hang onto someone for dear life just because you think you cannot do any better, but to let go of people who do not treat you well so that someone can come along who will love the real you. A big piece of what you are to learn and to share with others is to be real, to be who you honestly are, and to tell the truth about how you feel and not hide behind a mask of niceness. This is because you have no idea who is out there who is going to love the real you the way you truly are. For you see, they cannot find you if you are wearing a mask, pretending to be somebody that you think is what everybody else wants. Becoming genuine and teaching other people how to become genuine, how to be real, how to tell the truth and fearlessly be who they really are—that is a major piece of your work. As part of your life work you may even begin to write magazine articles for online magazines as well and reach many people that way. Eventually, the plan is that one day you are going to have a forum where people can come and talk about their issues, offering each other support. There will not be meetings in person, although there will be a few small groups of people in different locations who will get together in person, but primarily it is to be an online support group for developing self-love. This is a very high calling, AnneMarie; it is a very high calling indeed.

Another big piece of your life plan was to be a mother, and you have done that. I do not know if you are through doing that. You may actually have one more child. I am seeing that as a possibility out there, but that is up to you. So you need to know this is part of what you came to do and having children is a very important part of your life, and raising them to be loving adults. You accept people for exactly who they are and do not try to change anyone. That is a hard thing to teach – to accept people the way they are, to love unconditionally and stop trying to change people. Children need guidance. I am not saying you should just accept however they behave that day, because they do need structure and guidance. That is what you are there to provide: love, structure, guidance. And here is another thing that is interesting: they will learn to love unconditionally and accept people just as they are by being your children; they will learn by example.

In your later years I am seeing you getting involved in building hand-built houses out of bricks made of mud and straw. I would highly recommend that you look on the Internet at the concept of straw bale and hay bale houses. I am seeing you leveling the earth and helping people build houses. There is no reason to become an indentured servant, you see, to a bank, in order to have a home. People can build little communities where they hand-build houses themselves. For about $5,000.00 in today's dollars, you can have a nice little house that is hand built. Maybe somebody wants mud and straw bricks or hay bale houses with stucco on the outside. Some people may want a mix of the local dirt with cement to make extremely strong blocks. There are all kinds of natural building techniques all over the Internet now, and people are experimenting with them. I can see you becoming involved in that. It is not in the immediate future, but I see that ten to fifteen years down the road you are going to start becoming involved in something like that.

I am being told that is all you need to know about your life purpose at this time. If you know too much too far in advance, it is overwhelming. That is your complete reading. Thank you.

AnneMarie did not have any questions after the past life reading. Almost a year later, I emailed her asking how she was doing and if she had any feedback regarding changes after the reading. Here is her response:

Dear Lois,

Everything you gave me was fantastic. It has been somewhat of a struggle to let go of the trust issues with my boyfriend Chaz, but I've made some major progress. I can't believe it has been a year already!! I still have some things that pop up here and there, but once Chaz and I worked through the karma, the energy really became positive, and we rarely have any issues. You've helped me tremendously, so thank you. Everything you gave me was clear cut for me to use.

I did have one question that I did not think to ask after the reading. I have had my tubes tied, and I wonder how it is that I might have another child. I would like to have one with Chaz. I keep seeing a red-haired child. I suppose I could adopt, but I believe anything can happen!

Sincerely,
AnneMarie Nelson

Lois' Notes: *I was happy she and Chaz were still making it work. I agreed with her that in fertility, anything can happen from surgical reversal of the tied tubes to adoption to in vitro fertilization, to a miracle or the creation of a new technique that we have not yet imagined. I was delighted she and Chaz had understood the karma and worked through it to find greater peace and trust in their relationship.*

Past Life Reading

Babette Benson - January 21, 2013

Some people do not have any questions when they contact me; they just want to hear what their Guides want them to know. Other people have very brief questions. Here are Babette's:

Dear Lois,

My three questions are:

1) Have my husband and I been together in past lives?

2) I am adopted, what was the contract between me, my birth mother and my adopted mother?

3) Two of my children have said they "picked" me to be their mother, if so, when?

Sincerely,
Babette

After explaining to Babette why I do these readings, I began her session:

The Worst Natural Disaster in America

I am seeing you trying to stand up in an extremely powerful wind. At first I thought you were in a wind tunnel, but it is a hurricane. You are an adult female in Galveston, Texas. The year is 1900 and this event is in early September of 1900. There was a horrible hurricane in September that killed about—nobody was ever able to accurately count all the bodies—between 5,000 and 10,000 people. They died in the worst natural disaster that has, to date, ever hit the United States. In all my years of doing this, even though I formerly lived in Galveston, I have never seen a past life that had anything to do with that hurricane or even one that was in Galveston, so this is interesting. Your house has been blown completely away by a tornado at the time I am seeing. There are many tornadoes contained within each hurricane—sometimes hundreds. Your husband disappeared when your house blew away, and you are trying to get your two children onto a door that is afloat. You are doing that so that you are able to remain on top of the water, because it is rising. This was a Category Five storm, compared to the one that hit the East Coast this past year, dubbed Superstorm Sandy, which was a Category One—a very wet Category One—but the one in Galveston in 1900 was a Category Five, making it unimaginably worse.

I am relating this as I watch it unfold. You are holding them onto the door as best you can. The children are just five and three years old, both girls. It is a solid wood mahogany door as they had in those days, and it is tossing about violently. The wind is smashing it into things, and the girls are holding onto the edge of the door with their fingertips and you have your arms wrapped around them, holding onto them with one arm and the door with the other—rather holding onto the door with both hands and the two of them under one arm. This was an impossible situation you three were in. It was such an overwhelming storm—if you can imagine between 5,000 and 10,000 adults, including big, strong men, died that night. There was no way you could save your little girls; in fact, it was nothing short of a miracle that you survived. Some big piece of a tree limb came flying through the air and clunked you on the head, and you did not know what happened after that. But you did know that you never saw your little girls again, and you blamed yourself for that.

Waking up the next day on top of a pile of debris, you initially had no idea where you were. Some people survived and some did not. Your Guides had a reason for your survival. Your intent in that lifetime was to start an orphanage, and the storm was the catalyst that was supposed to get you started. In heavy shock the morning following the storm, everyone was looking for family members and friends or anyone alive at all. The entire island of Galveston was just like a giant debris pile, with broken slivers of wood piled dozens of feet high where houses used to be. There were bodies mixed in there, too. No one could even tell where the streets were, due to the fallen trees mixed in with that massive debris field which used to be houses and carriages and people and horses.

Ultimately, the rescuers and those who survived piled the bodies they could find onto barges, then set them on fire, sending them out into the ocean, Viking-style. There were too many bodies to bury. Many had been swept out to sea during the storm, as well. Your response, though, was that you were blaming yourself for letting go of your girls even though you were knocked unconscious. It was survivor's guilt. Nobody knew what to call it in those days, though. You went into a very deep depression and ended up in bed, being cared for by family members. To make matters worse, it took a month before anyone could identify any of your family members because you were almost psychotic with grief, as you might well imagine.

Mental healthcare was not good in those days, and it took about a year for you to even come up for air, so to speak. At that point you decided you would personally take in children who had been orphaned by the storm. This was not what your Soul had hoped would be the lesson or outcome of the storm. The plan had been that you would open an orphanage that could care for far more children, with that institution continuing to function long after your own life span.

So, in that lifetime, instead of starting an orphanage, you took in a few orphans, swearing you would never have another child again as long as you lived. That was something that, by the time you were an old woman, fortunately changed for you. You found yourself taking care of great nephews and great nieces, having moved in with family in a small town in central Louisiana. You began to get over the loss by taking care of your great nephews and great nieces, so that vow of never having a child ever again did not carry forth into your next lifetimes. However, you were so traumatized that it created certain issues that did need to be worked out in later lifetimes. One of those would be that you wanted to experience what it would be like as an orphan, which is the flip side of having taken care of orphans. I do not know if I am wording this in a way that makes sense to you, but sometimes you will experience one side of an issue and sometimes you will experience a different facet of the issue for balance.

In this current lifetime, you chose to come back to experience what it would be like to be adopted and cared for by someone who is not your biological mother, as part of your healing from this past life of losing your girls. Your biological mother in this lifetime had her own lessons that she got from having a baby and giving that baby up for adoption. That is not in our purview here; we do not have permission to open her Akashic Records, but know that she agreed to do this for her own reasons. She has had other lifetimes with you. She was okay with agreeing to give you birth and adopting you out. At the Soul level, she did this as a favor for you—she gave you your life, gave you a body—but the adoptive mother was always supposed to be your mother. She just was not to be your physical mother because of the lessons the two of you would learn from that type of relationship. She had her own lessons, as well, to learn from being an adoptive parent. That is another of the reasons why you experienced adoption in this current lifetime.

Slave Owner

I am seeing you as a female on horseback. This is in the late 1700s in far South America. You are the wife of some important Spanish official—like a governor of a state or something like that. Spain had a lot of colonies at that time in the Americas. You are riding because you are the mistress of this large estate. It seems you have a lot of slaves who are Indians; these are the native people who have been enslaved by the Spaniards. You are not a particularly compassionate slave owner, either. Growing up with a lot of money in Spain, you had a sense of entitlement and the feeling that the Spaniards were superior to the indigenous people. You were rather cruel to them in this lifetime.

One day you were out riding in a mountainous area, with cliffs, caves, and gorges—rugged country—and you saw something in the distance and decided it must have been a runaway slave. It might have just been a vision of some sort…Oh! Now I see. That was what it was. You saw some mirage or vision, and you were chasing after it quite fast when your horse tripped. Falling off the horse, you were injured badly and lost consciousness.

Your injuries were severe. A few of the local indigenous people who were free, not slaves, found you there, a good distance away from the house. They carried you to their healer, a medicine man, who took you inside the cave where he both lived and did his healing ceremonies. He immediately began doing a healing ritual for you. Waking up in the middle of it, you were in a lot of pain. The thought of resisting it all crossed your mind, but you thought, "There's no way I can get up and get out of here by myself. Let's see what is going to happen." You had awfully serious injuries, especially around one particular broken leg, a damaged foot and ankle, and massive bruising all over your body. Had the locals not rescued you and taken you to their healer, you would surely have died out there, and you knew that.

While he worked on you, this healer gave you a treatment using a dose of a teacher plant, a healing plant similar to peyote called San Pedro. When people ingest teacher plants, they have spiritual visions. The plants allow people to commune with spirits by seeing into different densities or dimensions. These plants open one's vision to things which are always present, but which normally cannot be seen. Because of the teacher plant, you had a very profound physical, emotional and spiritual healing experience.

A couple of days later, they returned you to your home area when they felt you were stable enough. They took you as far as they safely could. They dared not come too close to your home, knowing they faced capture because the Spaniards were in the habit of seizing them and turning them into slaves. The indigenous people had a go-between, someone at whose house they knew they could safely leave you. And so, carried back on a stretcher pulled behind your own horse, you were brought to safety. This was a deep and profoundly moving experience for you; your whole attitude toward the indigenous people changed.

From that point forward you continued to tell everybody, "Hey, this is not right. . .being mean and enslaving these people. They had a culture of their own when we got here. They are kind and good."

People thought you had lost your mind defending these "savages." They had no idea what had happened to you out there. They knew you were gone a couple of days and came back patched up. But the words you spoke were heresy—abolish slavery, and so on. Your own people began to ostracize you and treat you like you were, well, a crazy person, or a witch or something. It got so bad finally that you just packed up what you decided you needed most—like your jewels and things like that, small, portable important things of intrinsic value. You took your horse, plus a couple of extras, and went to live with the indigenous people. Finding that shaman was easy because you actually remembered how to get there. Immediately, you indicated to him that you wanted to help him in his work. He easily allowed that because he knew, before you ever got there the first time when you were injured, that you were coming and that you were going to leave and return. Spirit had told him his apprentice would be a white woman who would come, leave, and return. Eventually you were trained as a shaman yourself, and as an older woman you went back into white civilization and spread the word and the healing.

Your life was fulfilled by acting as a bridge; one of the very first bridges between those two cultures. This was a very powerful thing you did, and you needed to know about this accomplishment. You also needed to know that you have practiced shamanism before. You did not have children in that lifetime; it was not part of the plan. That is all you need to know about that lifetime. *[pause]* By the way, that Shaman who taught you is your husband in this lifetime.

Pleiadian Visitors

I am seeing you on a spacecraft. You are a man and coming to Earth to visit. This is a very long time ago—maybe a couple hundred thousand years ago—and you have come here to teach. You are actually teaching building techniques to the people here on Earth, and you are also here to share DNA. You are one of the many people from other star systems who have come to Earth periodically to work with human beings in terms of teaching and/or sharing their DNA. You were doing both. You helped the people of Earth evolve more quickly by sharing the more evolved DNA that came from your race. You were not alone; there were other people, but you were the leader of a Pleiadian group that came here.

You interacted in a very helpful and healthy manner with the people of the earth. You did not incur karma; that is not how you ended up here. You came here of your own free will to experience spiritual growth through the Earth School. Your guides want you to know that you have had a lot of lifetimes in the Pleiades.

Did My Children Choose Me?

This was one of your three questions. I am being told to tell you yes, your children picked you before they were born—picked you as their mother. Everyone does that: they do it in the planning stages before birth, just as we plan our lessons before we incarnate each time. We look at several different possible lives, we review different bodies that we could inhabit, and we study the parents and their circumstances and how they can help us achieve our goals. Then we choose the situation we think will benefit us the most—including the parents with whom we most want to be.

Aquatic Farming

What I am seeing, and I have not seen this before, is a farming technique I never knew existed. It is aquatic farming; this is a long time ago, maybe back around Atlantis, or even earlier. You have enormous tanks—somewhat like fish tanks. Part of each tank is under water and part of it is up on land. The part that is on land is made of glass. The part in the water is some sort of mesh so the ocean water can flow through there freely, bringing more nutrients to the plants. What you are growing is a lot like what we call duck weed, which grows in aquariums, long skinny stuff that moves in a lovely, lyrical way when the water currents and waves move around it. The plants undulate and wave softly in the water.

It is grown for several reasons. There are medicinal uses—in other words, if you prepare it in a certain way, it is a medicine. These are vast tanks—they are as huge as fields on land would be. You also can pull the plants out. They are processed on the land inside the glass part of the tank. This is a big operation and you have many employees; it is definitely a business you are running. The process is to pull the seaweed out and dry it. Right before it gets really dry, you roll it into little tubes and twist it so that it is like a long strand of something that can then be woven into pieces, like baskets or furniture. So it has many purposes.

I am wondering why I am seeing this. I am going to pause until I find out why they are showing it to me.

They are saying that because you have this experience, you can apply it again. Now, I do not know which part of the experience—maybe multiple parts. One might be running a business. You had a lot of employees to help you with that venture, so you can manage people. Another might be if you are interested in hydroponic or any form of gardening, know that you would be really good at it. It would be easy for you whether you just did it for pleasure or for profit. Also, if you do not already have fish tanks in your home, they might very likely have an extremely beneficial de-stressing effect on you, because that was a very peaceful lifetime, working with aquatic plants. As a business owner, you did a lot of good for people in the world. It was a very positive lifetime. You not only made medicines that healed people—because if you think about it, seaweed has iodine and all kinds of good nutrients—but you also created jobs for hundreds of people. You made affordable furniture so that lots of people could have nice things at a good price. So, for some reason your Guides want you to know about that because there are some bits and parts of that you can reuse if you want to—you can access those skills.

I am going to pause the recording and see if there is another lifetime.

I do not know if you believe in fairies or not, but you went through a period of time where you were not incarnating as a human, and you became a fairy. In that capacity, you could appear and disappear at will and you acted as a Spirit Guide to a lot of people at that time. The Guardians of the Records definitely want you to know about that. They also want you to do a little research on Spirit Guides and fairies.

This completes your past life reading. Thank you.

Babette sent the following email after the reading:

> *Dear Lois,*
>
> *I listened to the reading twice last night...many ah-hah moments!! Am I supposed to practice shamanism in this lifetime? I woke up this morning and there were blue spots all over my husband's face—I could see them, but knew they were only a "vision." It was very exciting!*
>
> *And the orphanage! I never mentioned this to you before, but I have been compelled to open an orphanage in Haiti for quite a few years. Is that something I am supposed to do in this lifetime?*

You had also stated I was a fairy and a spiritual guide before. Can you tell me anything else about that?

Thank you Lois!! You have helped me immensely! I have always known there was more to life than what we know. This journey of my awakening has been a long time coming. I have only recently begun to explore. Thank you again!!!

Babette

Here is my response:

Dear Babette,

Certainly you can study or practice shamanism in this lifetime if you wish. There is no requirement to do so, though. If you feel compelled to do something like opening the orphanage in Haiti, that kind of sense of being compelled is almost always a "spiritual calling." I would do it if I were you.

I cannot tell you more about fairies or spiritual guides—the Guides and Guardians of the Records already told me what I was supposed to relate. I suggest you study up on them if this is an interesting topic to you. That is what the Guides asked you to do.

I hope this reading will be a springboard to greater and deeper discoveries for you.

Blessings,
Lois

Past Life and Life Mission Reading
Dirk Richardson - March 8, 2012

Here is Dirk's email to me, giving me the photo and information that I needed to do his past life reading:

Hi Lois,

My name is Dirk Richardson. Please find attached my photo. I live in Wooten, British Columbia, Canada.

Here are the questions for my session:

1. Last year I decided to go back to school to pursue a new career path and would like some guidance on this new direction and if/how it relates to my purpose for this life.

2. I often feel a sense of sadness and disappointment that has been with me since I can remember. As this feeling likely originated in a past life, I am asking to know the origins of it and any guidance on how to let go of it and move on.

3. I was born with a muscle problem that I have never received a diagnosis for, and as I have gotten older it has increasingly prevented me from participating in some of the things I love to do in life, such as run, bike, and play tennis. Is there anything you can tell me that would help me understand the meaning of this in the context of my past lives, and if I can heal my muscles in this life so I can enjoy more physical activity?

I would also like to get the life purpose/mission reading, please

Thanks!
Dirk

Here is Dirk's reading. Frequently, I see things in peoples' past lives that shock me, and this first lifetime is one of those for sure.

Ancient British Coven

I am seeing you as a female in the 1840s in Great Britain, where you were a practicing "white witch," meaning you practiced magic only in order to do good works in the world. Part of a very large and powerful coven, you were practicing in secret for the most part. This organization was not known about publically. Having existed from about 1100 CE, this was a coven that actually went all the way back to the ancient Druids in continuous operation. Because of this, there was an extraordinarily strong and powerful morphogenetic field around this group of witches. Unfortunately, there had been off and on witch wars between your group and a similar group.

You were a prominent person in this coven. The identities of the members were kept secret from everyone outside the group. However, the other group had a fairly good idea of who you all were, and you also had a good idea who they were. One of the reasons you tried to keep your identities secret had to do with public perception of witchcraft at the time, and the other was that you all were participating in a group consciousness project to steer the future of the British Empire. The two groups were in disagreement about what direction the Empire should take, so you were cancelling out each other's efforts to a significant degree. Both groups had the best interests of both the world and the British Empire at heart, but very different ideas about what actions should be taken in order to make the world a better place.

In frustration at the blockage of their efforts to affect change in the world, the opposing group decided that, rather than come up with more potent spells to influence the political leaders, they needed to cast "interference" spells on the members of your team. This was clearly against all the rules. The spells they cast upon the members of your coven were designed to make you feel unwell, so that you could no longer continue to compete with them to direct the course of events. You were one of the people attacked. A strong version of that spell was put on you to make you tired, listless, and weak, with muscle aches and pains, so that you would just have to rest most of the time. Hence, you did not have any energy to get things done. No one ever did figure out what was wrong. No one in your coven dreamed for a moment that the others would attack the people in your coven, because that was just strictly forbidden. It was against all the moral and ethical rules of the white magic you all had vowed to practice. All of you were under the impression that if you did something like that, it would backfire on the perpetrator, and it actually did backfire on them, but you never knew of it.

We cannot concern ourselves with their problems, however. What we must focus on is that there is still there a certain element of that spell affecting you in this current lifetime.

Lois' Notes: *At that point, I paused to ask the Guardians some silent questions for the purpose of clarification, and there were specific instructions from them for Dirk. He was asked to get certain kinds of energy medicine healing sessions which could remove this kind of energetic implant we were calling a "spell." He was also told to break all vows he had made in past lives. He was told to research "vow breaks," techniques for which can be found all over the Internet, including all Wiccan vows, white witch vows, vows to control political outcomes, and so on—all his past life vows. He did not need Wiccan vows, since he no longer practiced that in this lifetime. I relayed that information to him. Then I continued with the reading.*

You spent the rest of that lifetime laid up, sick in bed. Your brain was working just fine, but you were too exhausted to participate in group meetings or do anything that could help the group work. There are things that you are to take away from this past life, aside from what has already been stated. Another thing to take away is that it is not only unnecessary but improper to attempt to use magic or willpower to manipulate the outcomes of events involving others. The reason for this is because everyone has their own Higher Self, Spirit Guides, life mission and free will. Because of that, to use any kind of group consciousness to manipulate others is wrong and damaging—you do not know what their life mission is, after all. You have seen the wrongness of this from someone doing that to you personally. The lesson is about why it is not okay to get together in a group and manipulate others (or even to do that one-on-one), because it absolutely is possible to use consciousness to manipulate people, and one way you can use your consciousness is through a magical spell. It is wrong to manipulate people to harm them or even to heal them without the person's permission, no matter how well-meaning you are. Since they did not adhere to the rules of the craft, they had their own karmic issues to balance as a result. At a soul level they are not happy they did this. However, for you, it was a great lesson. Now all you need to do is clean up the residue by following the instructions given. After you complete that, your muscles should begin to function properly again.

I am going on to the next life....

Negligent Nanny and the Checkout Point

I am seeing you as a very happy little girl skipping along on the sidewalk. Your nanny is behind—this is in France in the 1700s. Skipping along, having a great time, you are being given too long a leash for such a little girl in those days. Your nanny is busy flirting with a footman, keeping an eye on you but not standing as close to you as she reasonably should. There are very tall residential buildings all around. Someone is on the roof and they drop a very large stone; it has an appearance like masonry.

This is done in an attempt to assassinate a public figure who is also walking down the street. But something happens and a horse pulling a carriage comes by too fast and splashes water upon the promenade, people scurry every which way and, confused, you dart underneath that large stone after it begins to drop.

The public official was not hit, but you were killed instantly. At the time your Soul said, "Oh my God! Something horrible can come out of the blue and destroy a person even when they are feeling happy and bouncy." At the moment of impact, you were just bubbling over with joy, you were so full of happiness and the joy of living. You were only about five or six years old and were just having the greatest time.

Excited that you had freedom that no other child you knew had, since your nanny let you walk about a half block in front of her, you were so happy, and then zap! You were dead. So in the moment of death, your Soul is running through all these, "Oh, my God. It is not safe to be joyful, it is not safe to be happy and skip down the street, it is not safe to get very far from the people who take care of you and protect you."

Thoughts, and especially conclusions, drawn at the moment of death make a profound imprint on the Soul. This was an incorrect conclusion, of course. It was just not logical. From a worldly standpoint, this was just an accident. But from a Soul level standpoint, it was not. It was a checkout point. In the planning stages prior to incarnating we all create checkout points so that if something severe—a lesson, a growth experience—is coming our way and the Soul feels the personality is not ready and damage to the Soul would be too great, the Soul can leave that lifetime. This might happen if the personality has not developed to the point that it was hoped that the personality would—or if the personality is not ready to handle this big lesson that has been planned. The Soul might also check out if the personality does not have the support system in place that was supposed to be there to help them through that experience or that lesson. So in this particular case, that was what was going to happen had you not been hit by the stone and killed.

The nanny was allowing you to get too far out in front of her, rather than doing her duty, which was to stay close enough to protect you. There was a kidnapping which was about to occur, and the nanny was supposed to be taken right alongside you, because she was there close by to protect you. But because she was having this dalliance with the family's footman, she was not doing what she had agreed to do prior to that incarnation, which was to remain close to you and be kidnapped with you, lending her support through this experience. Without her, you then would not have learned what you had planned to learn. There was no stopping the kidnapping, which would have been too horrific for words and very damaging to you on a Soul level were you taken alone. For that reason, the Soul said, "Well, we are going to have to take her out, as we cannot stop the kidnapping."

Knowing about that should feel like an incredible relief. That is why there is this resistance to letting all the stops out and feeling happy and joyful—at least this is one thing from the past that feeds into that. Of course, the reality is that you were just being saved further trauma, so it seems pretty self-evident that joyfulness was not a causative factor—it had nothing to do with the demise of the child. Yet it was imprinted on the Soul due to "last minute thoughts/beliefs."

I am going to pause the recording while I wait for the next lifetime to show up.

Test Pilot

I am seeing you piloting— this is the 1950s in the United States—and you are an Air Force test pilot flying a jet attempting to break the sound barrier. You are having this intense rush—there is something, I guess it is adrenaline, this intense rush you get from doing the work that is addictive, actually, and causes people to push the envelope to get ever-greater highs. The long and short of it is that you tried to get this jet to do something it could not, but you did not know it could not, and in fact no one knew it could not. You were testing to see what it could do, and you did not pull back when common sense told you to pull back. The error was because of the intense, ecstatic feelings that you got from being a test pilot. The plane just sort of exploded; it seems to have blown apart into pieces, and you did not see it coming. You were at such a high altitude that your body seems to have exploded and of course, in the moment of death, the Soul again goes, "Whoops! Here is another instance of how it's not safe to feel fantastic." Of course, they never recovered a lot of those pilots' bodies. They were just scattered everywhere in small bits and pieces, and this was the case for you. Look at what you could do. Wow! You were at the top of the heap in a very competitive arena, and you were married with two children, as a matter of fact.

Apparently, they lost…it looks like a lot more pilots were killed trying to break the sound barrier than survived. I am hearing…it is hard with names…Wayne or Duane, Damon? I do not know if that was his name or the town he was over when the accident happened, but anyway that is what I am hearing…so this of course helps explain your decision to stay stuck in sadness maybe? Perhaps to avoid being crushed when you are feeling joyous? This was a Soul level decision and not a conscious decision.

Spiritual Ecstasy

I am seeing you in a caravan of camels in the desert and I am hearing that Sting song…"I dream of rain," http://www.songlyrics.com/sting/desert-rose-lyrics/ "I dream of rain, he-le, he-le, I dream of God who's in the desert." You were extremely happy in that lifetime, very joyful. It was an all-pervasive thing. You were some sort of, like an Imam…you were very spiritually oriented and because of that—ahh! You were a Sufi and you danced all the time, you know the swirling dances which, I am not quite sure how they do it, but they experience extreme states of ecstasy and bliss. Well, it is like a shamanic ecstasy, is what I'm hearing. And you loved that Arabic music, which is why I probably heard Sting singing that Arabic song, "Desert Rose," which he recorded with Cheb Mami.

You need to know about this because you have past lives—not just this one, but others as well—in which you are deeply and profoundly spiritual. Actually, that is where your bliss lies. If you wish to experience bliss, then that is the direction you need to go. You do not mention what your new career path is, you said you went back to school to study something and I am not sure what it is. Where your true bliss lies is in some sort of spiritual practice—whether or not you have the muscle strength to do the whirling dervish thing, I do not know, or whether you want to do shamanic ecstasy states, or find a group of people who practice shamanism. They go into ecstatic states. Or see if you can find other spiritual ways to achieve ecstatic states. Drumming will take you into an ecstatic state. That is where you will find your happiness—through ecstatic pursuits.

I suggest that you might want to make a study of spiritual ecstasy and how to attain those states. It is this for which you long, whether you are consciously aware of that or not. Your Guides say to do some research on the attainment of ecstatic states.

Basketball and Pool

I am not sure why I am seeing this. I am seeing you as a basketball coach, and yet I am not seeing where or when. I am seeing you coaching boys between the ages of ten and fourteen. It might be volunteer work you are doing. I do not know if it is future or past and I am not being shown that, which is really unusual. However, I am definitely seeing you helping young men understand very subtle movements, which make a huge difference in whether or not they evade the other players who are trying to keep them from moving through to hit the basket, or reach their goals.

Apparently, you are not to be doing that for very long, but it is a very important thing, whether it was this lifetime or another lifetime or if it is even in the future. There is something about what I am seeing that is odd—I don't understand it. But they are saying that you can apply the same principles as pool or basketball to other disciplines; you are gifted at that. You can apply the same principles as shooting pool. Why are they telling me that? Shooting pool? I do not know. I am putting it out there because that is what they are showing me. Shooting pool may be literal, or it may be symbolic of molecular action for all I know, that one thing hits another thing, and that hits another thing and so on until there is an outcome that most people could not predict ahead of time, but you could. I am hearing that it is like playing chess with moving objects. I do not know—I am confused. My personality does not want to go down this road, but apparently I am supposed to be telling you this. I am hearing that you will understand it at some point if you do not right now. This is about the relationships between moving objects whether they are people or things: interrelationships.

I am going to pause the recording until I can see what comes next.

Another bit I am getting about that lifetime in the desert is to remind you that anyone who has ever reached that point spiritually—the point that they can go into near perpetual bliss—they can do it more easily again later in another lifetime.

Repairing Nets

Next I am seeing you in a fishing village somewhere, and I think it is up around where Vancouver is now, or maybe slightly north of there. You are repairing nets and everybody goes out in a group and some people catch the fish using nets to do that. Some people repair the nets and some people create the floaters that help the nets' edges stay on the surface so if somebody drops them into the water they do not get lost. You are a net repairer because of an injury sustained to your leg while hunting. You are male, older, and your injury makes it impossible for you to go fishing in the boats. It looks like a pretty bad break just above the left knee. So you have that leg straight out in front of you all the time, even when you are sitting, and that makes it impossible for you to sit in a canoe.

Besides doing repairs, you are also teaching children how to repair nets in case anything ever happens to you. This new technique you have created to repair nets is really fast and strong. You enjoyed the heck out of teaching kids. You loved the basketball coaching, and you loved teaching the kids to repair the nets. You delighted in teaching children, and you have done that in many lifetimes. It brings a lot of joy, peace and satisfaction to you. That is all I am being shown on that lifetime. Ah, here is the point. You got hurt and you could not do the "manly" things anymore, and at first it really got you down, but you adjusted. The way that you adjusted was very healthy. You decided that there were other ways you could contribute to the welfare of the community and one of those ways was teaching. Even better, it was something that you actually invented—a new way of repairing nets. The technique was highly effective. It was fast and efficient to do, and the nets were far stronger when you finished with them. Passing that on to the children, they in turn passed it on to their children. It also gave you a lot of pleasure because kids are so much fun—seeing the world through their eyes is incomparable fun. The Guides say that you need to know about that experience of successfully adjusting after losing physical prowess.

Okay. That is all for the past lives. Much of your life purpose is implied through the past lives. The life mission segment of the reading is to cover anything that would be useful for you to know that is not implied in the past lives.

Life Mission

The first thing I am getting is that you are on track with making a career change. The reason for that is that you came into this lifetime to experience not being able to do what you wanted to do and then finding a way to be happy with something else. In other words, you found a substitute. There is more than one way to be happy and fulfilled, giving life meaning as in that last lifetime; that was a great example. That is what you are planning to do in this lifetime and you are right on track. Whatever it is you are doing in this new career, you are finding a way to meaningfully impact the next generation and at the same time, heal your own life.

The Guardians emphasize to me you are going in the right direction, reminding me that the spiritual path is a pathless path. You cannot see where you are going until you put the next foot down. That is because we create the path as we walk it. Decisions that we make affect where that path goes, so it is important to check with your Spirit Guides and follow their advice. Part of your life purpose also is learning to check with your guides and follow what they are nudging you to do. Some people just do this naturally and automatically, but for you it is harder because you are not sure what is coming from the ego or from spirit. That is one of your challenges and one of the things you wanted to learn in this lifetime: how to discern between the two and how to follow what guidance/Higher Self wants of you.

I am also being told that there are other lifetimes that are keyed into the sense of depression that you have always felt, and there is a limit to how much can be accomplished in one past life reading. I rarely tell this to anybody, but I recommend that you get more than one past life reading. However, you must wait at least three or four months before you get your next one—if you do choose to get another—so you can fully integrate this group of past lives. I say this because there is always more, but it is especially important for you for some reason to finally dig out all the depression. However, you should be feeling better than you were within the next three or four months. Let me see what else they want you to know.

Working with or in nature and with plants is one of the things you wanted to do in this lifetime. Maybe you might have a greenhouse or a garden in the summertime when that is possible where you are up north...but you intended to commune with nature even if it is just going for short walks or sitting by a stream. That is another place where uplifting feelings can come for you—by connecting with nature. That is one of the major things you wanted to do as part of your life's mission: to learn how to connect deeply with nature and experience its restorative qualities. It is also possible to camp out and really get into the nature groove without even going very far from the car, up where you live.

I am being told you have a special relationship to clouds. Now, again, this is strange and does not make sense to me, but you have a special relationship to clouds and the more time you can spend outside looking at them, the better. I do not know if you can do this in the winter or not, but lying on your back...I am seeing you with your hands behind your head lying on your back looking at the clouds and studying them. You will get messages from what you see in the clouds. Cloud gazing is a form of scrying. Instead of looking into a crystal ball, you can look into clouds and see things. You may have realizations that hit you from out of the blue. It is like, "Oh...I now understand such and so!" just because you are looking into clouds. I am being told that is everything you need to know at this time.

Lois' Notes: About a year later I heard back from Dirk that he was studying psychology, and he intended to work with children, which seemed to fit well with his mission. He did not mention spiritual ecstasy, nature immersion or cloud scrying. Dirk also said he had not had the funds to get any energy medicine from anyone or further past life work because all his money was being spent on medical doctors, going even down from his home in Canada into the USA to work with specialists to get help with his mysterious muscle fatigue. He never mentioned the spell or getting it removed.

Periodically in doing these readings, I meet people who do not accept all my findings or follow what I hear for them from the Guides/Guardians of the Records. Of course, there is a limit to what I can do, and that limit is just to tell what I have seen and let go of what they do with the information. I have learned to respect the sovereignty of their Soul. They will get where they are going in their own good time.

Past Life Reading
Donna Canelli - March 16, 2013

Donna, a pretty woman who appeared to be in her fifties, seemed to have an unusually long, sad tale of woe resulting from what she believed to be an unfair lifetime that had been one painful situation and relationship after another, including problems with medical personnel who had failed her, one after the other, in a very long string of what she thought to be errors. She had had divorces and bankruptcies as well. Additionally, she had a horror of being alone, and implied that too many people had abandoned her one way or another. In every situation, she saw herself as a victim. Many recent years spent in a particular location seemed to her to have been worse than the rest of her life, and she felt stuck there.

Donna even said that her entire lifetime had felt like a punishment. Looking into her eyes in her photo, the energy coming from her seemed so different from that message. Her lovely eyes were not those of a tortured victim, but her words were. I was curious as to what would come up in the reading to explain this incongruity.

Spoiled Royalty

The first lifetime that I am seeing is. . .you are female. I am seeing you as a young woman. They are telling me it does not matter where or when this was other than it was a long time ago. The Guides are saying that you have worked on this issue in various lifetimes off and on, since we do not necessarily work on the same lesson in consecutive lifetimes. Yet this is a particularly important piece that you wanted to work on this time and you really arranged a lot of difficult lessons around this. You decided before you incarnated into this current life that it was really important to get this business handled. You had been putting it off for quite a few lifetimes, because this issue is so difficult for you as a Soul.

When first I see you in this lifetime you are about eight years old, and your family is similar to royalty. This little girl does not have to do anything for herself. Surrounded by servants, people who, if they displease you, will be crushed—even at eight years of age, you had been given incredible power to harm other people. If they did not do exactly what you wanted them to do, you could rain down a lot of pain on them. That is a terrible position to be put into if you are a child. You can destroy the lives of other people simply by their not saying the right thing on your whim or doing what you want them to do, whether it is possible to do or not. An only child, your parents doted on you to the point of neglect. Not teaching a child right from wrong, not teaching empathy nor how to do anything for oneself, giving the child too much power and control over others, is actually neglect, which is a form of child abuse. These two had tried for a long time before they actually had a child. Producing an heir was crucial to the entire extended family. So they unfortunately spoiled you rotten.

Sad to say, things did not change. You never had to lift a finger for yourself even into adulthood. Somebody bathed you, cleaned up after you, someone coiffed your hair every day. Somebody else helped you dress, they prepared exactly what you wanted to eat and if you changed your mind at the last minute, dozens of people would scurry around to make sure you got what you wanted. Some people in your situation would be grateful for all the help, and then some people embody the opposite extreme of gratitude. That would be someone who has a sense of entitlement and is abusive to others because they are not doing whatever is wanted done well enough, fast enough or correctly, and in that lifetime, you were at that particular far end of the continuum. Your parents did not understand how you got that way, because they were not like that—but they grew up with siblings and other children to interact with. They in effect buried their heads in the sand, hoping you would simply outgrow the unseemly behavior. But you did not. Inheriting the throne at a relatively early age, in your early thirties, you were quite unprepared for the responsibility. Your parents had suddenly fallen ill and died. Well, wait, one of them died and there was an illness of the brain…ah, I see. Your father could not function anymore, so he was kept comfortable and you took over.

Yours was a reign of terror. From the beginning you were unkind to people and lacked empathy, thinking of no one but yourself. You were as unreasonable a ruler as you were a spoiled eight-year-old child. Hundreds of thousands of people in your kingdom suffered as a result of your inability to put yourself in other people's shoes. Because of your sense of entitlement, you held the notion you were somehow vastly more special than everyone else and had the right to be horribly cruel. You did not see yourself as a leader or a person who was there to help others, but as someone who was superior. You never married because you never met the guy you thought was special enough. So you did not have children, which might have mellowed you a bit, because it can do that for people. A mother's hormones can sometimes put her in a situation where she can identify with someone else. When you finally did pass, there was great rejoicing in the kingdom. A cousin of yours took over, a younger male. He had watched you carefully and learned from your example how not to rule. He changed everything and was very kind. That person is your son in this current lifetime, by the way.

This is material you wanted to work on in your current lifetime and in your email to me, you remarked that this lifetime has felt like a punishment. Well, no lifetime is ever a punishment. It just does not work like that. This lifetime is a result of lessons that you yourself planned ahead of time to learn this very difficult lesson, which is that you are responsible for every decision you make. No one is going to fix it for you, no one can fix it for you. There is so much here. Part of the lesson is taking responsibility for your decisions, for your life, and not expecting to find someone who makes things all better for you, as with the dentist and the doctors you mentioned in your letter.

You know, continuing to believe that allopathic medicine could help you when it clearly was not...that was one of the things you wanted to learn—to take charge and do things for yourself, not wait for someone to do it for you as they had in the lifetime of royalty. It would have made more sense to say, "Okay, I had better try something different here. Perhaps I should try alternative medicine, or try going to John of God in Brazil or my local acupuncturist." You needed to take the initiative and try something other than dentists and doctors after it became obvious over the years that it was not working. Now, the fact that you are getting a past life reading—pat yourself on the back, because that is considered alternative and *out there*. It is certainly a move in the right direction.

Since you wanted to learn to empathize with other people, you planned a group or series of lessons in this current lifetime in order to learn empathy. A divorce will make us empathetic with other people—at least there lies an inherent potential for that within the experience of divorce. Bankruptcies can do the same thing. The big picture in this lifetime you wanted to reverse from that lifetime of being spoiled royalty was the idea that you could not or did not need to do anything yourself. The idea that you are being tortured because no one is fixing things for you is the stance of a victim. As a Soul planning this lifetime, you had wanted to become independent, to become the person in charge of the details of your life. The desire was to become one who does things for herself, makes her own decisions, and does not expect someone else to be there to resolve solve her problems. This also explains your fear of being alone, because if you are by yourself, you have to do everything for yourself. So we will look at other lifetimes, as there may be other dimensions to that aspect. Still, this is what you wanted to learn in this lifetime: independence and taking responsibility. But that is not a punishment. And you are not a victim. You planned these lessons before you were born—we all do.

Alien Mining Project

The next lifetime I am seeing is very interesting. I see similar things occasionally, and this happened long before our recorded history. I am seeing you as a human, but interacting a great deal with beings from other star systems who came to Earth in spacecraft, but immediately went into hiding in networks of caves. Your party entered these caves through the ocean. Their spacecraft dove smoothly down into the ocean, entering caves along the coastline where they had an intricate system of underground homes and work spaces. I am seeing human beings come in and out of there as well, who work with them. This network is off the coast of North America...located at, well, North Carolina and whatever is north of that...right in there—the northern edge of what is now North Carolina.

One of the things they are doing is mining gemstones to take back to their home world. Planet Earth is very rich in minerals, and you were one of the humans who worked with them. I am seeing you swimming out through the underwater entrance coming up to the surface to sort of, um…it is recreation. This is during nighttime, and the starlight brightly illumines the water and shore. You are out at night because no one is allowed to go swimming in the daytime. There are many humans on the surface who do not know about these alien miners or about you at all—the group of humans who work in the caves. On this particular night, while you are swimming in the clear, crisp starlight, a tiny meteorite comes streaking down through the night. You do not see it until it is almost upon you. It lands in the water next to you and is red hot when it hits the water. This is a very dramatic event, causing the water to sizzle, steam, bubble and get scalding hot all around it. Believing in omens, you take this as a sign something bad is going to happen. For that reason you are afraid for anyone to know that this occurred, that this meteorite has come. You swim back into the underwater cave and resurface inside, climbing out to go back to your quarters, trembling. You do not tell anyone about it, but you knew that should have, because you were instructed to report any and all anomalous events.

Trouble did come, and it came because you made the decision to withhold information from the beings for whom you were working. Unfortunately, that meteorite was artificially created, sent by another group of beings from another system who were preparing to attack your station. These were ancient enemies of the extra-planetary beings you were working with.

This event was taken by you as an omen rather than something that should have been reported. You thought the event was personal, that it was about you and meant something bad would happen and everyone would turn on you. In fact, the meteorite was rather like a robot spy. It was measuring, observing, and picking up on certain things, like communications from inside the cave, relaying it all back to the people who had sent the device. Later, there was a full-on assault to take over the mining operations, destroying these off-world people you were working with. At some point, the aliens you were working with realized that there was a spy mechanism somewhere nearby, and they lined all of you up and said, "If you brought anything inside from the surface please tell us. We told you never to do that. Now somebody is spying on us." Then you said, "Oh. Could it be in the water? Well, there was this thing that landed in the water, and I thought it was a falling star and a bad omen."

That is when you got into big trouble, because you had not told them as instructed if anything unusual occurred. They were able to find and disable it, but in the meantime there had been a lot of death and destruction to them as well as to your people. As a result, you were exiled for withholding information. Everyone had been told to never withhold any information about anything important that comes to the surface of the Earth and to never bring anything from the surface into the caves for that reason. They knew they might be spied upon.

You were sent to the land's surface and had to leave everyone you knew. They went on without you. You had to function on the surface of the Earth without any help from anyone. You were isolated; you lost a lot of weight. Your clothes became ragged. There were small communities on the surface of the Earth, but they were not nearly as sophisticated as your group had been. Your clothing and food needs were not taken care of as they had been in that organization under the ground.

On the surface of the Earth you knew no one, so this was a very lonely, isolated, painful time. What would have been perfect was if you had stopped wandering and looking for someone who made you feel like your former community, and instead found a way to fit in to one of the surface civilizations by adapting to your surroundings. It was important to adapt to a completely different way of life and hang in there with the same group of people until they got to know you. They could not figure out why you were so strange and different, but because you kept wandering from one village to another looking for someone like you so you could fit in, no one ever got comfortable with you. Because you were not adapting well you only lived another ten years. Another of the things you wanted to learn in that lifetime— to adapt—carried forward to this lifetime. There is also that piece of not withholding information from other people based on fear. Transparency is important.

Telling people the whole story and not just pieces of it is being trustworthy. This is an appropriate word because when you withhold bits of information that are important to other people, especially when you have a relationship with them, it makes the relationship less solid. I think there are many more things from this lifetime that are going to pop in for you later as being significant. This is part of why you feel isolated, and yet another reason why you feel so terribly afraid of being alone. One of the things you wanted to accomplish in this lifetime was to learn how to be alone and to be perfectly fine with it—content within yourself. So remembering this past life will help you heal to a place where you will get closer and closer to being content within yourself without feeling like you need somebody else to make things okay. You do not have to be afraid of being alone. We are never really alone. We have angels, Spirit Guides and other loving spirits around us all the time.

The Art of Being a Clown

I am seeing a lifetime not all that long ago...maybe about a hundred years. You are male and in that last lifetime by the way, you were a female. I am not sure whether I said that or not. You are a circus clown who ran away from home because it was an abusive environment. When you were fourteen years old, you joined a circus. It started out that you were cleaning monkey cages, and then you worked your way up to cleaning up after elephants. Eventually a much older man—old enough to be your grandfather—took you under his wing and taught you the art of being a clown. When you were in your clown costume was the only time you were really happy. It was a way of hiding from people. No one could see your true face, because it was painted. It was easy to act goofy and make people laugh. When you were out of costume, you were very isolated. You never got close to anyone because your childhood was so...it was very cold and isolating. Nobody was ever close or affectionate with you. What you had hoped to do in that lifetime was to turn that around, to open up to people, be loving and warm and eventually have your own family to form real closeness. In a way, you did that in the circus in that you had a group of people you traveled with, but you never really opened up to anyone, though others tried to reach you. Very much a loner, you stayed in your own gypsy wagon when not working.

You got pneumonia in your early forties and died because your Soul recognized that you were just not getting the lessons, and were stuck in a pattern. Again, you were not adapting to a new environment. I am not sure what else you will get from being a circus clown and traveling in a gypsy wagon, but some of that will pop in later, I am sure, or maybe you have already realized it. Much of this is revealed over time to the client, and I am not privy to it unless they share it with me.

Happiness as a Bird-Breeder!

Now I am seeing a lifetime in which you are married to a gentle and quiet man. You had two children. It seems that they are school-aged at the point I am seeing. You live far out in the countryside in an almost tropical...I guess it was a subtropical region. It gets cool in winter but never freezes.

You had hundreds of birds in your care. It appears to me as if you were breeding them, but for the most part they were not in cages. Well, the doves were in cages, but you let them out from time to time. You collected their eggs. Doves were used like chickens—their eggs were collected. You had a huge hummingbird area with acres of open pasture, with a profusion of flowers in the pasture. There were different flowers for different times of the year for the hummingbirds to feed on and pollinate. There were blooming, climbing vines in the trees around the pasture. There were certain areas for certain types of birds. This was what you did for a living: breed and take care of birds, and occasionally you sold a few birds for other people to keep as pets. You taught them how to keep birds around, but not in cages: how to feed them and nurture them. You had information we do not have. You knew what to do so the birds would stick around, and you did not have to clip their wings to keep them there. They were beautifully-colored birds, one that especially gets my attention is purple and red, with a very long tail and graceful movements when flying.

There were all types of tame birds around. I think you did something to keep the predator birds away; there do not seem to be any. This is a very happy, peaceful lifetime and the Guardians wanted you to know about this because you have been hearing some really rough things, some hard things to listen to, and they want you to know that your lifetimes have not all been harsh or difficult. They wanted you to know that there have been some of what we call *vacation lifetimes,* where we just get to enjoy life. This was one of yours.

Sometimes we take on a lifetime that is just relaxing and pleasant so we do not get to the point that we are saying, "Oh, no, no, I cannot go back to Earth School again. It is so hard." Because it is not always hard and there are ways to see the beauty in life no matter what is occurring. One way to do this is to focus on being in the moment…not worried about tomorrow or feeling sorry about yesterday. An easy way to do that is to focus on nature. Go for a walk in the park, or in your yard if you are lucky enough to have one, and watch the birds. Gaze upon bugs crawling on leaves; lie on the ground and look at the clouds; walk barefoot and make contact with the Earth; study carefully the dewdrops on leaves...if you can, just be in the moment without thoughts about the future or the past. This is how we can experience the beauty of life in every moment. This is something really important that you knew how to do in that lifetime as a Bird Breeder, as we will call her. She was also an animal communicator. She could talk telepathically with the birds. This is something that would help you in this lifetime, to focus on being in the moment, being joyous!

Lois' Notes: Soon after the reading, I heard from Donna. She thanked me for the reading, said that the first one was a bit hard to hear at first, but that she was processing it well. I wrote to her the following:

> *Donna,*
>
> *Regarding the Royal Lifetime: Most totally unsupervised eight-year-olds have the capacity to be little tyrants or worse— just re-read "Lord of the Flies." Parental guidance or caretakers with the authority to correct the child were missing for you in that lifetime. As you grew older, you had planned to realize on your own, by watching effects of your actions on others, that you needed to make changes. You wanted a chance to develop empathy for others. But it did not occur. It was just one lesson the Soul did not get in one lifetime. Don't blow it out of proportion. Again, no judgment is necessary here— the Guardians and Guides do not judge us. We do not need to judge ourselves, either.*

Compassion and forgiveness for self are also important attributes to develop—for all of us. I hope you will consider this as you work through the lifetimes over the next few months.

Loving Blessings,
Lois

<u>Lois' Notes:</u> *Quite surprisingly, six months later when I asked if I could use her reading in this book, Donna reported she was still upset about that first past life of the spoiled child, and that it had done her no good at all, so she did not see how it could do anyone else any good, either. It seemed she was implying the reading had somehow harmed her.*

I was stunned and initially upset. The last I heard she was doing fine and processing the reading. I wanted to use her reading in the book because it beautifully illustrated what is called "victim consciousness," which I so often see people struggling with. It is a common thread that runs through many people's lives. And I now know that people can heal by reading about the lifetimes of others with similar issues. For that reason I wanted to include this reading in the book—to offer healing to others with victim consciousness issues.

Because I felt badly about her reaction to the reading, I wrote her again, underscoring that we are actors on a stage who have forgotten that we are actors. We come to learn so we can evolve as Souls. I was okay with not using her story in the book. I let go of it. A while later she wrote back. To my surprise, she gave me permission to use her reading in the book.

A couple of days later, I had to laugh at myself. It hit me that after many years of studying and applying Transactional Analysis, I had again been briefly sucked into the triangular "victim/rescuer/perpetrator" game myself. I rushed in to rescue her when she felt like the "victim" of my reading.

If the reader takes away one thing from this case, I hope it will be that we often choose to be a victim when there is another choice. I am not talking about victims of violence here, but rather those who often choose to adopt the posture of the victim in interpersonal interactions. This is a game we are not aware we are playing in which we become the victim so someone will rescue us. Then when they do not rescue correctly, we treat them as a perpetrator—it is a triangle in which you are always one of the three if you play the part of any one of them: victim, rescuer or perpetrator. This is an inadequate summary of a complex study, but it is not within the scope of this book to go into this in great detail. Transactional Analysis is a fascinating yet complicated theory, and it definitely bears looking into for those who find themselves either frequently rescuing others or feeling like victims.

Past Life and Life Mission Reading

Hank Benson - February 23, 2012

Hank Benson requested a past life reading and life mission. I had no information about him except for his queries. His three questions were:

1. *What can you share with me about the purpose of my relationship with Darrell Wilson?*
2. *What can you share with me about the purpose of my relationship with Christopher English?*
3. *Is working professionally counseling clients with astrology and Life Patterning a part of my progressive evolutionary growth? Everything else is gravy!*

The questions were short and sweet, giving no clues about the two men he asked about. But Hank was extremely easy to read; his spirit was open and trusting. The photograph of himself he sent made it easy to connect. And this is significant: there were no photos of Darrell or Christopher. Here is Hank's reading:

Lovers in the Dunes

I am seeing you as a camel trainer. Oh my goodness! You were with Lawrence of Arabia. I do not know what his real name was, and I do not remember the whole story, but I do know they made a movie about it. He was a real person. That is who you are with. You are Caucasian and you look a lot like you do now. I am seeing you in your mid-thirties, and you are operating in the background. You are acting as support, a person who does supportive work.

No, wait, you are not completely Caucasian—you are half-Arabic. You have lighter-colored hair and sort of olive skin and greenish brownish, not true brown eyes; they have a greenish quality to them. You have very striking eyes with long eyelashes. The work you are doing...it has to do with helping camels to be okay with being in battle somehow. How you do that I do not know, but it is what…what I am seeing is almost a circus-like atmosphere, working with the animals in a group, under a tent. So you are not working with one camel at a time, but groups of them, to teach them how to work in a group because apparently they tend not to do that so well—not until they are trained.

I am seeing that your mother was an Englishwoman but your father was Arabic, and you grew up there, so you spoke both languages. I think you fell very much in love with Lawrence. There was a love affair; you were absolutely head over heels with this man, yet I think he was bisexual. It does not appear to me that he was open about this with anybody. You know, being gay was seriously not cool in that culture at that time. So here you were just deeply, profoundly in love with the man, and he did not acknowledge you in public.

The long and the short of it is that you went along in some battle-type situations as a support person, and you ended up putting yourself in harm's way to protect someone else. I do not think it was Lawrence, but someone you did not really need to put yourself in harm's way to protect. It was not your job, but you did it because on a subconscious level you did not want to live anymore. This was because you knew you could never be with this man in the way that you wanted to be. I get that this is Darrell in this lifetime—he was Lawrence of Arabia or part of the life stream as some people put it, part of the life stream of Lawrence of Arabia. The moral of this story, Hank, is that one must learn how to let go, and one must learn to go ahead and grieve their losses and move on. Whether you are learning that with Darrell in this lifetime, whether you have already learned it with him, or whether it is a lesson you are learning with somebody else is not clear. But that is one of your major lessons: knowing when to cut your losses and move on and not grieve yourself to death. It was a quick death. You did not suffer. I believe it was a sword through the upper left chest, not through the heart but above it. A major artery was severed and you died quickly from exsanguination.

In that lifetime after you met Lawrence, you did not allow yourself joy because you could not have the one thing you wanted the most. And that is the lesson in this current lifetime. Sometimes you—I am hearing the song, "You can't always get what you want, but if you try sometime, you just might find, you get what you need." That lesson, the distinction between what you want and what you need to be happy, that is a big one for you. Maybe you have already learned it, but you needed to know about that, and later I think it will be clearer to you why. This is important for you, because we get those lessons again and again until we deeply understand this on a Soul level. Of course, you were recognized when you went to the spirit world as a hero for putting yourself in harm's way to save another, and that person was saved. The reason for doing it, though, that was the object of the lesson you came back to learn this time. Why did you put yourself in harm's way? Because you did not want to live because you could not have somebody you loved? Or was it because you were doing it to save another person, because it was an act of pure heroism? The line was blurred there because of the undercurrent of, "I do not want to live." It was not treated in the afterlife as a suicide, though.

Monastery Above the Clouds

Now I am zipping through space above the earth, moving through clouds. Ah! That is because I am going to a monastery above the clouds, above the tree line in what is now Bhutan. There I see that you are a woman masquerading as a male so that you can be a monk. This is because you are in hiding, and there is another woman there with you. The two of you have previously been prostitutes, and you were best friends since early childhood. You decided you were going to completely change your lives, and I am hearing that it was like a waking daydream. You thought, "What if we did something different? What if we did this? What if we did that?"

The history is that you two grew up next door to each other in a poor neighborhood, and you decided at some point that you needed to be able to support yourselves, because no one was marrying young women who. . .nobody but poor men wanted to marry women from your neighborhood, and neither of you wanted to live like that.

You did not want to live with your noses to the grindstone, a life of nothing but drudgery, with nothing pretty to wear—like you saw the women around you living. You decided to go to another place. . .you were in a small town or suburb or something so you went to the big city and the two of you worked as courtesans because you were smart, and you were highly adaptive, like chameleons. Let us put it this way. You knew how to watch other people, mimic them, and fit in.

However, the two of you were present at a private party of some sort and this was not in Bhutan, but in a neighboring country. This was about 500-600 years ago. You were at a party in which some very prominent man committed a murder, and the two of you saw it and knew that you better "get the hell out of Dodge," so you ran away. Then you changed into a different kind of costume like peasant girls wear and crossed the border to escape the powerful man's reach. Somewhere along the way you both decided to dress like men, as you realized you were being tracked. You both were still pretty young, not ready to die, and finally you realized that there was a very safe place to go—and that would be to volunteer to be a monk in a monastery.

The plan was hatched on the fly, so to speak. So dressed like men, you shaved your heads and went to a monastery claiming to be brothers. You asked them if they would please take you in and let you become monks. They decided to accept you, and so you became monks. Talk about bobbing and weaving! Apparently nobody ever thought to check and see if you were really men.

The two of you stayed for a really long time...this is Christopher by the way...like a sister to you, at least in that lifetime. The two of you became monks and honestly, you realized later that was where you were supposed to be all along and why the whole prostitution and witnessing the murder had happened at all—you two put yourselves in what we would now call "witness protection" actually, in the monastery. You liked it there, and stayed and became "old men" together, because by then you did not care if you ever had sex again. You'd had your fill, both of you. You enjoyed the company of men, but this way you did not have to be sexual at all. It did not bother either of you to live like men, so you became seriously involved in this and became very nearly enlightened. You meditated all the time and did regular monks' duties of cooking and cleaning and milking the yaks or whatever else you were asked to do.

That life is something you need to know about because of how flexible the two of you were in that lifetime. Flexible, adaptive, creative, able to reinvent yourselves—and you need to know this because you can still do it. It is also why you are so good at helping other people do it.

Ultimately, even though it was a very weird path, you wound up where you were supposed to be because they did not offer anything like that for women—not at the level that you guys were able to do it—that level of serious spiritual studies…they taught the men things they did not teach the women. It was not until the one who is now Christopher passed and they prepared the body for burial that they found out he was a woman. Then they looked at you and said, "Are you a woman too?" You said, "Yes, I am. Do you want me to go into exile?" They said, "No, we are just going to keep your secret because we do not want to look foolish." They never really told anybody, only the monks who prepared each of you for burial and the head of the monastery ever knew. They kept the secret because they thought it would besmirch the reputation of the monastery. It was quite an accomplishment and one you need to know about. I am going to pause until I see the next lifetime show up.

War and Orphans

Next, I am seeing you as a soldier in a WWII battalion. The war is ending and it is not safe for former soldiers, and you are in…I am not sure what the country I am seeing is…is it Austria perhaps? It is across the Alps from Italy. It is wintertime. You are barefoot and dressed like a woman to avoid detection as a soldier. You are good at this disguise stuff, Hank! You are hiking across the mountains and when people ask you what you are doing, you are telling them that you are on a pilgrimage, a religious pilgrimage.

Nobody bothers you because you do not make a real pretty woman in that lifetime. Your face is a tad rugged-looking. There comes a point where you just cannot walk any farther and you see a cave. You must bend over to crawl in, and as you get inside and your eyes start to adjust to the darkness you see a group of children. The eldest is about ten or twelve and they are further back in the cave trying to hide from you. There are still some embers from the fire they built so you went back toward them…they were terrified because they did not know what you were going to do with them. There were five of them and all from the same family, cousins. Some were brothers and sisters. They had been hiding out there for months and months.

They did not know the war was over. Talk about hungry. Lord have mercy, they were hungry. They were waiting for their parents to come and get them, and what they did not know was that their parents were dead. They were told to wait until they came back for them, so they have been foraging at night, but by this point it had started to snow. So you had a choice. Were you going to get up the next morning and go on and leave those kids there or were you going to stick around and be at risk yourself? You knew if anyone found out that you were an Italian soldier you were at risk since you were not back inside Italy yet. You did not know what they would do to you; Italy had lost the war.

You helped the children stoke the fire, and went out and got more wood since you were able to carry wood and they were not. They were quite weakened from hunger and barely hanging in there. They had a few tools their parents left with them. A pot to melt snow in, also to cook game in and the ten-year-old boy was able to catch the occasional rabbit, and so on. You decided you would stick around for a while and get these kids in better shape, then have them walk down the mountain with you. That night it snowed, and you all were stuck there for a couple of days finishing off the last of the rabbit and roots and bark that they had managed to gather. That gave you time to think carefully about it, and you decided you would take them home with you. You would tell the world these were your kids and that you had been on a pilgrimage, and you were trying to get back home. So you did this, walking in the direction of your home, which would take you past the town they lived in. That is when you found out for sure that their parents were dead and the town was destroyed. You had already suspected this, since their parents were so overdue.

Gathering up what you could from the rubble of the town, odd things to help on the journey, you proceeded on toward your home. The five children and you walked over the Alps to Italy, foraging as you went. When you finally got back to where you lived, your family still had some moderate means. You kept these five kids and raised them. Of course, after you got home you let them know you were really a man. Again you took up your trade, which was watchmaking, and opened a watchmaking and repair shop and jewelry store, then married and had children of your own while raising those five kids as well.

The reason you need to know about this is, if you had not had any desire to have children or if you had questions about whether or not you should have children, you left that open-ended when you incarnated this time. It is like you not only raised your three kids, but some total strangers' five kids. This was an awesome thing to do—and out of deep gratitude to you, they took care of you in your old age. This lifetime is coming up for you to know about so that you are clear that you have "been there and done that" where children are concerned, and you are good at it. You have a good heart and some very positive karma around children. It was not necessary for you to have offspring yourself in this current lifetime, but it was okay if you did.

So if you have had questions one way or the other whether you were supposed to have kids—"Am I supposed to adopt? Am I supposed to have biological children? What was supposed to happen here?" The answer is: whatever you want to have happen. It is open-ended.

Recovering Balance

In the next lifetime I am seeing, you are in Atlantis and you are a healer. You specialize in emotional disturbances and helping people reclaim a healthy emotional balance. You were well aware that if a person suffers enough losses, they will become depressed. At that time, you were a highly gifted "psychologist," or the equivalent in that day and age. But especially you were great at diagnostics. You were really gifted at helping people transform their lives, helping them understand what it was that they "tripped over" that got them where they are and how to recover their balance and transform their lives.

As a very old soul, Hank, you decided that since you had this powerful, amazing gift, that as part of your current life you would be doing that again…in some way. This is such a crucial time in history, you knew that it would be important for you to do that for a while; however, it is not written in stone that you should have to do it the rest of your life. Should you get interested in something else, go for it.

My sense is that if you have not already seen the next phase forming, you have a sense that it is about to. When that comes, do not tell yourself no, I am supposed to be doing this thing I am already doing; just know that there is more than one thing a Soul as old as you can do, and there are different phases in this lifetime for exercising different facets of who you are. This is because you are extremely complex as a Soul.

Tropical Waters

Here I am seeing something having to do with tropical waters. I do not know if you are thinking about taking groups to swim with dolphins or whales, or traveling to sacred sites, some of which are underwater; I do not know why I am seeing this. But if you are thinking about doing this, it could very well be travel or giving lectures and teaching, so that more people can do what you do, but also just having fun, so do not be afraid to be expand or morph—it is like you are going to expand or morph into something else, and it will be quite easy, but you will not totally ever give up what you are doing now. Your career will morph into something similar but not exactly the same. That is all we need to know about that particular lifetime

Avalanche

Now I am seeing you skiing. You are a woman and extremely athletic. You certainly give the men a run for their money. This is somewhere in what we are now calling Scandinavia, quite some time ago…perhaps 200 to 300 years ago. There is an avalanche on the day I am seeing, and you are able to stay above the snow but you slam into a limb of a tree. The snow is so high you are pushed up where the limbs are. Your back is broken right about where the shoulder blades are—right at that level of the spine. You are not paralyzed, but you are—I want to say somewhere between your early forties and forty-seven when this occurred. If you have been having back pain, you need to know about this lifetime when your back was broken while skiing. The avalanche was nobody's fault; these kinds of things just happen sometimes.

Yet if you do not know what happened, or if you somehow blamed yourself for this avalanche or for skiing someplace where you probably should not have been going, well, you need to know it was not your fault. Accidents like this are usually planned before incarnating to learn specific things.

It could have happened to anybody, and it could have happened anywhere you had chosen to ski. This was not anything that could have been predicted. Again, you were not at fault, and you did a good job of surviving…it appears you were doing swimming-like movements—crisscrossing with your arms and legs to stay high up in the snow as it was moving, and then got flipped onto your back. The bones got crushed, or cracked, but the spinal cord still worked.

Yet it was because of that and self-blame and guilt for skiing someplace you normally did not ski that you thought you were at fault for taking risks. That is what you need to know in order for the back to heal fully, so I do not know if you started to feel that back pain between your shoulder blades or not. How this will manifest I do not know—or if it is going to happen in the future. There are many ways these things can appear in our lives.

If that kicks in, assuming that it has not already, you need to remind yourself that you were not doing anything wrong and can let go of this back pain. If you have already started to feel this back pain, then knowing about it is going to begin to heal it. You have a tendency to blame yourself for things that you really did not do wrong because you are trying to make sense out of things, and you have decided in a couple of lifetimes that it is better to blame yourself than to never figure out what happened. At least that is what you seem to think, and it is really not true. Sometimes it is just easier to say, "Stuff happens. It does not have to be my fault."

I think you had some experiences in this lifetime in which people tried to lay blame on you, and you took responsibility when it was not your fault. Hopefully now that we have mentioned this, you will begin to get a handle on that tendency.

Not Human

This is going to be brief, it seems. It is just a little piece. I am seeing you on a spaceship and you are not human. You are from another galaxy; they are specialists in energy adjustments inside the bodies of biological creatures. Interesting. I have seen this in energy medicine sessions. Your people have a theory about there being energy cords that need adjustment from time to time; like, there is one that runs from your right shoulder to your left hip, and another that goes from your left shoulder to your right hip. I see that they perceive them as being like guy-wires. There is one between your sphenoid and your coccyx, and so on inside the body. This species are masters of balancing this energy.

They did various experiments on different life forms in various galaxies to see what would happen. They were explorer scientists gathering data. This is fascinating. Your species was doing basic research. Ah! That is what we call it, anyway. They did basic research on multiple different life forms to determine how their energy manipulations affected people and animals and so on—with the intent to help. Yes. You were doing this during a period early in Atlantis when people's knowledge was extremely advanced. But you all got caught and in effect, your ship was tractor-beamed down. This was against your will and you guys were hopping mad and you said, "We are scientists. You cannot bother us." The locals said, "You are in our airspace and we can do whatever we want with you, because we have you now." They wanted to understand your technology, and you would not share it because you were not supposed to do so. Part of your edict was not to interfere with the development of other cultures. You put up a fuss and finally ended up in the Earth's incarnation cycle…oh! You had a little fling with somebody—an Atlantean cutie. Because she got pregnant…this is how you came to be drawn into the incarnation cycle of planet earth. Altiburon, or something like that, is where you were from before you came to earth, although I think you have lived in many different galaxies. Altiburon is what it sounds like. I am getting that is all you need to know about this for now. It was just for your information.

Hank's Life Mission

Let us now talk about life purpose or mission. In the course of this reading, we have discussed life purpose some—being a healer, helping people get their balance, helping people to balance their emotional energies and decide whether or not to raise children. I am going to pause and see if there is anything further that your guides want you to know.

They want you to write. At first, I saw an envelope, a white envelope from the back. Now, I am feeling that means you are supposed to write something that has to do with individuals, maybe some form of case studies? Writing up the kinds of healing experiences your clients have experienced, to help other people understand how to heal. It is something like that. I sense that if you play around with that thought, it will come to you exactly what it is you wanted to be doing.

You deeply wanted to do some things having to do with tropical water and being under water because your Soul longs for that. You have not had enough lifetimes where you were in the water, and you want to experience that in this lifetime. However you want to do it is okay. Nice, warm, tropical, pretty turquoise blue water. You have a Soul-level longing for that. It does not mean you have to go and live there, just take some groups there or take some vacations there or have a vacation home where it is tropical. Maybe do some healing work under water. Let's see…what else?

Travel is a big piece of what makes your Soul sing, so do not be afraid to go out there and see the world. You need to do that to be healthy so you can do your full mission and leave behind your legacy. Part of your legacy is to leave behind written materials as well as videos, recordings, that sort of thing, about whatever is unique about the way you heal people. You may not be ready to do that until you are in your fifties or sixties, but you may want to begin to take notes now.

I am also seeing you doing some gardening—with a purpose. I am seeing zinnias, but I think those are just for fun, and I am seeing you growing herbs and plants for medicinal purposes and preserving them somehow, like tinctures and whatever and spagyrics. That may be later in life, too. The study of healing properties of certain plants was part of your plan in this life, and I think you are going to start seeing Devas if you have not already. Plant Devas. You left this lifetime pretty open-ended. You came to serve and there was not a whole lot of karma to balance. You came to serve and to have fun. Do not forget to have fun. It is one of your assignments—to really have a lot of fun and to help other people figure out how to have fun; to cut loose and click their heels together and have a good time.

This completes your reading for today. Thank you.

The feedback from Hank was extraordinary.

Dear Lois,

Thanks so much for this. I don't have any questions, but I'll make a couple comments which I'm sure you've gotten before. The first life you spoke about where I was the "camel guy" for Lawrence of Arabia, who seems to be Darrell in this life, felt spot on. We always knew we had been together in a past life and that we had been untimely separated. We were together for twenty-seven years and had an amazing life together, filled with laughter and fun, very creative and we inspired many people with our relationship and our creative projects. Interestingly he was the bi-racial one in this life and older than me. He was a great man and incredibly charismatic and I often worked to support or direct that energy out into the world. There were still some issues for him about being comfortable being out and open in public together. He died five years ago after breaking his back (very high up neck and between the shoulder blades) while we were surfing in Hawaii (something we did every winter for 2 months—we loved tropical places) when I was forty-eight. It is still difficult letting go of him and all the joy we had together, so what you had to say is very helpful. A side note is that we both loved the movie "Lawrence of Arabia" and watched it many times together and often shed tears while watching it.

Christopher and I were together for the last two years. He is a spiritual guide and psychic channel doing amazing work in the world. Our connection is warm and very spirit-oriented, but I ended the romantic aspect of our relationship because I had come to realize that I felt more brotherly to him than romantic. And I still haven't totally let go of Darrell, so can't be fully present for anyone else. Your read of our past life together seems laugh-out-loud perfect.

The WWII story is interesting simply from a timeline perspective. I was born in 1958, only thirteen years after the end of the war, so living into old age in that life presents some timeline challenges, but I am quite comfortable with multiple-timeline perspectives. The child thing is interesting, as I never wanted to have children but taught hundreds of them over the years as a dance teacher and choreographer. I have always gotten along easily with kids, as I have a very expansive sense of fun and don't look down on them.

I've gardened and grown plant medicines for most of my life and the spirits in the plant world communicate freely with me, though I look forward to even more in the future.

Most people who know me would say that the thing I am expert at is having fun. Of course in the last five years that ability has been challenged, and I know it's my assignment to fully find it again on my own. I continue on that path.

I am very flexible and have always been able to blend into any group, but have more of a challenge really standing out as myself without trying to match. Your reading shows reasons why I may unconsciously feel the threat of exposing who I truly am. In this life nobody wants to kill me for who I am, and I continue to become more willing and able to freely fly my freak flag.

I am aware of my galactic heritage and have been told by a number of people that I came from a star starting with the letter A. Always the letter A.

Thanks for all the detail and nuance in the reading and your warm spirit. It helps!

Blessings and Love,
Hank

Here is my reply:

Dear Hank,

Yeah, I agree that the overlapping lifetimes are hard to accept in a way, but old Souls do it all the time.

I am still so surprised at the details these readings bring out that I could never in a million years have guessed. Thanks for the confirmation.

While my freak flag is slightly different than yours, I still fly one. I may have to borrow that phrase one day, if I may?

I suggest you listen to the reading at least once a month for the next three to four months to maximize the integration of all the material.

Much love,
Lois

This is Hank's last message:

Dear Lois,

Thanks I will do that—listen to the recording several times. Oh yes, the one thing I forgot to mention about the reading. Zinnias!

They were Darrell's favorite flower and we grew huge quantities of them on our 200 acres in Northern California. They became a favorite of mine, too, and I always have them in my garden wherever I live. Zinnias also symbolize fun and happiness. There couldn't have been a more significant flower to mention. I also let Christopher listen to this and he agrees that you are very gifted.

Freely borrow all flags and phrases. Oh, and I found you through Summer Bacon, who is also a friend. Keep up the wonderful, creative and healing work!

Hank

Lois' Notes: *In this reading the coincidences (or parallels) were just amazing in that I had not known about them beforehand. In the "Lawrence" lifetime with Darrell, Hank was of mixed race. In their current life, Darrell was of mixed race. They were still both males and lovers. Darrell was once again in this life shy about public acknowledgement of the relationship; clearly still an issue he was to work on again this time around.*

Hank was urged to grieve and let go as a lesson from that same lifetime. As it turned out, in this current life Darrell had already died, which I did not know, and Hank was having a hard time moving on.

In the second lifetime as the female prostitutes who hid out as monks in the mountains, Hank and Christopher were like siblings. In the current lifetime Hank had broken off the romantic part of the relationship since he realized that Christopher felt more like a sibling, again, something unknown to me.

With the lifetime as a woman skier who broke her back between the shoulder blades, I was concerned whether Hank was having back pain starting at the same age when his back had been broken while skiing in the prior lifetime. He was making swimming motions to stay above the snow when I saw the accident. This happened in the prior life...and I saw it to have happened between the age of sometime between his early forties and forty-seven.... But when Hank was forty-eight not Hank, but his partner Darrell, broke his back between the shoulder blades while also making swimming movements—in a surfing accident. Hank needed to hear that this was no one's fault. It would seem that one way of balancing the back pain issue was for Hank to minister to someone else who had a broken back.

Hank had previously been told by other readers that in a previous life he was from a star that started with the letter "A". I got that he came from Altiburon.

In the Life Mission section, he was told to spend time in tropical waters, which again, unknown to me, he and Darrell had done two months of each year when Darrell was alive. Since his Soul longs for this, it is hoped Hank will start going to the tropics to swim once again.

Also in the Life Mission section, gardening and working with healing herbs was mentioned. Hank has been doing that most of his life, working with plant devas, too, as recommended. It is very gratifying to see that what shows up in the Life Mission, the person has already often been doing. It is confirmation for the client, and for me.

The part about zinnias specifically was very touching to me. Was it confirmation that Darrell was there with me when I was doing the reading?

Past Life Reading, Part One

Lydia Easton - September 6, 2011

I got to know Lydia while visiting in England in 2011; we had friends in common. One day she mentioned that she could swim, but had a horrible fear of putting her face into the water, and wondered if it might be from a past life. Because she had done an enormous favor for me while I was visiting, I told her I would do a reading as a favor for her just about that subject, to see if we could uncover something about that phobia. Here is that reading:

Mysterious Comings and Goings

Here is the past life that I saw when asking The Guardians of the Akashic Records about why you experience difficulty putting your face into the water. Knowing about this lifetime will help begin to heal that phobia. It's not a pretty story. However, in looking at past lives we begin to heal the damage or scar to the part of us that is immortal—that part which comes back repeatedly in many different lives. Here's what happened to you:

This was a very long time ago—before recorded history, as so many of our lifetimes are. I am not familiar at all with the houses or the clothes, but I will say that these were very plain people. No matter how much money they had, they lived in approximately the same size house as everyone else, based on how many people were in the family. Their houses looked like stucco from the outside with no sharp edges. The houses do not have any consistent shapes…some rectangular, some square, others would have amorphous shapes; all the corners are slightly rounded. The roofs look like a vegetable material—rather like thatch. From a cultural standpoint, they were fairly evolved in that they did not believe in being ostentatious with their wealth, so as not to hurt anyone's feelings. Some families were more stable, was how they put it, because they had more holdings, and wealth was represented by land. People did not wear fancy clothes or fancy jewelry or anything, but some families had more land holdings than most, and others had none, but they all lived approximately the same. Those who had no land paid rent to those who owned the home they were living in and yet that rent just might be a small percentage of a crop.

In this lifetime at the point I am first seeing, you were a ten-year-old boy whose father came from a family that did not have much stability… in other words, holdings and wealth, whatever. He married a woman who really adored him, and she gave him a lot of freedom because she knew it was hard for him that her family had more holdings than his family.

They did not have machines like cars or so on, no flying machines or machines that traveled across the ground. Most people walked everywhere they went. I do see they used certain animals to help with moving around farm equipment like plows. They did not use animals for personal transportation very much, for some reason. So here is what was going on in your family.

You are the eldest of three children. There is another one on the way. At the time I am seeing, your father had this habit of disappearing for a couple of weeks at a time every other month, and no one ever spoke of it. You could tell when he was gone that your mother was worried, but if you asked about it, she changed the subject. She just said, "Your father has things he has to do, and I allow him his personal freedom to come and go as he wishes because he is a man. Women are not supposed to tell men what to do, just like men are not supposed to tell women how to run the household." She was clearly disturbed by it, but never did anything about it, and neither did any of the other adults. They all thought it was strange, but looked the other way as he did his periodic disappearing act, because he always came back. He never told anyone when he was leaving, but you decided that one day you were going to find out what was going on. You packed a little traveling bag with food and a water container and a change of clothes and you were planning to follow him the next time he disappeared, or try to anyway.

Early one morning you heard a stirring in the house. Peering out the window, you saw that your dad was creeping out, so you climbed out a window with your bag, following him for a day and a half. He was about two-thirds of the way to where he ultimately would end up when he stopped, went into a pub, and changed clothes. He apparently stored clothes there. He put on a hat—a stocking cap with oddly colored hair hanging out of the bottom edge of the hat. He was putting on a disguise. You were really puzzled at this point and unable to discern what he was up to, but continued following him. The entire trip took about a day and a half to two days of walking. You observed him from a distance and darted behind a tree or bushes if he turned around. This was mostly a rural area, and part of the journey was through a very old forest with massively tall, ancient trees with thick trunks. He slept outside and so did you.

Finally, your dad arrived at his destination. The town where he had been headed was significantly far enough from your home that no one you knew had ever been there. People did not wander far from home in your world. You were not even familiar with this town; you did not know it existed. Your father stopped, went into an abandoned hut, put away his disguise, and then walked the rest of the way—almost to town. As you observed all of this, he walked up toward a specific house calling joyfully out to the inhabitants before he even got there. As you watched from the woods, a woman and two small children came running out and they were screaming, "Daddy, daddy! Oh, daddy is home!" Lo and behold, to your utter dismay your father had another family!

Wisely, you found a place to stay in someone's barn saying, "I am traveling through, may I do some work for you to pay for my room and board?" They were happy to have you because you were a friendly, helpful kid. The location allowed you to keep a watchful eye out for your dad. When he left one morning heading back up the road toward your home you began to follow him once again.

Reaching the outskirts of that town your father remembered he had forgotten something. He turned around suddenly to go back, and that was when he saw you. You were not expecting him to turn around to go back, but he reversed direction suddenly and saw you—there was no time to hide. You froze. He said, "What are you doing here?"

You replied, "I followed you and I know about your other wife and children and I am going to tell my mother."

He snarled, "No, you are not."

You insisted, "Yes, I am. She has a right to know where you are going and that you are taking her money..." because the father did not do much of anything. He did busywork; he helped with the horses that pulled the plow. . .and worked with oxen or whatever those draft animals were, and pretended to be an overseer in the fields, but he really did not do very much. That was hard on him, actually, and your words struck a deep, painful nerve.

He needed to be someone's hero, which is why he created this other family, actually. As you two spoke, he became more and more enraged because he knew if your mother found out, the money he was taking to his other family would dry up and he would be out on his ear and not have two wives and two sets of kids, rather he would have nothing and no one at all. He snapped and went berserk. There was a water trough nearby that looked like a large metal tank. He shoved your face down in it, and you were squirming, trying to get loose. He realized what he was doing and pulled you back out but it was too late. You had already inhaled water and died. Oddly, nobody else saw any of this. The tank was behind a wall next to a barn or shed. So he picked you up and carried you into the woods, found a cliff or edge of a gully, and he tossed the body and went home. He walked back to your mother's house, anyway. That was the end of you, but you need to also know that this man is not in your life at this time. You may bump into him later, but you do not know this man yet.

The other thing you need to know is that it troubled him horribly. He just snapped and went crazy for a moment, and it was too late by the time he came to his senses. He never intended to kill you; later he told himself that he was trying impress upon you the fact that he was stronger than you were and you had better do what he said. But in his rage he held you under far too long.

He was never the same after that and ultimately ended up killing himself over it. One of the times that he went to his other family he hanged himself, and they never understood why. Your mother never knew what happened to him nor did she find out what happened to you. Your body was found but the people who found you had no idea who you were. Knowing about this, gradually you may have some emotional releases, and you may want to take the apple cider vinegar bath. You might have some memories come up on their own while awake or in dreams, and it may be that little bits and pieces of this click into place over time.

Part Two of Lydia's Drowning Reading

After I turned off the recording I started getting more information, so I turned it back on continuing the reading:

At the moment you were dying, you were really furious and quite terrified, as you had no idea that anyone would ever do a thing like that to a child. Your innocence was damaged at the Soul level. Your ability to trust was damaged because anything that happens while you are in the process of dying is imprinted on the Soul...and you were also running through...a lot went through your mind in a short period of time. You were running through: where did I go wrong—should I have just let him go where he wanted to go and ignored his movements?

Should I have lied to him and said, "No, I will never tell mother?" All these things went through your head like, "How am I responsible for my own death? What should I have done differently?"

One of the main things that you need to understand is that you were trying, as a ten-year-old boy, to take on the responsibility of a grown man for protecting your mother and your family from this person whom you had come to see as a con artist. So you also had doubts in the moment of death about whether if, sometimes, is it better just...how can I phrase this...to allow someone to do something bad to someone else without saying a word about it? Is the lesson to just keep your mouth shut because it is not safe to try to set matters right? Yet that is not true. It is important to set matters right when you see wrong being done, but it is also important not to take on more than you can handle based on your physical size, your maturity level and all that. All those conditions need to be taken into consideration before we get up on that horse and raise that sword and go to battle over something.

You have been getting lessons in several lifetimes over when to take a stand and when to be quiet, and that may be something you are still dealing with to a certain extent.

<u>Lois' Notes:</u> *After I sent this reading to Lydia, she emailed me asking where the father had been holding the boy. She wanted to know precisely how he had been held underwater long enough to drown. I replied that he had held the boy by the back of the neck. At that point, Lydia replied that when she heard the recording of the reading she knew it was by the back of the neck, because her neck stopped hurting right after I said that he shoved the boy's face into the water. Unbeknownst to me, she had had unremitting neck pain since she was about ten to twelve years of age, which no one had ever been able to heal. After the reading, the pain in her neck just stopped. But she needed to hear independently from me that the boy had been held by the back of the neck—just for confirmation. Otherwise, she was not sure she would have believed this really was her past life. The neck pain having spontaneously stopped along with my telling her where the man had held the boy (by the back of the neck) were necessary for her to believe I was really doing a past life reading, and not just making up an interesting story. She also reported something I had not known about her, which was that she had a profound, deep sense of the importance of "children's' rights," almost at the level of being a crusader. Her work in this lifetime has to do with children as well. She felt sure that*

had to do with her rights having been abrogated as a ten-year-old boy in that lifetime, murdered by his own father.

After that, Lydia scheduled a full reading with me. I waited three months so she could fully assimilate that prior traumatizing one, and then did the following full reading.

Full Reading for Lydia Easton
December 15, 2012

A Friend's Betrayal

I am seeing a lifetime in Scotland. You are a man and Alma is your wife…I mean your daughter in this lifetime, Alma—she was your wife then. Her name in that life was Evelyn and they called her Eve or Evie. You had three sons: Craig, your son now, was one of them, and the other two—I think your brother, yeah…was one of your children, and I am not sure who the other one is. Maybe it will come to me later. Geoff (her current husband) was your dad in that lifetime. You had quite a few acres of land and a nice house…it looks sort of like adobe or mud, and it is big. The roof is thatched.

When you were young, like twelve or thirteen years old, you were hunting with…it looks like a falcon. Not too many people did that sort of thing, and while hunting one day you met another boy about your age. He was doing the same thing, and you became very good friends. He was traveling with a group and was from a nearby area. This young man's family was very wealthy, but you had falconry in common, so he became your friend. You two hung out together every day for years until he finally went off to boarding school.

Many years later, after you got married, he came to visit. He was very taken with your wife, who was most delicate and beautiful. On the one hand he was your friend, and on the other, he surely was attracted to your wife. In the beginning, you never suspected that anyone would do anything inappropriate with a friend's wife. However, he was gradually over time coming to visit too much until it started to bother you. You thought, "Doesn't this guy have anything better to do than come to my house?" This especially bothered you when you came home from working a distance away from the house and he was there. Your wife seemed uncomfortable with his being there. The short of it is this fellow was trying to take your wife away from you, and ultimately you had to do something about it. You needed to stand up to him, which was not easy because he came from a powerful, wealthy family with political clout, control and power. This went on for years, and you felt very protective of your wife because she did not know how to handle it.

Evie did not know what to do because she, too, knew they were very powerful people. She was nice to him, but she did not know how to get him to back off. It took several years before you actually got a handle on it. He created a highly uncomfortable situation. What you two finally did was to distract him by finding a particularly attractive woman to introduce him to, but it took a lot of work to accomplish this. He was causing problems in your family, creating a lot of tension. Here was this powerful person pretending to be a friend while at the same time undercutting you. He never totally went away, but he did get distracted by this other woman and eventually lost interest in destroying your family. For the rest of your life he would drop by periodically, though not constantly like he had been, and flirt with Eve. She was repulsed by his attention, so it was an ongoing discomfort, but not the daily struggle it had been at one time.

As you were in the planning stages of this lifetime, the one you are in now, as Lydia, you decided you needed to work on that again, on getting the upper hand with him and be in a situation with different roles, different bodies, different relationships, but still stand up to this Soul and control the situation. This is why, when Alma was born, you felt like you needed to protect her, because she was so small and delicate. But also, when your eldest daughter Helena was born—Helena is the reincarnation of this male falconry friend of yours—into this relationship with Helena is built in the need for you to have the upper hand. This is just another way of learning that lesson—for both you and Helena. Geoff, in the other lifetime when he was your father, would say, "You have to get in control of this situation." But he never said how to do it. I suppose he did not know how to do it, either. So he wanted to be there in this lifetime, too, and watch and participate and be a support to you in this because he wished he had been more of a support in that lifetime. So that explains some of what has gone on in terms of trying to get a handle on all that boisterous energy Helena brings to the family.

Spooked Hunter

Next, I see you as a man, a Native American in the Pacific Northwest, hunting alone in the woods, walking in complete silence. This is a damp, silent, primeval rainforest, and appears to be near the current location of Seattle or Puget Sound—up in there. The woods I am seeing are breathtaking. They are gorgeous, rich with color, the deliciously earthy scent of composting leaves on the forest floor, and teeming with wildlife.

You were fairly young, not married yet, and as you walked softly, you saw what we would call today a Big Foot or Yeti. These are beings that come easily in and out of different dimensions or densities. They can effortlessly disappear back into their dimension or density or frequency or whatever you want to call it. You saw this particular one grab up a deer under its arm and vanish. It was as though he walked through a fold in space—he just disappeared into a slit in the air. You felt as though you were looking at a backdrop instead of reality. It freaked you out very badly, because you assumed if he could pick up a deer and disappear with one of them, he could also pick up a person and vanish. (Native peoples still know about these creatures and what they can do with the fabric of space/time. Our indigenous people just are not talking very much to mainstream folks about it. Yes, even today, many still know about the Yeti.)

After witnessing that huge creature, you were so terrified you would not go into the woods again. Your family ultimately took you to the local healer to find out what was wrong with you, because it was seriously dysfunctional for a male to refuse to go in the woods and hunt. A man had to hunt to eat unless he had other skills. You wanted to stay in the campground around people where it felt safe. Of course, it was not any safer; you just felt safe there. The Shaman determined you needed to participate in a shamanic plant ceremony for your healing. It was during this ceremony that you realized you were destined to be a healer like him yourself.

When you came out from under the influence of that plant, you asked about studying with him. He agreed to this. So the end result of this terror of going into the woods was that you never went hunting in the woods again, but did go walking in the woods with the shaman in order to collect herbs. As far as the others knew, you were cured. You spent the rest of your life healing people, which may be why you had that traumatic experience in the first place—so that you would become a healer. You married and had three children.

Persian Goldsmith

This next life I am seeing is in ancient Persia, and you were a goldsmith. Again, you were a man. You made beautiful, delicate, small things out of gold-like beads, ornaments for jewelry both for women and men, and sometimes even for animals. (Oddly, people put these decorations on their animals sometimes, too.) You were a highly successful, gifted goldsmith. You were extremely gifted and well known, far and wide. People came from very far away to look at your objects of art. I am not seeing anything negative or upsetting in that lifetime. I am seeing that you needed to know you have certain abilities when it comes to metal-working. If you ever wanted to do that again for fun as a way of relaxing, you would find it very easy to do. It is one of those gifts you can draw on if you wish. Oh, and in that life you also married and had children. That is all you need to know about that lifetime.

The Painter's Model

Now I see you as a painter's model, and this looks like it is happening around the turn of the twentieth century. I do not know who this painter is. I think perhaps he is French—not very well known, though he may have been moderately well known at the time. He loved to paint things in water, and he painted you floating in water with your hair flowing out around you, and flowers floating in the water, your dress billowing about you gently in the water. (I think I have seen this painting somewhere.) Your eyes are closed, but you are alive, just floating in water. He posed you in a lot of different ways. In fact, I think you were his lover. But I do not believe you know him in this current lifetime.

Eventually, you became pregnant and moved in with him. I think you were only about twenty-one. When the baby arrived, you died from complications of childbirth. So if you had any fears about having babies, this would explain it. That was one of the reasons you decided you wanted to have several children in this current lifetime. It was because you had not…the baby did not live either. He died in the delivery process. I believe that it was not supposed to happen that way. There was a problem with the presentation, like it was not breech, but instead of being face down, it was face up—or something—but definitely it was too large and died during delivery. The midwife did not get there in time, and eventually you both died.

Egyptian Perfumer

Next, I am seeing you in the Middle Kingdom of Egypt. You are a member of the upper class, and I think your father was a priest of some kind. They knew how to do certain spiritual or mental practices we do not know how to do any more, mainly utilizing sound. If you have a strong attraction to ancient Egypt or even any interest in construction, this would be why, because your dad used spiritual technology to build or to assist in building some ancient structures. Born to a life among the very privileged, you amused yourself with growing flowers and creating essential oils. These were not for healing purposes, but for perfumery. You created some exotic oil blends, so if you have any interest at all in aromatherapy, which, by the way, can be used for healing and especially for calming people down—that would explain it. Yes, and homeopathy, too. It looks like you had a past life as a homeopath not too long ago, too.

Okay, I am getting that is all you need to know about today. Thank you.

A few days after I had sent the past life recording, I emailed Lydia.

Dear Lydia,

I trust you have received your past life reading. It may be obvious to you, but I neglected to say that the first past life mentioned is the reason for all these things happening that you asked about, issues with people coming to your house and imposing, and your not being able to say no to them. This again is about protecting your family, home and personal space, just like in the Scotland lifetime.

These are all lessons to help you get to the point that you will protect yourself and your family first, and create stronger boundaries between yourself and others. While it is not easy to say, "Oops, sorry, our guest room is already spoken for at that time" (as in the visitors from Australia) or "Goodness, it is getting late, and I need to get some things done before supper time, so we need to say goodbye to our play-dates for today. It's been fun!" (instead of inviting them to stay for dinner when you really want them to leave), that is just what you need to learn to do, or else the lessons keep coming until you finally do this, and the lessons keep getting harder.

Big Hugs,
Lois

The next day Lydia emailed me. I answered her by returning the email with the questions answered inside her email. So both the questions and answers are below; my answers are in bold.

Hi Lois,

Thank you so much for this! I got it! I've listened to it a couple of times and I'm trying to work out if I need to ask any questions. When I was the artist's model, did I definitely die in childbirth? I think I know who I am but if I am this person, then I survived for about a year after and then couldn't handle the grief so took an overdose. Is that who you saw? If so, it would explain why I'm so interested in art (especially when I was younger). When I first moved to London, I used to wander around the National Portrait Gallery. I have no interest really in modern art. It would also explain why when I googled some random phrase it brought up a picture of a guy/artist who I know I recognise despite never seeing him or hearing of him in this life.

Lois: **When you were the artist's model, the feeling and image I got was that you died as a result of childbirth and the baby died, too. The exact details I do not know for sure, but if your spirit was so devastated by losing the baby that you never got over it and you took your life, I would say that could be easily what they were showing me as well. The result of the childbirth and the death of the baby killed you; it just took longer than what I assumed was meant by what I sensed.**

Interestingly, I do have a good nose for perfume. I can recognise a person's scent so when I smell it somewhere else I can always place it. Makes sense.

Lois: **I know we carry forward things like that. Abilities and gifts can be carried forth from lifetime to lifetime. I see this all the time, and have experienced it as well. Personality traits may carry forward, too.**

I also like jewelry and designing bits and bobs. Maybe I should give jewelry-making a try. I got really frustrated a while back when I inherited some pink pearls when my dad died and wanted to turn them into a necklace but the jewelry-maker didn't do what I wanted because he said it wasn't possible, when I just know it is.

Lois: I would agree that designing jewelry would be a lot of fun for you. I would encourage you to try your hand at it. There are probably some classes somewhere to get you started—just to remind you of the various techniques.

Next Lydia refers to a dream she had and asked me about much earlier:

I also think I've worked out my mystery dream. Do you think it is possible to escape time in dreams? You know how you described our friend Aaron flying to New Zealand in a dream? I'm wondering if when I see things that happen in the future, it's just me wandering about in time, bored. I never see things in the past, which is why I was confused. I'm now wondering if it wasn't me looking back to the lady in the black dress but me (the lady in the black dress) in the past looking forward and seeing me now. Does that make sense? I think I kind of caught her off guard by catching her seeing me now which is why she smiled at me and why I knew it was me in the black dress. Anyhow, I suppose it doesn't really matter that much, I'm just intrigued as to why I remember that dream so vividly.

***Lois:* I feel pretty certain we travel through time in our dreams. It shouldn't be too hard to do, since there is no time in the first place, once we get out of space/time. Time is just an illusion, which is an artifact of being on a spinning planet, anyway. All our lifetimes are interconnected. She may have been saying hello to you, to let you know we are interconnected with our other lifetimes.**

Right, getting late, better run and get to bed! I'll email again soon and thank you again for this.

Lydia

Lois' Notes: *Lydia later emailed me with a link to a photo online of Rossetti's Ophelia, and asked if the painting looked familiar. It did, and I think he did more than one painting of her in the water. I feel certain that this was the model I saw in the reading—except the woman I saw was more robustly healthy-looking, but the painter may have taken liberties with her appearance, too. The story of her life was slightly different in the one detail, but the theme and the experience of the Soul was the same. She and her baby both died as a result of childbirth. The suicide of a depressed mother a year after childbirth is today considered a complication of childbirth, which was what I had initially called it while in trance.*

She was a red-haired artist's model who had been painted floating in water, had become the artist's lover and moved in with him, had a baby who died, and then she herself died from "complications of childbirth." I would say that what I had seen in the reading was stunningly close to what historically is reported to have happened.

Past Life Reading

Marlene Dennison - January 15, 2013

Marlene Dennison contacted me about a past life reading with the following questions:

1. *What am I to learn from my daughter, Kaylee's, death? Did our Souls agree to experience this for a reason? Is this a repeating pattern for me of losing children? How do I complete this process, learn from it, and not have to repeat it? How am I working with Kaylee now, after her death? I don't know how to word my question; I hope you understand what I am trying to say: Why did this happen and what now?*

2. *Relationships: I have had patterns in the past of victim/perpetrator/ rescuer and co-dependency. Being in controlling relationships, where*

I make myself small and don't speak up, I even choke, cough and get laryngitis. I try and please and have a hard time saying no. It doesn't feel safe. I feel powerless. When I get triggered, I feel dizzy, confused and apologetic. In other relationships, I am the caregiver and decision-maker. It feels unbalanced and I feel "too big." The relationship I am in now with Nolen does not trigger me, but I still have trust issues and do not want to get married; I like to feel independent...If I have to interact with my ex-husband I feel uncomfortable; my hands shake, my stomach hurts, I panic. I want to resolve this... find my own voice. How do I have healthy, balanced relationships?

3. *Extra Weight: My health is good except for a tendency to retain extra weight...when I am heavy I feel disgusted...but there is a comfort in the buffer it creates around me. When I lose weight...I feel nervous and not safe...At times when I look good, I feel powerful, but afraid of my own power. Is there something from my past that I need to resolve to be at a healthy, comfortable, safe weight?*

Lois' Notes: *While I do not believe a past life reading can cure absolutely all the client's issues at once, I still know it can make a difference in a person's life. So after reminding Murlene why I do past life readings, I begin to relate to her the past lives I see after opening her section of the Akashic Records:*

A Problem Selling the Virgin

I am seeing you swimming in a sea, an ocean—oh, actually, I am seeing your spirit doing the swimming prior to coming into a female body. I see that you are born on an island in the Pacific Ocean, south of present-day Japan. It is not very far south, either. This lifetime was quite a long time ago. The first thing they are showing me is...I am seeing you working as a slave, actually, from the time you were a small child. You were born into slavery, and as soon as you were big enough you began gathering wood for the fire, learning how to build a fire and carrying out the ashes—simple tasks. As you got older, you helped with cooking and with taking the food into the eating area, serving it to the slaveholders. You actually were not miserable, accepting that this was how life was supposed to be. By the age of fourteen you had gone through puberty. Had you not been a slave, you would have married then. The nephew of the slave owner visited and decided he was going to seduce you. This he did rather easily by saying how pretty you were, and giving you some much-needed positive attention. Of course, he was manipulating you, but you believed his lies. You willingly gave yourself to him, believing that he was going to take you out of slavery, since that was what he told you. This rogue promised to take you home with him and make you his wife; you believed him because he seemed sincere. But you were also deeply naïve and badly in need of love and attention.

When his visit was over, he just went home without saying goodbye. When the slave owner discovered you were pregnant, he was livid and wanted to know with whom you'd had sex. He was planning to sell you as a virgin to someone else. Out of both fear of the owner, and loyalty to his nephew, you would not tell for a long time. The owner's wife came to you thinking perhaps she could get the information out of you, and she tried a more compassionate approach. Finally, you told her the truth, that your lover was her nephew. This was not what she expected to hear. Enraged, she grabbed you by the throat and began strangling you. She stopped right before you died and said, "Now, you tell me the truth. Who was it?"

You said, "That is who it was. That is who it was. He said he would marry me and take me home with him." She started strangling you again and when she released your throat, you would cough and sputter and cough and sputter—yet not change your story.

Ultimately, she just strangled you to death because she finally believed you and thought, "Oh, we cannot have this. We cannot abide a slave having a baby of ours like this." They could not have a slave bearing a child who was related to them. That would be dishonorable in the extreme.

Strangely, they did not bury slaves who displeased them; they burned the bodies in a shameful way, which was horribly upsetting to your family. You watched all of this last part from outside your body. At the moment of death, you were distraught that telling the truth had got you killed, so this created a form of scarring to the Soul so that when it reincarnates, it picks up the effects of the damage again until it is healed while you are in a body. You have experienced this effect again when you reincarnated, many times. We choose which things we are going to work on in each lifetime, and that is when you experience those effects again, when you choose to work on it. What you need to know about this is that just hearing about the past life will cause it to begin to heal. Do not be afraid to think about it. Do not be afraid to feel it. It explains why you cough and sputter when you try to speak up for yourself in a situation when you perceive yourself as "less than" because culturally, at least, you were "less than" the person who strangled you in that lifetime.

This is also one of the pieces of why it is hard for you to trust men—or to give up your independence. Another piece of that lifetime's ending was that your mother was completely devastated by your death. Now, there is no cause and effect, by the way, but after your own daughter died, you understood better how your own mother had felt. That is not the reason for or cause of your daughter's death, but that is a piece of your greater understanding as a Soul that resulted from that experience.

Revolutionary War – Seeing Both Sides

In the next lifetime I am seeing that you are a male, a British soldier. You are marching in a parade and wearing a full regimental uniform, including the red coat. This is the time of the Revolutionary War in what is now the United States, but you are in Britain.

When marching, your job was to play the drum so everyone could keep in step. At the point I am viewing, you were a very young man, hotheaded and desirous of glory. After begging and pleading with your commanding officer, you were allowed to go to the new world, to America, to help put down the insurrection, the traitors, the American Revolutionaries.

You boarded a ship bound for America, and there was a storm. The ship capsized in the storm, hmmm…or perhaps a few of you were washed overboard—it is not clear—at any rate, you and a couple of other people ended up floating on top of some wooden planks and managed to get to the nearby coastline. In fact, it was an island just off the coast of the United States. Taken in by American Indians who were friendly to the revolutionaries, your rescuers were not particularly trusting of your group. Because you wanted to live, you cleverly made friends with the Indians who were guarding the three of you. One local you made friends with ultimately came in the middle of the night, set you free and set you on a footpath with a sack full of food. He gestured which way to walk to escape, because the next day you three were slated to be executed, but you did not know that. You took off and thought, "I will just go get help."

When you got to white civilization, you ditched your uniform, knowing that if you told the revolutionaries who you were, you would be killed and the other two would not be rescued—and quickly you heard of the fate of your companions. So you decided to blend in. Soon you began to see the world from their point of view. It was not long before you found yourself fighting with the revolutionaries against the British. You were torn because you knew the revolutionaries were right, yet you felt a certain allegiance to the British soldiers. You felt especially compassionate for the Hessian mercenaries, since they were only there because they had no other way to earn a living. Their families would have starved had they not fought these essentially innocent Americans. This was how you fell into a pattern of victim, rescuer, and perpetrator. This is how that pattern got started, and why you needed to know about this lifetime. Finally, you were killed in battle. The issue of victim/perpetrator was not resolved in that lifetime, so you came in deciding to work on it in this current one. Knowing about this lifetime will contribute to the healing of this issue.

A French Woman in Turkey

Next I am being shown a version of you in Turkey, even though you were a French citizen. This is in the 1700s. You were kidnapped and sold into the sex slave trade. As you would expect, you were miserable. This was especially demeaning and sad because before this you had been a member of an aristocratic family. That is why they wanted you…you were so genteel, poised and beautiful. The person who owned you made a lot of money when he rented you out. Realizing that you would never go home or see your family again, and that you would be doing this until you died or got too old to be desirable, after which you would be turned out to starve, made things much worse for you. You had seen that wash-out happen to other women.

This lifestyle caused you to become clinically depressed. This meant that you put weight on and after you put the weight on, you noticed they were not renting you out any more. Fortunately, they could not decide where you were getting all the extra food. It did not occur to them that someone they trusted, the person in charge of this harem of prostitutes, a certain eunuch, loved and was trying to protect you. Being a eunuch did not mean he could not have sex, it just meant he could not impregnate anyone. He wanted you and figured the way to accomplish that was to overfeed you, let you get fat and release you, because he had seen them release overweight women before. So that is exactly what happened. You got fat, and they told him to get rid of you. And he did. He took you home with him. Unfortunately, that did not end the depression, and you did not lose the weight, but still this nice man kept you alive and loved you just the same.

You did not love him back, however. After about five years, you decided to attempt escape and when recaptured, you were executed. That was the unconditional legal penalty for slaves escaping. That lifetime was where your pattern of eating to avoid attention came from, and the one in which this behavior was the most pronounced. That was not the only time it ever happened, but this was the one your committee of Guides and the Guardians decided would most help you to heal by knowing at this time.

My Life for Yours

I am seeing you as a cousin or perhaps a close childhood friend of Abraham Lincoln—you knew him growing up. You were male and continued to live out in the countryside where you both grew up. You loved him and he loved you, but the world he inhabited when he became an adult was so different than yours! Hard as you tried, you could not figure out how that happened; how you were still a mere farmer, and he was so prominent and successful. By comparison you felt you were a loser, because you could not elevate yourself like he did. As children you were close buddies who, when you had the chance, went fishing and hunting together and played alongside each other. Yet there he was as a grown man running for political office and winning, and for the rest of your life it was traumatizing for you that you were unable to do anything to lift yourself above the situation you were born into. By contrast, there he was: known and respected all over the world. Even when Lincoln was assassinated, you thought, "I would still rather have had the life he had than the one I have." You were obsessed with his living what seemed to be a glorious, wonderful life while you were struggling to put food on the table.

The reason you needed to know about that was because thinking like that, over and over and over again, perpetuated your situation. You have had a tendency to do that in several lifetimes, to think about the same thing repeatedly, blaming yourself for something that is not your fault, and imagining yourself in a different situation or someone else's life. This prevents your inhabiting your own life fully. Hearing about this will help you begin to let go of that escapist tendency and focus upon your own life and what is good in it, forgetting about the people whose lives seem better. You had a long life, so that you had more opportunities to change and grow, but even at the end, you still were wishing you had had his life. This misdirected focus blocked your growth and change.

That is the last past life you need to know about at this time. I know that you asked the question about your daughter, Kaylee, and why she died, and if that is a pattern in your lifetimes. We did not get a direct answer from the Akashic Records as to if that is a pattern in your lifetimes. I am not sure why they chose not to answer that directly. I cannot look into someone else's Records; I cannot look into your daughter's, so I do not know why she chose in that lifetime to die so young. To look into her Akashic Records without her permission is a violation of her rights as a sovereign Soul. You are certainly not the first person who has ever asked the question such as, "Why did this happen?" so of course, that is not wrong.

My sense of it is that I do not think it had anything to do with you so much as you generously agreed to be the host on earth for this beautiful person who had a job to do and something to complete. This was something she wanted to experience, and I think that is the only interpretation you can put onto it right now. It may be that later you will get more information. I suspect that is true, but you have received all the information that your Guides, the Guardians of the Akashic Records and your Angels feel is appropriate for you right now.

Sometimes the farther a person gets away from an event that was traumatizing, and the more time that has passed, the more ready that person will be for more detailed information. They are telling me one thing more. They say that her lifetime was supposed to benefit you in that after she left, you would be triggered to go deeper into your own spirituality in a way that you otherwise would never have done. That is not the reason she died, that was just one of the planned benefits to you. She had her own reasons that had nothing to do with anyone else at all; they were her reasons.

That completes your reading. Thank you.

Here is Marlene's feedback. My answers are in bold, below:

Dear Lois,

First of all, I want to thank you and honor your precious work.

Lois: **You are welcome; I appreciate your acknowledgement.**

Some of my questions are general to receiving a reading and some are specific to one of the lives you observed.

I'm feeling emotional. Stomach, breath, heartbeat. Is this a common response? Is this simply my soul integrating the reading? Is there anything that I can do to help me integrate?

Lois: **Is this a common response? No. Normal? Yes. Your Soul/Body is integrating the feelings of the lifetime. Please take an apple cider vinegar bath to expedite the release of emotions. The instructions are in the appendix of the book "Akashic Records," but I am sending it as an attachment to this email, too.**

Can you confirm if any of the people from these lives are people from my current lifetime? Some feel familiar, some don't.

Lois: **If they are in this lifetime, you will know it. Your first hit is always the right one. Some of them may not be incarnated at this time.**

First Life: I totally related to all of it. It felt very familiar. I cried like I was feeling in it the moment. I recognized all of it. In my current, I was raped at fourteen, so I related to that as well. I related to being manipulated, lied to, and not wanting to tell anyone. Related to doing what I thought I was supposed to and being punished for it. The nephew who seduced me felt very familiar. Is he my current ex-husband? I can relate to choosing to marry him in this life and learning that marriage did not make him not manipulate/lie to me. It didn't make me happy. Now that I know of this life, will it help me to heal my choking and trust issues with men?

Lois: **If you think that was your ex-husband, then it was. Part of this process is in trusting your own guidance, your own gut, about these things. Yes, it will probably help to heal choking and trust issues. You may need more readings to fully heal it, but you will begin to see a change in these things.**

Second Life: I related to this life too, but it did not make me emotional. What I related to was being a part of contrary groups and empathizing with them even though the groups contradicted each other. I can sympathize with different groups. I tend to see both sides and be in conflict as to which is 'right'. Both sides feel justified to me. I will allow this to assimilate and accept the healing. Did I also identify with the Native Americans? It feels like I was torn in three directions.

Lois: **Yes, absolutely. You saw everyone's view.**

Third Life: Again, related deeply to all of it. Sexually objectified. Depressed. Is the guard someone I know from this life? Again, feels like my ex. Will knowing about this life help me to feel safe and shed my excess weight and keep it off?

Lois: **Knowing about this should help with the weight issues.**

Fourth Life: I didn't relate as much to this life. Is that common? I related to the over analyzing and blaming myself. I don't think of myself as wanting to be anyone else. I do deliberate on a general sense of injustice as to why some people have it so hard and others have things come easy. I can accept that it is good for me to focus on my own life. I'll let it sink in.

It doesn't surprise me that they chose not to explain why my daughter died. I feel like it is something that I have to experience and figure it out. It has definitely changed my spiritual perspective. I have also taken classes in mediumship and am learning how to be a bridge between the spiritual and physical worlds. I don't think I would have studied or pursued this path if I had not lost her to physical death.

Lois: **Right. More will reveal itself as time goes on. Just keep doing your spiritual work. Start meditating daily if you do not already do that.**

I don't know if I missed it, or if I am just still integrating or if it isn't time to know yet, but I'm not sure about if my question regarding maintaining balanced relationships was answered. Perhaps, I need to integrate these lives first, before I can understand. Start with breaking patterns and trusting before building relationships.

Thanks again.
Love, Light, Lucidity,
Marlene

About a week later, I got another letter from Marlene. In it, she spoke of Lincoln's losing his son while in office. Here is what she wrote:

Dear Lois,

I've been doing the apple cider baths. They do help. Thanks.

The life as Abraham Lincoln's cousin did not resonate with me. I have never been particularly interested in him in my current life. This week while processing it, I remembered discussing him in my grief group for parents who have lost a child. Lincoln lost his son while in office. At the group meeting, in the midst of my sorrow and feeling like life didn't make sense and not being able to focus on complex tasks, I thought of how difficult it must have been for Lincoln, grieving during the Civil War with all his responsibilities.

After listening about my life with Lincoln and feeling envious and obsessed with him, I did not relate. I thought perhaps remembering this life involves feeling his loss and my loss and feeling his pain and appreciating my simple life as his cousin. From my current vantage point, I would not have wanted to be him. Perhaps this is part of my healing from that life to make me understand.

Love,
Marlene Dennison

<u>Lois' Notes:</u> *Many months after doing the reading, I contacted Marlene again. I wanted to know if her physical issues had budged any after the reading, since in my experience they usually do. Here is her answer:*

Dear Lois,

Thank you for writing. Interestingly, I re-listened to my Past Life reading this week and was processing some of it. [It is] synchronous that you emailed this week.

I have greatly improved upon my past tendency to choke or cough when I had difficulty speaking up the truth about how I felt in confrontational situations. I now find that I respond in my authentic voice before I even have a chance to think about what to say. I even find now that I can't tolerate lies, manipulation, or suppression of the truth. In the last few months, it has come to light that my mother has been lying to manipulate people, and I simply cannot tolerate it. I've stood up to her and have told her that I will not put up with it. I've had to limit contact with my mother. I feel stronger and more confident. I no longer doubt myself like I did before with my mother.

The victim/rescuer/perpetrator issues are in a way connected to the current dynamics with my mother, sisters, and brother. Whereas in the past, I saw all of their points of view and got lost in it without knowing how I felt about it. I was getting overwhelmed and confused as to what to do. Now, I've been able to live/speak my own truth and feel solid in who I am. The more authentic and real I become about who I am and what I want to feel in my own life, the more peace and grounded I feel.

I have lost weight since our reading, but last month I was re-triggered regarding a few things. It was the anniversary of my daughter's death and a lot of other stresses all happened at once. The past week or two, I have felt a definite shift and a letting go of the past. I am more at peace and feel more at home with myself. And as such, I have been losing the few pounds that I had gained while depressed last month. It felt like I had to revisit it and re-let it go. I hope that makes sense.

With regard to my life with Lincoln, it was more complicated and trickier for me to process. Yes, we both lost children, but that is not why I lost my daughter this lifetime. I had a tendency to feel that life is not fair, or that "bad" things should not happen to "good" people. I have slowly processed that I am where I am supposed to be on my path. [I know] that I planned it this way, that I had a choice, that there are no such things as "good" things and "bad" things; that things just are what they are. [I know] that when I surrender and let go of trying to force things to be a certain way and let go of my attachment to outcome, then I can feel the natural flow and align to it. I am at peace with my flow and the movement of my life and realize that I can connect and align to my Divine Purpose, and that every experience is a blessing and an opportunity to learn and grow. My Soul's Desire and Divine Purpose are mine and mine alone. It will not look like anyone else's. It is special and unique and precious to me. Other people's lives are just that. Their lives belong to them. They are not better or worse. We are all where we are supposed to be for our own Higher Good. No one can live someone else's life for them. It wouldn't fit.

Many blessings to you and much appreciation for your being you,
Marlene

Here is my answer to Marlene:

Dear Marlene,

Your letter is just stunning. I love how much you got out of your reading, and how much your life has changed in such a short time. Some people get a lot from the readings, and a few people refuse to accept change or growth at all. Most are somewhere in the middle. And it is all up to the person whose life it is to choose what to do with the healing offered. I am constantly amazed at how differently people process these readings. I long ago accepted that it is always their path, their life, their growth, their journey to the Light, and I do not judge, but I can still be surprised.

I am so glad about the positive changes in your health and your emotional/family life.

About the toxic people, I agree. Sometimes we have to limit contact with toxic family members, friends, or co-workers, for self-preservation. Have you ever read, "The People of the Lie" by F. Scott Peck? It is a great tutorial on this subject—a major eye-opener.

Luminous Blessings,
Lois

Past Life Reading

Michelle Lange - June 27, 2011

Michelle was a beautiful, dark-haired woman with delicate features. She was a vulnerable-looking, sweet, young, newly married woman, and her mother was a student/client of mine. I felt protective toward her. She only wanted to know about any past lives she might have had with her much-adored new husband, Joseph. Here is what I saw when I opened Michelle's records.

The Detective and the Singer

The first thing I am seeing is...and I do not usually see a disturbing image right off the bat like this, but if I do not start to narrate, I will not get to see the rest of the lifetime—the pictures just stop, so...here we go. You were a young female in this lifetime, and I am seeing you as already deceased.

Lois' Notes: I then became quite upset at what I was seeing, and worried about how this would emotionally impact the client, who was such a young woman. I hesitated and because I did, the scene began to fade from my sight. So I started describing what I was seeing again...

Your spirit hovered around, not going to the light at first because you had been murdered. This was in the 1930s in the United States, during the Great Depression. A serial killer had shot you in the face with a shotgun. Your hands were removed to prevent identification, and your body thrown into the water. It was several days before the body was found. The reason your spirit remained in the area was that you were hoping to make sure the murderer was caught for a couple of reasons. One, you were really upset that your life was taken early. The other reason was that you did not want him doing that to anybody else. Therefore, you kept trying to talk to people...with your mother at first and then with a police officer, a young man who was fairly sure there was a serial killer on the loose, because he had seen this killer's pattern before. He had seen another person killed and disposed of in precisely the same way.

The detective was a little bit clairaudient, but in the 1930s it was broadly accepted that if you heard voices, you were crazy. So, when you would try to talk to him as he was trying to solve the case, he would hear what you were saying like a thought inside his head. You began to consider him your partner in this, because you could tell he was listening. Sometimes you would amuse yourself by moving your hand through his body, stopping at the heart, and he would get a flutter in his heart. He sincerely felt that your spirit was present with him; he also thought that if he told anybody, they would think he was nuts. And he was right, you know, they would have.

He began to learn all he could about you. A farm girl who came to the city and had become a singer, you had independently traveled around a good bit of the time for singing jobs. Coming home after a performance late one night, you were walking toward your hotel room. Someone you did not know was watching you and had quietly hidden in the shadows observing your travel pattern for weeks. That was how he abducted and killed you—he was stalking you and appeared seemingly from out of nowhere. You never saw him coming and didn't have a chance.

This young policeman would study pictures of you as you were before you were harmed, and gradually he fell in love with you. The more he learned more about you, the harder he fell. He began to grieve your loss. The detective fell in love with your courage. He fell in love with your desire to entertain people. You sang songs that you actually composed yourself and they were so hopeful! You were striving to uplift people during those really hard economic times of the Great Depression, when most people were truly suffering and many going hungry, unable to find work.

Eventually this detective did solve your murder. Yet he was almost killed himself when he tried to apprehend your murderer. Oh…I am seeing now that the killer was mildly schizophrenic. He was also somewhat psychic, as schizophrenia sufferers often are. When the police detective approached the killer, your spirit was at your champion's side and the killer saw you!

At the sight of your spirit, the killer drew a knife and threw it at the police detective, barely missing. The policeman then shot him through the heart. At that moment the light tunnel opened up again, and you wisely went on into the light which takes all Souls on to friends and family in the afterlife, where you were welcomed with love.

Because you had remained in the area and helped this man solve your murder, he went on to become a very well-known police detective. Later he was hired in a bigger city in the 1940s, going on to make a name for himself as a great detective. He also wrote some semi-successful crime novels. His name was Jansen, Johnson, or something like that in it. The police officer who solved the murder is your husband now, Joseph. Because he fell in love with you, and because you stayed around and helped him to solve your own murder, in between lives you two decided to come back and have a lifetime together. The beauty of this lifetime was that he set you free so that your spirit could go on into the Light. You decided to come back to be with him and resolve certain issues, including being a real partner with him instead of a fantasy.

I have a feeling that as a couple, there is some sort of quality to your partnership having to do with justice, with bringing in fairness, or with problem solving, perhaps. You two intended in this life to work on behalf of others somehow. I almost want to apologize to you for seeing that kind of difficult life first, but I am not in charge of this. It was very hard on me to see this one. The Guides are...your Guides and the Guardians of the Akashic Records want you to know that the reason you experienced having been the victim of a serial killer was that it was karmic balancing for you. You had decided to do that in that particular lifetime as karmic balancing for lifetimes you had as a soldier. Yes...you had more than one lifetime as a soldier, in which you followed orders even when you felt like you were doing the wrong thing.

Soldiers in a Circle

As a Russian soldier in WWI, you have too much responsibility, as at only seventeen years of age you are put in charge of guarding a group of prisoners. They seem to be speaking German. Orders were to kill any of the captives that got outside a circle that your people had drawn in the dirt.

The prisoners had their hands tied behind them. You were instructed to first hit them with the butt of your gun if anyone got outside that circle, no matter the reason. If they passed out and fell outside the circle, you were supposed to hit them with the butt of your gun until they got up again. It was bitterly cold outside and they had not slept nor eaten for days, so many of them did simply pass out.

As ordered, you slammed them with the gun, even though you thought it was wrong and you felt horrible about it. But you were following orders, mainly because the people who gave the orders were old enough to be your father. Yet you were deeply conflicted, as you were told if somebody did not get up after you hit them with the butt of your gun a couple of times, you must shoot them dead and then drag them to a nearby ditch to be buried together in a mass grave. You and your fellow soldiers followed orders, but you fell to your knees crying and threw up again and again, because it upset you so much to kill unarmed captives like that—men your own age who were just accidentally caught, and who had simply been following orders, just as you were.

The guilt at doing something so horrible was unbearable, so much so that when troops came to rescue these men you did not put up much of a fight. You made yourself more vulnerable to them than you should have as a soldier, and you got shot in the chest. Their searing hot bullet went straight through your heart, and you died within minutes. While sad at leaving, you were also relieved to have gotten out of that murderous conundrum. When you got to the other side and were conferring with your Guides, you decided the thing to do was to experience being on the receiving end of deadly injustice the next time around. That is why you planned one lifetime as a female murder victim.

When you got to the other side after the warrior lifetime in WWI, you were thinking, "Well, gosh, why did I not tell my superiors 'No, I am not going to kill people. I am not going to kill people who are not armed.'?" You said, "That was a mistake. I was only a few days shy of the age of eighteen, but I could have said, look, I am not going to do it. You can shoot me instead if you want, but I will not do this."

So to achieve some balance of experience, you came back as the victim. We come back again to experience everything—both sides of the equation—and we exist, we Sparks of the Divine, so the Creator could come to know the Creator better. Our experiences are God's learning experiences as well as our own, because we are all infinite sparks of light coming from the great Source of Light which is called God, Prime Creator, or the Zero Point Field. So as we get to know ourselves through experience, Prime Creator then knows Self better, as well.

The True Wild West

The next lifetime I am seeing is one in which you are a Native American man...I take that back...you are an actor pretending to be a native. This is in the 1830s or 1840s. You are on stage pretending to do a war dance—part of a play being performed. This was in Philadelphia. At that time the people in the eastern USA were fascinated with the Wild West, Indians and the Indian wars. A local playwright wrote a piece about people who rode in a wagon train off to experience the wild, wild West when the Indians captured them. After their capture...interesting...the native warriors put the settlers in the middle of a circle. They tied the captives' hands behind their backs. That is interesting as it mirrors the soldier lifetime we just saw.

In the play, you were dancing in a circle around them along with a couple of other pretend Indians doing silly war whoops—silly because you had never seen one, none of you had, so you had no clue what they were like. Yet you were having great fun as an actor while making enough money to put food on the table. You were an unmarried man of about twenty-three, still trying to figure out what you were going to be when you grew up.

After the play was over each evening, people would congregate at the stage door and tell you how great you were, giving you flowers and asking for your autograph. You thought that was all great fun. Then a man approached you one evening at the stage door after you finished signing autographs, as you were preparing to walk home. Walking along beside you he told you he worked for the Bureau of Indian Affairs. He wanted to tell you that he felt it was a disservice to the American Indians for people to write and participate in plays about them, making fun of them, as this play did, and portray them as foolish or bad people. He suggested you should come out and learn about Native Americans so you could return and write truthful plays yourself—plays which would teach the people about reality instead of disseminating misinformation, as you had been.

He wanted you to experience what the "Wild West" was truly like. You thought that sounded like an exciting proposition. The man said he needed an assistant at the Bureau of Indian Affairs and offered to hire you and to travel with you to where he was working out west. There was a fort there and an office of the Bureau of Indian Affairs was within the fort.

The two of you traveled by stage coach most of the way. He hired a couple of horses after reaching the point where stagecoaches did not go any nearer the fort. When you arrived, the fort had been overrun by members of local tribes. Many people who resisted were either injured or killed. People who did not resist were uninjured. Provisions were taken.

This was terrifying. You wanted to turn around and go home, but he pleaded, "No, your help is needed here. We must get communication going between the soldiers and the tribes so that both sides understand each other. You are a good communicator. You can help with that." Impressed with your skills of oratory, he convinced you to remain and help rebuild the part of the fort that had been knocked down. A few days after you got there, more troops arrived, bringing provisions like blankets, food and water. Although there was a small well inside the fort, it had been poisoned. So the soldiers were digging another well. As all this was going on, you just woke up one morning realizing this was where you belonged. You saw you could make a difference, and you preferred that to doing something frivolous, as you had been previously.

This was a place where real things happened, and what happened mattered; it was not just pretend. You truly did help with communication between the tribes and the soldiers, brokering a peace between them for a long period of time. There was great preservation of life because of your efforts.

You need to know that you have the capacity within you to broker a peace, an important one, and to create community. You also have the ability to make a ninety-degree turn, or even a one-eighty, and go in a completely different direction, making a difference in the world as you did in this lifetime.

Lemurian Organizer

The next lifetime I am seeing is...in the South Pacific, and I am seeing you at the top of a mountain on what used to be the continent of Lemuria. Today all that is left are some islands in the Pacific. This one I am seeing is not one of the Hawaiian Islands, but another island that I do not know the name of...oh, it is an atoll actually. The time I am seeing is not that long after Lemuria slipped beneath the sea. There are a quite number of people on this tiny atoll. It appears they have been through a horrible trauma in that an entire, gigantic continent has gone underwater because of earth movements on the sea floor. Most of the people drowned. Only a few survived, and they are at the top of what used to be a mountain. There is not much vegetation there and these people had previously lived inland; they did not know how to fish. There was nothing to eat, and chaos reigned. People were starving, desperate and trying to build shelters out of what little they could find. The ocean was very stirred up and dirty with a nasty mess of debris, as you might imagine in the aftermath of a continent going under. The sea was muddy for a long time.

What you decided was that everyone needed to get organized and do something, so you started talking to people. You said, "Look. We have to survive and the only way we can do it is if we pull together and create some sort of community where there is structure. Right now, there is chaos. Let us talk to everybody to see if we can get people to come together and create rules and consensus about what is needed to help each other survive." At the time people were just killing each other over the tiniest little thing—even twigs to make a dwelling.

They all had severe Post Traumatic Stress Disorder—everybody did. They had seen thousands of bodies floating in the water until the sharks, crabs or other sea life ate them. All of them had lost everything, including many family members. Yet you had somehow managed not to let that overshadow your deep humanity. What you did was to create a new form of government different from anything that had existed before. By the way, you were a man creating government, which was unusual, because Lemuria had been dominated by women.

You organized people to create a new set of rules where men and women were equal, and you scratched out a very new and different form of relatedness, where people got together and cooperated. This made their lives functional, so that most people actually did survive this chaos. This later evolved into a tribal system that exists to this day. You were sort of like George Washington in a way, you know? Or Thomas Jefferson—you created a new government. You need to know that you have abilities to organize people and to create social structures, and if you decide you want to do anything like that again, you have that to draw upon in your past. You are also a very old soul, Michelle.

Okay. That completes your past life reading. Let me know if you have any questions. I suggest that considering how many traumatic past lives we have talked about, you might want to take an apple cider vinegar bath after you listen to this just because emotions may be coming up. I recommend that you listen to this again several times over the next few months.

Lois' Notes: When I heard back from Michelle, she was not at all upset about my seeing her murdered and dismembered. She simply thought it was a sweet love story between her and the detective. She was concerned with my feelings, because I'd had to re-live the trauma and feel it in her place. She was grateful for my work on her behalf.

Two years later, as I was putting the book together, I wrote her to ask if she had any feedback about how the reading affected her. I sent her the semi-edited written transcription of her reading, so she would not have to listen to the recording again. Here is what she wrote to me:

November 11, 2013

Lois,

Going over the reading and processing it by seeing the words and developing the pictures in my head as opposed to listening to the information actually gave me a richer experience. The first reading of being a singer pulled at my heartstrings all over again.

It is interesting you sending me this information at this time, as I am again looking to develop my goals with, essentially, what

I want to do when I grow up. Seeing that I have already led so many groups to prosperity and peace while also being fulfilled spiritually and emotionally is very encouraging.

I think I am going to pull in this strength to help propel me forward.

Wishing you all the best!

Warm regards,
Michelle Lange

Past Life Reading

Nicolette Kensington-Peters - December 8, 2012

Nicolette wrote that she was interested in knowing about any past lives she had with her brother, Marcus, for whom she had purchased a past life reading as well, and if her two children had been with her before. She was also curious about whether she had been with a certain fitness coach who had recently been in her life, since he felt very familiar to her—there was an intense attraction from the beginning. She was having trouble letting go of him after the sessions were over and it was time to move on; she wanted to know why she felt this way. She hoped the reading might shine some light on that. Nicolette was also concerned what she would do with her life once her children were finally going off to college. Her whole life had been devoted to raising them, and she was not sure she even knew who she was out of the current context.

South African Recall

The first lifetime I am seeing is in the 1930s. You are playing tennis in your back yard on what looks like a clay court. This is somewhere in, I almost thought it was Europe, but it is not. This is South Africa. You are

European with three children. Two of them are the same two children (the same souls) you have in this lifetime, and the third is your brother Marcus. I am seeing that your husband is being called back to Germany, which is where your family originated. He had had a great job in South Africa for twelve years; he was very happy and successful, making significant amounts of money. Then there was this sudden recall with no warning, and no time to pack—most things went into storage. Everyone in your family was knocked completely off guard. It all felt almost sinister, but neither of you were sure why.

When you arrived in Germany, you discovered that all the Jewish people—and you and your family were Jewish—were being put into a ghetto. You were in a state of shock when you found where these people wanted you to live, and even deeper in a state of shock that you had to wear Stars of David on your coats and clothing. Plus the government confiscated all the money in your bank account.

Childhood friends who were gentiles then tried to hide you, but quickly were discovered and shot for their trouble. Immediately your family was put into a concentration camp. Dachau. Well, you were moved around several times, but the last one you were in was Dachau. After being there a few months you were all gassed—all five of you. At the very end you huddled with the two smaller children in the gas chamber, crying, holding them and rocking them, swearing that you would rectify this one day. Sadly, you felt like a failure as a mother that your children were not going to get to grow up and live full lives. You felt responsible for not somehow preventing this horror. Surely thousands and thousands of parents felt the same way.

When your children each came back to you in this lifetime and you looked into their eyes, you remembered that promise to give them a good life. Clearly their premature deaths were not your fault in that last lifetime. You deeply needed to know about this experience so that you understand from the perspective of being in another body/personality that the gas chamber was not your fault. At this point in your current lifetime, you have done everything you had wanted or intended to do for these kids, which was to provide them with the best life you possibly could.

At a Soul level, though, there has been an ongoing feeling of responsibility for how they died, though you did everything you could to save them. There was no way you could have convinced your husband not to go back to Germany, even if you had tried, because no one would have believed what was to come. You had both allowed yourselves to hope he was getting a promotion; that is what they had told him. None of your social circle had any idea of what was going on back in Germany. Word was not getting to anyone on the outside at that point about what was being done to Jews. It was being kept absolutely secret to the outside world, almost until the end of the war. The war actually ended before people outside of Germany fully knew about the worst of the atrocities; many of the ordinary German citizenry did not even know.

This is why you felt a strong responsibility to give your kids a great life, and you did. They are going to be fine, both of them. Every lifetime has its ups and downs and lessons to learn and experiences provided to learn those lessons, but you have done what you set out to do now, and in two years when Minna goes off to college, you can then focus totally on yourself. And, you know, you feel protective toward your brother, as well, because of this same lifetime, since he was your son. That is all we need to see, and all you need to know about that life.

The Tropical Matriarch

Next, I am seeing you in a tropical location. You are not on an island, but you are on the coastline of…many times I cannot tell the difference between New Zealand and Australia, but you are on the southeast part of whichever one…I think it is Australia. You are a woman (although we do go back between male and female through all our lifetimes). You mend nets and you catch fish, and this is a very matriarchal society, so you are the head of the household. You have a couple of husbands—but not husbands in the sense that we think of them. This was very long ago.

This is an indigenous culture where women run things. So in this particular lifetime, you do not need a man to take care of you—you are in charge. It has been a long time since you experienced that, but you do have that experience of independence in your Soul. For that reason, you could easily draw upon that energy—to be the person who makes her own decisions about her own life. The feelings you have about being lost when the kids are grown are normal and natural. Still, you have a stored experience of matriarchal strength you can draw upon. Malika was her name. You can call upon her to help you craft the next chapter of your life, and without input from anybody else. You can invoke Malika to help do that. She was very successful, by the way, making nets for other people with intricate knots that she created. She was well known, had many progeny, which was considered very important socially, and was highly respected in her community.

The French Tailor's Daughter

I am seeing that you are French in about the 1400s. You are the daughter of a successful merchant. Your family are members of the middle class at a time when that is a small minority. Ah, now I see that your father was a tailor. He would travel directly to the homes of aristocrats and measure them for clothing. He measured the men and had a female assistant who measured the women. They brought fabric samples along so the ladies and fine gentlemen could choose which fabrics they wanted to use. Nobody came to him at his tailor shop; he always went to them. His place was considered too humble for them to visit. These were very important people.

When you became thirteen or fourteen years old, he started taking you with him to carry the fabric scraps. You also were entrusted with the kit that held his tools, like the pins, marking chalk and measuring tape—all the tools used in those days. You were there to begin to learn the trade. He wanted you to have a trade—work that you could fall back on, or the ability to work alongside him as long as you wanted to do that.

One day you two went to the home of a particularly nasty aristocrat who had a son who was a real rogue. Your father sent you back out to the tailor shop to procure some more fabric samples. This aristocrat was turning out to be impossible to please that day. So, you made the trip. After you got back to their estate the son, who was about twenty at the time, grabbed you in the hall—jumping out from behind a large statue, laughing at your surprise.

This scared the daylights out of you, but you did not scream because you were afraid that you would cause your father to lose business. You were not sure what to do. This young man put his hand over your mouth and dragged you into a guest bedroom and raped you. After a time, your father went out looking for you and could not find you for quite a while. Finally he found you under a staircase, crying. What had happened would just not come out of your mouth, you felt such shame. Finally, he finished up his job measuring the father and getting the fabric selection. Your father packed everything up and took you back into the carriage. Trembling, you sniffled and cried softly the whole way back, leaning up against him. When you got home, you ran into your mother's arms, sobbing. Your gentle mother took you aside and quickly found out what happened. The entire extended family was livid, but they could not do anything about it, and they knew this. All prayed that you were not pregnant, but you were.

In a frantic flurry to protect you and your reputation, they found a young man who was a distant cousin in another village. They hired a scribe to write letters to his family. This kindly cousin agreed to marry you because you were pregnant. You were fourteen by then—by the time it was becoming obvious you were pregnant. Lovingly your parents sent you to his village, and the two of you were married, saving you from shame and disgrace. You picked right up on your father's trade and became a seamstress/tailor to women, and actually fell in love with this young man who rescued you from such deep shame and degradation.

The two of you had a happy life; he was good to you and your baby, whom you both loved dearly. Often you thought, "If the rape had not happened, I never would have found this man. He was the perfect man for me."

This former cousin is the younger man that you met recently in this lifetime, the man who helped you with getting back into shape. You have had other lifetimes with him as well. He just came into your life at this time to once again help you out, but this is not intended to be indefinite. The reason you are so drawn to him is because you have been married to him before—with children, too. So, this happens periodically. We bump into somebody that we have been married to before. It does not mean that we are supposed to marry them again. It just means that our souls wanted to reconnect for some reason, like support, in this instance. I am being told to say to you that when it is time for him to go, it is really important to let him go. You already have a husband. Just be grateful for the experience of having found the younger man again, and remain on friendly terms with him, if you can do that.

Roman Healer

Ah, here it comes. I am seeing you in the second century AD. You are a man living in Rome. You were a Christian, but of course that was a big secret, as it was not a good time to be out in the open with that. You were also a healer. What you did had to do with actually using ancient symbols; oh, I see, having to do with sacred geometry. This is interesting. I did not know that existed as a healing technique back then; I thought it had been lost by that time. They were still using sacred geometry at that time, symbols laid on the body, as well as poultices, unguents, herbs, that sort of thing. You were masterful at this. You grew the plants and processed them for healing, and you had studied with someone who was considered the greatest healer in all of Rome. This was your profession. You were like a doctor… and I think they also did some bloodletting, but not very much. There were certain little surgeries they did and you participated in those as well.

You need to know that you were not only a doctor and healed people, but that you were very good at it, using a lot of herbal as well spiritual healing methods. However, you had some very secret work you also did.

You helped smuggle people out of Rome to safer places once they were identified as Christians. Your beliefs were more along the lines of the Gnostics, who understood that God is within, or the kingdom of heaven is within, and that we are here to ascend one day. So, if you have not read any Gnostic teachings or what the Essenes have written, you might want to read some of that. I think it would trigger some memories for you. If you have a desire to heal or teach, since you were teaching healing techniques in that lifetime as well, that might be something you would enjoy.

Russian Fencing Instructor

Next I am seeing you in Russia, and it is difficult to tell just when this is. You are wearing one of those little cages over your face, like people who are practicing fencing—with a rapier. I see, you were a fencing instructor for the privileged class. You were gifted at this, which meant you had great reflexes and amazing balance; it requires a lot of balance the way that particular art form is practiced—fencing, I mean. You had a younger brother, who also taught this with you, and again, he is the fellow who was your coach, the young man you were attracted to. There is another experience you two had of great closeness; you worked together, you lived together, when you married, your wives and children all lived in the same house. In that lifetime, you two were involved in a business which involved athleticism, which is another reason that he was here to help you get you in shape, as you had done athletic things together before, so it was familiar to be doing that with him.

If you wanted to take up fencing, you'd be good at that, too. They wanted you to know about that...the Guides and the Guardians of the Records, that is.

<u>Lois' Notes:</u> *Nicolette wrote me one poignant letter—immediately after she received the recording of the reading.*

> *Dear Lois,*
>
> *Thank you so much for my reading—listening to you telling my stories was a very powerful experience for me. I feel already much of it making perfect sense to me. In reference to the first life in the late 1930s as a German Jew—I have always had a fascination with the history of that time, especially the concentration camps and hearing you say those things just resonated with me—of course it was mind blowing that my children and brother from this lifetime endured that with me.*
>
> *In my early twenties I had a very good relationship with a German man who wanted to marry me, we got along great, and I know he loved me very much. But as soon as he asked me to marry him, I panicked and literally ran away from him. The poor man was heartbroken, but I now see that this recent past life was the reason for my not wanting to live this life with him. He was very dark haired –I guess in a Jewish way. It is interesting that I was attracted to him in the first place given the previous experience.*

I am also grateful that you have helped me to put my relationship with Paulo [fitness trainer] into perspective, he has left now and it made my heart hurt very much to say goodbye to him although I think we will stay in contact via email. I am happy that he and I had this opportunity to meet again in this life—although I doubt he knows that because he is not very open to ideas such as reincarnation or past lives although I have tried to broach these subjects with him.

The relief I feel that I am on track, that I am doing my job where my children and brother are concerned, is huge. It all makes sense to me now why I feel so strongly that all three of them are always protected, loved and get the best of everything—so thank you so much for sharing this with me, those words do not fully express how much I appreciated hearing you tell me I am fulfilling my life's goals.

I will listen to the recording many more times I am sure and hope that with each time my emotional response will be a little less intense.

Thank you and blessings to you,
Nicolette

The next reading that follows this one is for Nicolette's brother, Marcus.

Past Life Reading

Marcus Kensington - December 8, 2012

Marcus' sister Nicolette paid for his reading as a gift. I am including his reading primarily because this is one of the rare occasions when I have seen the same past life for two people for whom I am reading—in two separate readings.

Initially, I asked her to have him correspond with me directly as I needed his permission to open his records, and when finished, I sent the reading directly to him alone so he could share it if he chose or not. When he sent his questions he wanted to know:

1. *Why do I constantly push myself to excessive extremes (professionally, personally, socially and privately)?*

2. *What is the source of straight men's attraction to me (Santoro, Travis–photos attached), and me to them? There are more examples, but these two are important. I feel I need to have contact with them.*

3. *Professionally (actually it's on many levels) why do I intimidate people and am unable make the next step to break through the barrier?*

Here is Marcus' reading:

From South Africa to Nazi Germany

I do not know if you heard your sister's reading or not. They are very personal and people may or may not share them; however, there was a past life in Nazi Germany in which both you and she participated. You were her eldest son. I am seeing your whole family, which included your father and your two much younger siblings. You were about seventeen years of age at this time, and your dad had been called back from South Africa to Germany where he thought he was going to be getting a job promotion. Instead, because you were Jewish, you were put into a ghetto at first, and then were moved from one detention center to another until you ended up in Dachau. Your younger siblings at that time were six, seven or eight years old—much younger than you. This is so strange.

It looks so completely different through your eyes than it did through your mother's eyes. You were put into the men's area, just like your father was, but your mother was allowed to keep the little ones with her. You guys were there probably eight to ten months; it is hard to tell. I think people lost track of time. It was not kept clean, there was not enough food. People were deeply miserable and desperate. Whispers were going around, and most everyone knew people were being gassed, yet not ever sure if they were next. Because you were young and strong, you were part of a work crew doing manual labor. Feeling responsible for the plight of your family, your father went into a very deep depression and was not much help to you. You felt like you were on your own, and for the most part, you were. You began to try to figure out a way to survive because you did not want to die in that concentration camp. Knowing that the war would come to an end eventually and some people would survive, you were absolutely determined to be one of those people who made it. It was irrelevant to you what it took to make that happen.

You observed that there were basically three types of people in a concentration camp, other than the guards. There were the people who were just neutral, who just took it, or who lay down and gave up like your dad was doing. They just moved like zombies from one place to the next. There were people that you judged to be completely crazy because they were constantly helping everybody else. They pretty much decided they were going to die like everybody else, but they wanted to do as much good as they could for others in the meantime. They were not fighting to stay alive, but they were giving their all to help others stay alive. Then there was the type of person who was going to stay alive come hell or high water, no matter what, and they did whatever they had to in order to stay alive. Those people were doing things like ratting out other prisoners; they had contraband, or stole food from other people. They did whatever they had to do—give the guard a blowjob, throw somebody else under the bus—it did not matter. All they wanted to do was to survive, and they assumed it was highly unlikely that those who were complacent or those who were trying to keep other people alive would be around when it was all over. From your point of view, it seemed that your best chance for survival was take care of yourself and be merciless doing whatever the guards wanted you to do, no matter what it was. And that was what you chose to do.

Your entire family was gassed on the same day including you. Even though you were heterosexual with no attraction to men, were only seventeen and still a virgin, you died alongside them. Even though you had performed sexual favors for the guards and ratted on other people, in the end you were gassed the same day as the rest of your family. This came as a profound shock. You could not understand how this could possibly have happened. You had a plan to survive and went into that gas chamber kicking and screaming and clawing and finally one of the guards just bonked you on the head from behind, dragged you in, and threw you on the floor, where you were gassed like everybody else.

And this is really important—what happens at the moment of death, what you are thinking when you die, that stays with you. You did start to awaken while you were lying on the floor before the gas actually got to you. You were thinking, "Well, I must not have tried hard enough. I did not do a good enough job making myself available to the guards. I have to try harder to claw my way to the top, to bully other people. I should have lived. I was not supposed to die at seventeen." And this is a vow you took so that the next time, "I am going to fight harder. I am going to take care of myself more intensely." At the moment of death, whatever you are thinking is imprinted on your Soul, so after you got to the other side of the veil, you thought, "This is something I am going to have to work on in the next lifetime—to get past this idea that the way to survive is by bullying others or making them afraid of me or intimidating people into letting me have my way."

This is a hard thing to resolve, but it is something you decided to work on in this current lifetime. Surviving at all costs is not a healthy way to live and does not help the Soul evolve toward a spiritual place—a place where it can ascend and no longer be on the wheel of karma. In fact, it does the opposite. However, there is no judgment in the Akashic Records. And remember, you were just a seventeen-year-old boy. Yet, you have come into this lifetime with a tendency to be intimidating and brash in trying to get your way. The task is to notice when you are doing it, stop doing it, and apologize.

There are people who think intimidation is good. Somebody even wrote a book about winning through intimidation. But it is not good at the Soul level, so hearing about this lifetime will go a long way in helping you to conquer that tendency, which simply comes from fear. You were snuffed out in your youth in a very recent past life, so it is important to be able to reverse this and catch yourself before you perform intimidating acts. It is also your task to come from a place of helping others, instead of betraying them. This is one of the things you wanted to work on this lifetime, which is why you brought that tendency in—so you could work on it. Listening to this will help you begin to correct those behaviors, because it will help to heal you once you know about it, just like any other repressed memory. If you remember something you repressed from childhood, the very remembering of it will allow you to begin to heal that aspect. So when you find yourself intimidating people or being brash, it is not easy to apologize, but every time you do, it becomes easier. Give yourself time and be gentle with yourself.

The Jealous Russian Husband

The next one I am seeing is you as a man and a member of the Russian Army, about 300 years ago. You had a very beautiful wife and were extremely worried about her. The problem, as you saw it, was that men were constantly flirting with her, trying to seduce her while you were gone. Your wife was extremely desirable and incredibly beautiful. This Soul is now incarnated as your friend Santoro in this lifetime.

You were an officer and came from money and an aristocratic family. You wanted to do something meaningful, so you joined the military. You were an officer because your family could afford to purchase a commission. That was how it worked in those days.

The jealousy caused you to go out of your way to have people keep an eye on her—not just servants, but friends of yours who would drop by, people you trusted to come and check on her and make sure she was not having an affair. The reason you did that was because you were actually the one fooling around. As you were traveling you thought, "Well, gosh you know, I am young and horny, and I have to do something about it." You would hook up with a barmaid or pay a prostitute or whatever it took to satisfy your cravings, yet still you expected that your wife was supposed to be faithful.

So there was some major distrust there. Your wife knew it and she found it insulting and offensive. She knew when people were checking on her, and she also knew the servants were being paid to report to you. The sad thing is that she really loved you and never looked at another man the entire time she was married to you.

About five years into the marriage, she became pregnant. You had to leave again, and as so many women did in those days, she died in childbirth. Her last thoughts were of you and how she wished you were there. She longed to be with you. For your part, you were heartbroken, utterly. There was no consoling you; you were just in a puddle on the floor, sobbing. The other army officers were shocked that the love of a woman could devastate a man that much...that anyone could love so intensely.

As your wife realized she was dying, she prayed that she would come back and be with you again. This current lifetime is the first time the two of you have encountered each other since then, and that explains the attraction between the two of you. There is something that is there on a soul level, so in this lifetime, since he is not attracted to men in that way normally, it looks like the best thing that can happen is just a nurturing, loving friendship, but that is up to the two of you. You two were passionately in love, and it was a very sexual marriage, very intense, passionate and physical. You did marry again, but it was never the same. She was your one true love. That explains the attraction in this life. What you two choose to do about it is entirely up to you, but that explains it.

Love and Rage

Next, I am seeing a life that occurred a long time ago. I am seeing a group of people who live inside caves—and there have been many civilizations like this. They are highly developed, though they live inside caves, coming outside to do their gardening, farming, wild crafting, hunting and fishing. I can tell you this is on the North American continent long before the people we call the American Indians were here. What I am seeing is several hundred thousand years ago.

You were the mother of twelve children. Good heavens! They were really populating the earth. There were not very many people then. There were other women who came to assist with childrearing. You had a husband, and that would be Travis in this lifetime. He was a respected elder at a very young age. He was only in his forties, but considered an elder because he inherited that title from his dad and as an elder he had the right to have other women. Therefore, he was also sleeping with a couple of the women who were helping you with the kids. You did not like that, but that was the way it was in this culture. You were still top dog; in other words, you got to boss the other women around.

There was still a great deal of jealousy and when you knew he had been with one of them, you would punish her the next day when he was gone. Of course, the women were not in control and could not help the situation, but the longer it went on, the more extreme you became with your punishments, because your rage kept growing. You were so much in love with your husband that you did not understand why he had to have relations with these other women. You continued taking it out on them until you actually killed one of them, and it was a really young one—a new one. He got rid of them when they got older or was tired of them. You were the only one he kept around, and that was because you were married. He was spending a lot of time with this new, young one, and that hurt you. In your fury, you overworked her to the point that she just collapsed and died. You were slapping her around a little bit, too.

The problem was that this was a terribly inequitable situation. There was nothing fair to you or the other women about it. You had absolutely no control in this situation, and your husband just laughed at you when you told him you were hurting. That is one of the things you came to work on in this lifetime…not pushing so hard in a personal situation, to just let it be. One of the things you could have learned in that lifetime is that we do not always get to control our environment. Life is easier if we accept what we cannot change, and it seems that you are being given opportunities in this current lifetime to work on that issue of social inequity and private unfairness.

This explains your attraction to Travis and gives you a few things to work on, which will be easier now that you know about this past life.

Mountain Climber and Guide

In this next lifetime I am seeing, you are a male mountain climber in Austria. This mountain range is called the Dolomites, or at least that is what they are called now. It is hard to tell what the timeframe is.

You were leading a group of people. Weather was bad, and the climb was not recreational. You were hiding from someone. This is prior to

WWI—let us put it that way...somewhere in that era, maybe the 1800s. The time is not clear to me yet.

You were taking these people to a remote cabin. It looks like there were five people in the group and one of them was very frail and sick. They were your friends, but they had also paid you to do this dangerous thing to help them survive. Somebody was looking for them, and it was not the government. There were individuals who were coming after your group. You were becoming impatient with the sick, frail person because she was slowing everyone down; she was having a problem with her lungs, exacerbated by being in the high altitude and the cold.

Everyone was pleading with you to slow down and give her an opportunity to continue with the group, yet you were concerned that no one at all was going to make it if you did not cut her loose. There was a storm coming, and you were pushing the group very hard in order to arrive at the cabin on time. They were refusing to leave her to die because they were close like a family. So finally you said, "Look, I am going on without you; I am not dying out here because you will not let her go. I will leave markers behind so you can find your way to the cabin, but I refuse to freeze to death out here."

So you left markers and arrived at the cabin, built a fire and got everything ready for them if and when they did get there. Finally, three of them did arrive, which meant they finally did leave her behind. And even though they did do this, they all felt like had you been there, you could have helped them with your physical strength. You were very, very strong. They were so upset when they got there that the three of them set upon you and killed you. You did not understand; you could not figure out why they were so upset with you. You had the fire going, the place was warmed up. You had food on the stove for everyone when they got there, but they blamed you for the death of the woman; they were just insane with grief. You died in sheer confusion, not understanding their reaction.

The problem was that you could not imagine how they felt leaving a family member behind to die so they could survive. Actually, everyone would have survived if you had slowed down and helped carry her, but no one knew that, including you.

That confusion about people, not understanding why they do what they do, is imprinted on your Soul, too. Not being able to put yourself in their shoes, or at least behaving as though you felt compassion for them, you would have lived. But you were just goal-oriented without any emotion or regret. And that was what got you killed.

So that is something you wanted to work on in this lifetime as well—understanding others and being compassionate.

Life Mission

A lot of people think life mission is about, "What is my career supposed to be?" It may be partly that, but it is not usually—and certainly not completely. More often it is, "As a Soul, what did I want to accomplish in this lifetime? What did I want to learn?" And you bit off a great big chunk, Marcus. You wanted to learn, first off, compassion for other people—walking a mile in their shoes, learning how you might feel were you in the same situation that they were in. That is not easy to do, because the natural thing for most people is to only look at things from their own perspective. But in this lifetime, the first and foremost thing you wanted to learn was how to feel what the other person is feeling in that moment, to empathize with them, to look at the world through another's eyes, or put another way, to step inside their skin just long enough to understand how they are feeling, and why they would do what they are doing. That is number one on your "hit parade," the most important thing you came to learn. If that were the only thing you came here to learn, that would be enough for an entire lifetime, because that one is not easy, but it is of utmost importance to your spiritual growth, as it is to everyone's. Part of that is asking, "Well, when I do this, then how do I look to them? What might they be feeling as a result of my words or actions?" In other words, if I am intimidating, then how do I look to them? How would it feel to be around someone like me? Imagine being them for a minute; see if you can feel what it would be like on the receiving end of that kind of intimidation. That will go a very long way in helping you cease and desist with intimidating behaviors.

In this lifetime, you also wanted to experience creativity. That could be dancing, it could be writing music, performing music. It could be painting, sculpting, photography, printmaking, drama, or acting— anything along those lines. All those are creative processes, and you wanted to spend a big chunk of your time, whether professionally or just for fun on the side, engaging in creative activities. Doing something like community theatre would be fine on the side, or even painting on the weekends. Creativity is something your Soul has not experienced in many lifetimes, and for that reason you wanted to dive deeply into it in this life. If you have not done anything like that yet, it is time to start playing like a little kid. Just play with paints or plucking a mandolin or whatever. Go join a community theatre or whatever excites you—whatever makes your heart sing.

Again, we have covered this already, but I am supposed to repeat it for you. One of the things you wanted to accomplish was to begin to accept what is going on at the moment, and to not push yourself so hard. Extremes in your private life, your social life, your personal life and your professional life are counter-productive. Relax and go with the flow. Control is an illusion.

Get in sync with other people and do not push so hard. It is not a matter of life and death in this lifetime, though it has been in other lifetimes. But in this one, it is not. Again, you came to learn to work in a group. Life is very different if you are not the lone cowboy, but a member of a group. That completes your past life and life mission reading.

__Lois' Notes:__ Marcus' initial reaction was surprise at the reading, and gratitude. When I contacted him a year later to ask if he had anything to add to his follow-up, he said he did, and he wanted to give it some thought, and that he would get back with me soon, but he never did.

Past Life Reading
Santha Bergeron - January 30, 2012

Santha just sent me a photo and her time zone in Australia. She did not have any questions, trusting the Guides and Guardians of the Records to tell me what she needed to know:

This is a past life reading for Santha Bergeron in New South Wales, Australia. According to the world clock website it is now 12:30am, Tuesday, the 31st of January. Where I am, it is Monday morning and the sun is just coming up. You are coming into my treatment room on the inner planes, Santha, getting onto the table, and I am sitting at the head of the table and putting the palms of my hand under the back of your head. Now I am going to pause the recording as I begin the process which allows me to see into your past life repository.

Isolationists: Underground City

This first lifetime I am seeing is in a very old community. It is a very established culture that, at the time I am seeing, has been around for 2,000 years. They still were doing things the same way they did 2,000 years earlier. This civilization lived inside the earth in caverns, but they collected food, tended gardens and kept their animals on the surface. Yet, underground there was a large city. Some interior spaces were natural and some they had excavated over the years. The reason they lived there was because they believed it was safer from not only the elements, but also from their enemies. This may be why they existed as an undisturbed civilization with no wars for such a very long time, unchanging.

You were born a female into this civilization, yet you were born with some sort of mental illness that expressed itself at a very early age. By the time you were three or four years old, people knew something was seriously wrong with you, and they did not know what to do about it. They had no way of dealing with mental illness.

People who went insane as adults were isolated. The governing body would remove them from the community, take food and water with them, and carry them to a remote area. They had special little caves, and they would just leave them there. These shunned ones were not allowed to come back; they were not allowed to see how they were getting to their remote cave, either. Why? This civilization was actually afraid of the mentally ill.

But at the time period that I am seeing, when you were a child, they had no record of anyone being born mentally ill, or becoming so in childhood. There was very little stress in this particular culture, so a lot of the mental illnesses we are familiar with in this day and age they simply did not have. Their normal state of calm prevented the formation of mental illness in large part. But this is why they could not handle people if they did go off the deep end. They did know about schizophrenia, though, and it terrified them. When a small child, like you were at that time, was exhibiting signs of serious mental illness, such as slamming your head against the wall repeatedly or running around in circles, everyone was helpless to handle the situation.

Actually, you were possessed by some sort of dark energy, and they were totally unfamiliar with this as well, and did not know what to do about that, either. So, because you were a child, they took pity on you and did not put you in a cave and isolate you, but they did keep you in the underground community and isolate you. It was like you were in a little jail. I am being shown this because you agreed before you incarnated to take on this task of helping this very old, static, established civilization learn how to deal with mental illness.

Remember that nobody had any record, and they kept meticulous ancient records in their libraries, of ever seeing a child act crazy before, and this turned them upside down and shook them hard. They convened a council of the elders, or the leaders, of the community and said, "What do we do about this? We cannot just isolate a child. An adult has a chance of feeding themselves. We give them a little food and water for starters, enough for a couple of months, and they are then alone." So they maintained you in this comfortable little jail where you could not get out and upset other people. They did not want the peace that they had established in their community toppled.

After about two years of not knowing what to do, they finally decided to end your isolation and take you to the nearest neighboring civilization with which, at one time, they had many wars. The primary way they had learned not to have wars any more was to isolate themselves from everybody else on the planet. They had thick, tall walls, well manned and protected at the edge of their territory on the surface, so no one could get in. Isolation was their solution to all problems, apparently. But because of your issues, they sent a delegation to the head of the government of their neighbors.

They took you to the nearest surface community, which was a couple hundred miles away, because in discussing your case, the council had realized they should not be isolating adults, either.

When the delegation arrived, the citizens of this other culture were in a state of shock. They could not believe they came out of their caves to actually talk to people and ask for help. It had been 1,500 years since an official delegation had left the caves to talk to anyone. They had to scurry to find someone who could even translate.

The neighboring culture sent you to their most highly regarded healer, who recognized immediately that you had what we would now call a demonic entity attachment. He removed it and you suddenly calmed down and started talking, and telling people how glad you were that the monster was not sitting on your back any more— because you had been telling people that. But they did not know what you were talking about, and would not listen to you. To get away from the demon you would run around and scream, or you would bang your head on the wall, trying to kill yourself to get away from it.

Your delegation wanted to pay their healer, but their reply was amazing. The people of the surface community said, "No, what we would like for payment is to have a trade route with you. Open your borders and begin gradually, at whatever pace is good for you, to rejoin the rest of the world, and let us train you in how to do this type of healing yourselves. Send some of your people here to learn how to heal in this manner so that you do not have to isolate the mentally ill any longer." So they did.

Your incarnating as a child with this problem accomplished a lot of things. It triggered these people to stop isolating the mentally ill, and eventually to stop isolating as a culture. Gradually, over the years, they trained healers, a trade route was established, and your culture became part of the world again. Apprenticed as a young adult, you were among the first persons trained to heal in the new way and went on to train many others in your community. This was a very productive lifetime which you needed to know about. One of the reasons you needed to know about it is that, as a counterbalance, sometimes we will come to experience being around people who are like we were in the past. You have come back, and this is part of your life purpose; you may have come back in this lifetime either to put up with someone in the family who is mentally ill, or you may also be here to work with disabled children. There are many ways to counterbalance this. You may be here to work with the mentally ill, and if you do not already do it, remove demonic entities from people, which is very powerful, important work. (But this can also be dangerous, so you would need to be trained by somebody who *really* knows what they are doing before attempting it.) Primarily, this lifetime was one of great accomplishment and heroism.

Ecological Disaster

I am seeing you swimming in very turquoise water. You are a young male in a loincloth swimming under water. You look like a frog as you swim. There is a knife in your mouth, and you are looking for something on the floor of this lagoon. It is not that deep, maybe twenty feet deep. Oh, I see. You are recovering something from a shipwreck; you are a native diver in the Pacific somewhere.

The ship went down a long time ago, and you are the first person who has ever even considered going down to see what can be recovered. Seeing something that looks like an enormous metal loop, you decide you are going to open it up. So you go back up to the surface, and get a good big lung full of air, come back down and you pull on this thing. It is metal and stuck, and you are scraping around the perimeter of it to loosen it with your knife. Finally you pull on it hard and it opens. An inky black liquid comes flooding up out of this hole and you are trying to close it again because it does not look like a good thing to be getting into the water. Now the hinge is stuck and you cannot get it to close. The black stuff, whatever it is, is burning your skin and so you get out of there, get back in your boat, row ashore, and say, "I need help. This is what happened and someone has to come down in the water and help me close this thing," but no one will do it. They were terrified. So finally this ship, it was some sort of – the liquid was some sort of experimental fuel. It was a French ship and I am not sure if they were carrying a lot of heating oil? Wait. They were going to…yeah, that is it. They wanted to colonize this island you lived on. They were carrying a whole lot of heating oil because they wanted to go up in the mountains. They were also considering doing some mining, and the oil would run their machines. The local Shamans could see what was about to happen as the foreigners came toward the island, and they warned the people on the island to sink this ship, so they did—in stealth, at night, drowning the sailors.

You got into the salvage disaster in all innocence. No one blamed you for it, but you did penance for the rest of your life due to the poisoning of the fish and the trouble to your people. The self-imposed penance was catching fish and feeding others all the time, and you never married or had children. You punished yourself and passed away early from overwork and grief, stemming from an inability to forgive yourself. Because you could not let go of the deed, you have carried it with you from lifetime to lifetime. What you need to know is that you are not guilty for something that you did in all innocence, trying to benefit your community. You thought there were things on that ship that people could use, and you were right. There were many other things. You happened to pull on the wrong thing.

But you decided that you were a bad person and that you had better not take any risks; better not try anything unless other people have already proven it is okay to do it. So the tendency to innovate, the tendency to try something new, has been scary.

Hearing about this past life will, hopefully, heal you gradually over time, so that you are not afraid to innovate. That is how culture advances; creative people try things that no one else has ever tried before.

Plus, forgive yourself for accidently causing an ecological disaster, and if you are attracted to cleaning up after ecological disasters, if you are somebody who really wishes she could go where oil spills have occurred and wash the oil off of birds, that could be why. So part of your life purpose is to learn to be free of the fear of doing something without knowing what the outcome is going to be. Also, let go of the fear of innovating, and get out there and forge new territory. That is something that your Soul really wanted to do in this lifetime.

Pregnant Quaker in Costa Rica

This life had a simple "check-out point" experience complicated by a misunderstanding. Living in rural Costa Rica in a Quaker community, you and your husband have been trying to get pregnant for years, and finally do. At about five or six months along, you are in a wheat field when you are bitten by a snake. Your husband comes rushing to you on horseback and tries to get you to a doctor, but he fails to do so in sufficient time. As you are being rushed to the doctor, dying in his arms, you decide you must have done something horribly wrong to die so young and be denied the pleasure of children.

Yet this was an incorrect conclusion. It was a check-out point taken because the Higher Self decided that something was coming that you would not be able to handle without damage to the Soul. The incorrect conclusion at the moment of death has stayed with you, and hearing about this, and knowing that you were not a bad person, will begin to allow you to heal from that.

The Boys' Choir

The next lifetime I am seeing, you are singing in a children's choir, and it is a very well regarded choir. This is in the sixteenth century in Italy. I am seeing a group of boys in a choir. Your family is poor, and the priests give your family money to allow you to spend your time in the choir when you would otherwise be working for money to help support the family. You were one of the very best singers, so the priests went to your family and said, "Look, you know we have a choir of adult men who have beautiful voices, too." These men were castrati, which means that before they went through puberty, they castrated these little boys so that their voices would not change. Thus, they could still sing the high notes beautifully. The priests went to your family and said they would give them a huge sum of money to relinquish their son to the priests for the adult male choir.

Your father did not really want to do it, because he thought it was a horrible thing to be castrated. On the other hand, the rest of the family desperately needed the money because once you went through puberty, you could not sing in the choir anymore. They would not be getting that stipend any longer, and sadly there were a lot of mouths to feed and very little money. At his wife's urging, your father ultimately did go along with it. The priests gave your family a great sum of money, and they were always moderately comfortable after that.

But no one asked you what you wanted, and you did not wish to be castrated. You did not want to be part of that choir. It never occurred to you for a moment that your mom and dad would go along with such an awful thing, because you heard them say how tragic it was for those unfortunate castrated men long before you ever started to sing in the boys' choir.

Only after the surgery did you learn your tragic fate, and you knew that meant you would never be able to get married and have kids of your own—something you wanted desperately. You wanted to grow up to be just like your dad in every way, and you would never be able to do that. Never to attain manhood, you were a livid, rage-filled eleven- or twelve-year-old boy, furious with the world, with God, with the priests, with your family. You felt betrayed and you know what? You were. You were betrayed.

Even though it was a common thing, and rarely did anyone ever turn the church down when they wanted one of their sons for such an honor, you had been certain it would never happen to you. You did not know that your dad cried for months; he horribly grieved that decision, knowing fully the depth of the wrong that was done you.

As soon as you were healed enough to walk or run, you did run. Thinking it through ahead of time, you gathered up as much treasure from the priests as you could. There were candlesticks made of gold, for example, and you knew right where they were. One moonless midnight you slipped away. No one ever dreamed a choir boy would do that. The treasures were not even guarded properly, at least not in this particular area of Italy.

Awakening a man at the livery station in a nearby town, you said, "I need a horse and some food and some water and I will give you something very valuable, and you can melt it down." You gave him a big, gold candlestick for all this, which he did melt down. He did not know who you were or that people would be looking for you, nor did he care. Never looking back, you journeyed direct to the coast on the far-eastern side of the country, riding your horse to the sea by back roads by asking verbal directions along the way. People were just so surprised by a little boy all by himself on a horse—thinking you must have been royalty or somebody rich on an urgent mission, they left you alone.

Making it all the way to the sea, you took a barge—traded the horse for a trip across the water, and got yourself another horse on the other side. Proceeding on to what is now called Croatia, you reestablished yourself. Eventually, you opened an orphanage for little boys because you wanted to protect other children. With the money you stole from the church, you changed your name and made up a story about your life in which your family had died and left you with everything. Citing that you were an orphan wanting to take care of other orphans, you did open a facility—a non-denominational orphanage—and you lovingly took care of other children in bad situations for the rest of your life. At some point a woman came into your life, and you loved her dearly. She loved you as well, and it was okay with her that you could not have children, because you could still have sexual relations. You got married, and running the orphanage together, you lived happily ever after.

That is an amazing thing to have done with the terrible tragedy and betrayal perpetrated upon a little boy. That is such a powerful and surprising thing for a child of that age to do. I am being told that this lifetime gave you a big "gold star" in your crown as a Soul.

Lois's Notes: *Here is Santha's feedback from the reading, which has many connections to the past lives I saw, even though I did not know these things about her prior to the reading. This is my confirmation that the reading was accurate:*

Hi Lois,

Thank you for the reading. I just thought I'd let you know as a matter of interest, I work as an employment services manager. We help people that have barriers to employment such as mental health, drug addiction, etc., and I have recently read a few books on entity possession and gave some people prayers to dispel negative entities.

I have always had a fascination with turquoise water and feel very at home in the south pacific region and with islanders. I have often thought that if I ever came into a great deal of money I would open up a haven for kids that are ostracized by their family or scarred due to cultural disputes or to escape "honour" beatings etc., and to try and educate those parents and communities.

When do you recommend, if at all, how long to wait for another reading? I obviously will be learning from this reading now but I like to grow and this is a peaceful way to know me better.

Santha

<u>Lois' Notes:</u> I asked Santha in a reply email if I might have permission to include her reading in my next book. As you can see, she gives permission and a lot more information having to do with the past lives and how they have impacted her current lifetime. Below is Santha's answer to me:

Dearest Lois,

I am most happy for you to use the information if it will benefit you and your readers. With this in mind I'll tell you a little more. I have never married, nor have I had children and I have always had a fear of giving birth. In fact when I was about twenty-three years of age, I had a nightmare that I was pregnant and close to giving birth. I was petrified in the dream that something was going to go horribly wrong.

When I was thirty I looked after another person's child when he was about twelve years of age, she was going to give him up to foster care due to behavioral problems, but the boy didn't have behavioral problems. The mother had parenting problems.

I do live with my partner's seven-year-old son now, and he also had behavior issues that were really parenting issues. Others have recognized this theme of my looking after other peoples' children but not having any of my own. Clearly this seems to relate to the boys' choir/orphanage past life.

As for the tropical island past lifetime, I won't eat fish, I like going fishing but I never keep them, I always feel very compassionate toward them, and often feel guilty about hurting them. I only go on holidays to places that are tropical such as Fiji and the Cook Islands. In the reading you mentioned in a life that I swam down to a French ship. This reminded me of an experience I had when I returned from holiday in Fiji. I was in my bed but I felt uneasy and had never felt that before in that room, I opened my eyes and saw in front of me a shortish skeleton in a 16th-19th century soldiers uniform (I'm not good with military uniform times). I went to work and described it to my boss who told me that it sounds like a French soldier's uniform from centuries ago. We discussed how I could run into a dead French soldier over 200 yrs old in Sydney Australia. She then mentioned that the French had tried to invade Fiji at one point, and I must have picked up a hitch hiker.

After your reading it makes a little more sense, that was my first trip to the South Pacific and I was so looking forward to that ocean, like it was special in some way. (I still do think it's special.)

As for the lifetime in the cave community, I am a qualified mental health counselor (I studied to get the formal qualifications, however I found it incredibly easy and didn't need to study, the information was in my mind). I do have the ability to understand and verbalize what others are feeling. If they are having difficulty doing that themselves, I seem to be able to unravel the emotions and help them clarify it mentally. I've always been able to do this and can pick up on emotions very easily. I don't really have to speak to them to know what emotions they are feeling, however I don't often do this because it's important people communicate, but if there is an emotion underneath that they are possibly hiding and it needs to come out, I grab it for them. I can also do this with animals if I am around them for a certain period. I can heal through my hands when I need to, and I can often work out if an illness is emotional, mental or spiritual or a combination.

In regard to the spirit attachment, I have always questioned whether multiple personality disorders and schizophrenia, among others, are actually spiritual events in some cases. I recall seeing an Oprah episode with a lady that had a huge number of personalities, and I just couldn't understand why nobody mentioned this may be spirits speaking through or taking over for her—or if a trauma in this life had caused her to alternate between different lifetime personalities either, in order to cope or due to a "short circuit" that had been caused via the damage.

And yes, I actually do have quite extensive experience in removing both discarnate and demonic entities.

In Gratitude,
Santha Bergeron

Lois' Notes: *I thanked Santha for her detailed, fascinating feedback. I also agreed with her that multiple personalities and some cases of schizophrenia seem to be instances of "spiritual events." For example, these forms of mental illness sometimes can appear to be one of two things. They might be some form of entity possession coming from a past life. Or, they may be one of the Soul's own past life fragments stepping up to help out a traumatized child but then remaining operational afterward. Remaining operational afterward is, of course, inappropriate. This would be the "short-circuit" to which Santha referred. I was both relieved and gratified at this confirmation of my suspicions by someone else with in-depth psychological training and, in Santha's case, vast clinical experience.*

Past Life Reading

Sandra Ballinger - January 19, 2013

Sandra, who is an American living in Western Europe, sent me the following message when asking for her reading:

Dear Lois,

For my questions, I would like information about my husband, Miles, in any past lives we may have had together. I'd like insight on the purpose of this lifetime. I have always followed the spiritual path toward Oneness and feel an overwhelming desire to express my true spiritual nature. But truly, I just want an objective look to know what is most important, and necessary, for me to know about that will provide insight into this life experience. Now this is funny, and I'm not being flippant, but an old song title suddenly comes to mind - "What's It All About, Alfie?"

Thank you so much.
Sandra

This is Sandra's reading:

Elephants in a Storm

In the first lifetime I am seeing, the first scene I am shown is you participating in some parade. This is happening in what is now called Pakistan, and I believe Pakistan was part of India at that time. This was quite some time ago. It was a very happy festival of a parade. Everybody was dressed in bright colors, their clothes sparkling, and there was joyful music. People were dancing in the parade and onlookers in the street were dancing as well. You were in charge of making elephants dance as part of the parade. Apparently you were an elephant keeper—they were actually trainers—yet they called them keepers. You were responsible for six elephants. In this life you were a male.

You were having quite the time of your life and fondly looked forward to this particular festival each year. The holiday had to do with the

Goddess Lakshmi. I cannot really tell when this was, but it was hundreds of years ago. In a way, the festival had so much going on it was like a Mardi Gras parade without all the sexuality and drunkenness. People were acting wild and crazy and having great fun. There was great revelry and everybody was on a major endorphin high. This parade, this celebration, happened to coincide with some very good news that your country had received about good fortune coming from over the ocean or something like that…trade routes were perhaps being opened. It seemed that it would be extremely profitable, and that everyone was going to benefit greatly from doing business with foreigners. The entire populace was giddy at the prospect of these great riches. The foreigners who had come to establish trade routes were European. These people had been handing out goodies to everyone. They were sparkly, fascinating things, which no one had seen before. It was rather like when the American Indians saw mirrors for the first time, how excited they were over such a small thing. You were over the moon over these things that seemed like trinkets to the Westerners.

Going forward a bit…a few months later…you were contacted by some of these foreigners to bring your elephants across the sea—these particular people are Portuguese, actually—to bring your elephants to Europe and show people there what you could do with elephants. Showing elephants at all was going to be a major event for them. They had not seen this particular type of elephant nor elephants with these particular types of adornments doing these particular types of dances and tricks.

You had a very special, close relationship with the elephants in your charge. You thought about it long and hard, asking for spiritual signs, and believed you got a clear sign that you and your elephants were to get aboard the ship and go to Portugal. To get the animals inside the belly of the ship, the crew had to create a special opening into the hold of the ship.

At one point the ship encountered choppy seas. There soon followed a very bad storm. The crew had closed that opening back up after the elephants were in...it was made its normal small size again so that in case of a storm, water would not quickly fill the hold of the ship. They did this thinking that they would have plenty of time to open that door back up to get the elephants out once they reached Portugal. However, this was a freak storm with huge waves, which happens yet rarely, out at sea. No one knew that it was coming—it was a woeful surprise. It was a freakishly intense storm.

What happened next was horrific. The elephants were of course extremely heavy, and they would not hold still but kept moving around nervously. The higher the seas became, the more the elephants got upset. They swayed back and forth and back and forth, walking to and fro, making it very hard on the people who were trying to steer the ship. Their movements even affected the handling of the sails. Ultimately the ship capsized. Most of the people managed to get into the lifeboats safely, but your elephants drowned. You were in shock, and kept trying to get back to the ship, and diving below the water's surface, hoping to get the elephants out. However, someone grabbed you and forced you aboard one of the lifeboats. There simply was no saving those elephants. It was monstrous to you because you believed the elephants were your life. You grieved inconsolably.

The lifeboats were picked up by another ship after a few days and you made your way back home—months later.

Upon your return, everybody greeted you with great joy and said, "Oh, we are so happy to see you. How did it go in Portugal? Do you want us to help you unload the elephants?" You had to tell everyone over and over again what happened. You felt responsible, yet there truly was nothing you could have done about that freak accident of nature. You were confused, since you had thought that Spirit wanted you to take your elephants to Europe. And actually, you were hearing your guidance correctly. You were supposed to learn a lesson from this—and as with all lessons, it was planned before you incarnated. The lesson was that we are not in control, and we have to roll with the punches. We must survive our losses, dust ourselves off and continue on with life. You intended to learn in that lifetime both how to survive great loss and to have compassion for people who are grieving. In doing that you could be an example for others on how to handle mistakes and grief and then to come out the other side of that kind of pain.

There were more elephants back home pining for you—missing you so much, and you finally went to those elephants and cried, grieving even more over the ones who drowned. But due to the guilt you felt, it took a while before you went to them. So unfortunately, at first you neglected the elephants you had left behind because you were so overcome by grief and self-recrimination and not forgiving yourself. Taking them on the ship was not inherently wrong. There was a lesson in the experience—and now you know that.

Now, I do not know whether or not this relates to your current experience living in France. There must have been things you gave up to move there, and the important thing to know is—I am hearing this and I have heard it before: "Bloom where you are planted." Finally, in this lifetime you did go to a foreign country to live, and one of the reasons for that experience was so that you could more fully learn that lesson of adapting to a new environment, how to make the best of what you have, and how to create a meaningful life wherever you are—letting go of what is beyond your control.

By the way, your husband Miles was with you in that lifetime. He was the ship's first mate, second in command to the captain. He was the person who forced you into one of the lifeboats when you risked your life trying the impossible task of getting back to the elephants.

The Leatherworker's Leg

What I am seeing now…is that you are in a very frozen environment. I am seeing you sliding down a slippery channel on what looks a bit like a luge—on some sort of device. You are sliding on ice going down a frozen, slippery path designed specifically for people to go super-fast—and just for fun. You are male, and I am getting that what I am seeing is in what is now Finland. They are not calling it a luge at this point in time but it is…I am hearing the word sluice. This is a narrow winding pathway made specifically for these things you are racing on, but it is filled with water in warm weather. I notice that you are lying down racing, because you go faster that way, since it cuts down on wind drag.

You were married, and had not been married very long. Your wife was pregnant, and she begged you to stop this sport because it frightened her. She was about to have a baby, and wanted you to be there for them. You told her not to worry; you would be just fine. You were not paying attention to her wishes, and one day when you were racing down this thing somebody else got onto the path ahead of you. The rules were strict; they were not supposed to stop at all until they got to the bottom. But the man in front of you dropped something, and thought that he had enough time to go back and pick it up, but there was not enough time. You slammed into him, killing him and maiming yourself.

It took a long while for you to heal, as you had broken a leg quite severely. For months you were totally laid up and could not walk at all—you had a compound fracture of the left thigh bone. Unfortunately, your wife had to take care of you as though you were a baby. She even had to diaper you, since you could not get out of the bed. To make matters worse, you were in searing pain—there is little worse than bone pain.

Sadly, you did not ever walk properly again. But fortunately your work did not require you to be extremely physical. You were not a farmer or woodcutter or anything like that. In your work you did something while you were sitting...let's see...oh, I see now. You did leatherwork.

This was work that you had always done from home, but due to the sustained period of incapacitation you became extremely far behind in your work. There were unpaid bills as a result of your accident and inability to work, and you became quite depressed. In other words, you did not easily get past this event. Again, this is the same lesson—getting past this mistake or perceived mistake and making the best of the moment. Making a fast recovery emotionally is one thing that you had wanted to learn in that lifetime, and you did a bit, but not nearly as thoroughly or as well as you had hoped you would. To the disappointment of your family, you were grumpy the rest of your life. You were so busy beating yourself up, you did not realize it was making everyone else miserable. Your leg hurt most of the time, too. There was always some pain— especially when the weather changed. So that is a partially learned lesson, since you were grumpy and took it out on everybody else. The family was not as happy as it might have been. That was rather the same lesson as in the last lifetime we saw: learning to make the best of what you have in the moment and bloom where you are planted.

Missing the Point

I am seeing you in a lifetime in which you are male and preparing the soil for planting using a hoe-like device to break up the soil, which is packed down hard. It is very dry, rocky soil—not a very good environment for growing food. Oh, I see, you were in Peru, located really high up where the climate was arid. All the water had to be carried in with buckets. These were extremely rough conditions. You grew crops acclimated to the altitude—at around 11,000 feet above sea level, you were scraping out a living on this harsh little patch of land where it hardly ever rains.

It is difficult to tell how long ago this was, but it was not recent, that is for sure. Looking at you, your eyes sparkle, but your face and lips are dry and cracked, your hands are dry and cracked, and you just work all day long, morning until night. . .year after year, and so does everybody else around you. At the time I am seeing you, you were an older man and your children were grown. Your wife was an old woman, and she also worked the fields. Everybody stayed in pretty good shape because they had to work so hard. Nobody could slack off or they would not survive. It was like forced exercise.

You began thinking toward the end of your life, what was the point of all of this? There was nothing hugely significant that happened in this lifetime; it was just a lifetime of constant subsistence-level work. Of course, you had a wife who loved you, you had children and grandchildren who adored you, but you were working for what? You found yourself wondering, what is the grand scheme—the meaning of life? Should not the gods have had something in mind for me besides this? You were missing the entire point, which was love. Love was the whole point of that lifetime, and you had enormous amounts of love in that life.

That is a great challenge in any lifetime. We struggle to remember to look around and notice what we have to be grateful for. You were not grateful for a life filled with people who loved you, since you did not recognize this as something some people did not have, even though you were happy because of all those who loved you.

And that love was something to be grateful for, because as soon as we are grateful, we get more of what makes us happy. With that gratitude, we give off a frequency that attracts more of what we want. Gratitude is probably the most important thing we can experience on a day-to-day basis, because it brings us more of what we want, and we can decide to be grateful for the tiniest little things, like the dew glistening on the leaves outside the front door. If we just notice the smallest things—a sparkle of sunlight on the snow, or the clouds moving through the sky—our own world becomes a better place. To notice small details like those we find in the perfection of nature, truly being present brings peace and joy, making our lives more fulfilled. As soon as we do this, it opens up the possibility for more beautiful experiences. That was an unresolved bit that seems to have carried forth from that lifetime—pondering the meaning of that lifetime into your old age, and not figuring out that the meaning of life was simply love.

The Seal Hunter

In the next lifetime I am seeing you as a seal hunter. This was a couple of hundred years ago. Once again you were male, and you lived and worked travelling around Alaska harpooning seals, skinning them, and leaving their flesh to be eaten by whatever animal came along. You were only interested in taking the skins. The money was quite good. But the longer you did it, and the more money you had stockpiled, the more killing seals bothered you. The attitude of your crew toward these animals and their suffering began to disturb you as well. They had absolutely no compassion whatsoever.

Finally you retired and sold your ship and your trade route—meaning the area where it was okay for you to sell the skins. Apparently you needed someone's permission to go to certain places to sell. You sold the trade route and ship to the same person. You took the money and retired to a location far from the sea, because you did not ever want to see the ocean again—it reminded you of killing all of those poor, innocent little seals. When you first started, it did not bother you. The older you got the more it bothered you because of the noises they made as they died.

Taking the money from the seal hunting, you bought land. It looks like a lavender field somewhere in what is now current day France, actually. You decided you were not going to do anything having to do with animals, because it was not something you ever wanted to be around again. You did not even keep dogs.

You planted lavender and other flowers, employing people who knew about this sort of thing to teach you. Hiring men to do the hard work, you became a lavender farmer. There were other enterprises on the side, too. You grew some grapes and had a very small boutique winery, selling wines locally. And you grew some other thing—a white flower—I am not sure what it is. That is what you did for the rest of your life. You kept absolutely no pets and told your employees that if animals that were pests had to be destroyed, you did not want to know about it; they should just take care of business and not bother you with it. I am being told that you are going to figure out why you need to hear about this lifetime. It may be obvious at first, or it may take a little time before that realization pops in, but anyway, this completes your past life reading today. Thank you.

Here is Sandra's feedback from the reading—a couple of months later:

Dear Lois,

I wanted to let you know that the Akashic Records reading you did for me mid-January gave me food for thought. And the last one resulted in an intense emptying process, with a sense of profound grief and sadness. You won't remember probably, but it was about a life where I was a seal hunter, and killed and skinned baby seals; later on in that life, not being able to take the cruelty of it, I sold out and moved to the south of France. When I first heard the life recall, I had a sense of total denial. It seemed so foreign to my current state of being that it took a while to digest it, apparently. About a week after hearing the reading, the emptying process occurred with tears, grief, sadness, and asking for forgiveness of these gentle beings. It has never come back to my conscious thought. I know that your work is done as part of your spiritual dharma, with absolutely no judgment. Just wanted to let you know it was a very powerful experience.

Peace and blessings,
Sandra

I replied to her with a question:

Dear Sandra,

Thank you for the feedback from your past life reading. That is so beautiful. Something healed deep inside of you, of course, and likely was at a subconscious level. Have you been able to attach that to any changes in your life?

Right, I have no judgment about people's past lives. If the Guardians don't judge us, why should I? I am certainly no greater than they.

No, I had not remembered that seal lifetime. I wonder if you found the South of France familiar when you first went there? Just curious, since you now live in France.

Thanks again!
Lois

Sandra answered:

Dear Lois,

No, I haven't been able to attach this healing (seal hunter) to anything in my present life, or to any changes. In the reading you said that your Guides told you that it was important for me to know about this lifetime, and that I would understand why later. So, I'll let that unfold. One thing that occurs to me is that it could be that it was necessary for me to face this buried trauma so that I could recognize the character trait of "getting money at any cost." The idea of doing something similar is physically repulsive to me. But, I'll let you know if anything happens to give me more insight. It really was a profound experience.

You asked if the South of France seemed familiar to me. I have an idea I know about where I lived, but haven't yet visited that region. I first visited France forty-three years ago, at age eighteen, with my sister, Karen. It seemed then that France was very "familiar" and that I "knew" it without ever having visited it before. So interesting.

Love,
Sandra

Past Life Reading

Tamara Mollinard - June 13, 2012

Here is what Tamara wanted to know from her reading:

Dear Lois,

First, it seems I am at a crossroads. My guides would like for me to choose my next vocation (divinely guided work in my definition). Catalyst is all I get. Serving my part in the divine plan is most important to me. Being multi-faceted, there are so many areas that attract my interest: music, writing, motivational speaking (never done it but those who know me name it a gift), math/science, some form of healing/medicine (crystals, color, light and sound are recurring themes here), starting a spiritual retreat in Montana . . . currently I sell real estate (and helped with Light/wireless sound devices) and as you say your work doesn't have to coincide with your WORK, but my calling is so strong. I have WORK to do. Is there a hint in my mission? Yes, I know, go inside!! My work on the inner realms is accelerating rapidly. Any smidge of info, if even in the form of a question is greatly appreciated here! I'm READY!!!

What is/was the contract between Earl Higgins and me? Pictures attached.

How can I maximize this opportunity of a lifetime?

By the way, I've been working slowly with your EDINA method and it's really interesting. So far, I've only worked on myself, and it's interesting what I'm told to do.

Thank you for your dedication to your calling. Bless you for recognizing your talents and putting them to use for the benefit of all. I am working on joining you.

Respectfully,
Tamara Mollinard

And here is Tamara's reading:

Fancy Flying

The first thing I am seeing is a WWI bi-plane pilot. I am hearing "Sopwith Camel." I think that is a type of plane and may be the one you are flying or one you have flown. I am hearing a name that sounds something like Bandera, Bandara…I do not know. I do not usually get names. You were a Canadian flying for the British, I think, although…I seldom get names and locations because that is not the point anyway. People get distracted by insignificant facts and don't focus on what happened to them.

I am seeing that you were seriously into fancy flying. You were more into that than the whole dropping things on people, like those early bombs. You were into reporting back what you had seen, which was your main mission anyway—to let people know about troop movements and supply. [At this point I am chuckling.] Okay, this is interesting. This is what your Guides are saying: you were "getting confused" about what you were supposed to be doing, You were having so much fun being an aerial acrobat and showing off for the people on the ground, even though they were the enemy and you would never see them. You forgot this was a military exercise. Even when you came back to base, you would do the same thing over the landing strip. You were having fun with your job, showing off.

You may have already guessed that some of that fancy maneuvering got you into trouble while you were flying into a mist— rather a low cloud. Lower than you thought you were, you caught a downdraft—I forget what they call them, but they can shove you down and make you lose altitude. Your craft crashed into the side of a big hill, and it took you a few hours to die and there was lot of pain.

The Guides want you to know about this life for more than one reason—because you were a good pilot and because you enjoyed performing. You would still get a kick out of performing, whether as a motivational speaker or in any other capacity. They want you to know that you have had a tendency in the past to trip over the purpose of what you are doing. In other words, you say, "I know I am supposed to be doing this, but I could also be doing that at the same time. I am sure it would be fun." They are saying do not do that again. As you were in pain and dying, you were fading in and out of consciousness—you had a lot of broken bones. Actually, your spine was broken.

It seems you had a co-pilot. There was a fellow in the seat behind you, and it was this man you asked me about: Earl. He did live through the crash. Somehow, the impact was softened by your body, and he lived. Fading in and out of consciousness as you lay there dying, you were thinking, "Okay. What did I do wrong? Was this an accident, or did I screw up?"

Whether or not you were at fault for the crash, the answer is: discretion is the better part of valor. In other words, if you were trying to be an amazing pilot, and you went down in history, it was much more important to stay alive so you could do that than it was to do all the aerial acrobatics you were notorious for. Taking care and staying alive was more important than being noticed. People loved watching it—your commanding officer did not, though. He was worried for you. You were confused when you died, and it seems that you sometimes still at times experience that confusion thinking. "What is going on here, really? Am I doing something wrong? Is this just bad luck, or is the universe trying to tell me something?" I am getting that you spend a lot of time confused, whether you are able to articulate that for yourself or not.

What you need to know is to focus on what you are doing. Focus on the task at hand and do not get sidetracked by the…I hear the word "glory." The task is what is important, not the audience or the applause.

In that lifetime, though you were hit by wind shear, which comes from out of the blue, had you been focused on returning from your mission and flying cautiously, it would not have shoved you down far enough to hit that hill. You would have been far above it.

A Spy in France

I am not yet sure when this is. I do not think it is very long ago. I am seeing you in a classroom and it is one of those…okay…you are in England and you are a woman. It is one of those auditorium-style classrooms where the seats are in tiers, with the seats going up toward the back. You are a university professor teaching history. I got confused because I saw you wearing judicial robes and a wig; you know those powdered wigs of which the British were so fond. Wearing it, you were just making the history lesson more interesting. At times you would come in costume.

This occurred in the 1930s, I believe. This was British and European History from a certain period to a certain period—like perhaps 1840s to modern times. This occurred at Cambridge, it seems, yet I am also hearing another word—Glacelle, Griselle—and I am not sure what that means. You were a gifted professor of history. Now what I am seeing is getting very interesting. You also spoke French and when WWII broke out, you were approached by a British spy group to foray into France. Since you spoke French growing up, the accent was impeccable; your father was British and your mother, French.

Because of this, you were sent to parachute into France, oddly enough, to masquerade as a French woman. The objective was to gather intelligence and then send information back using Morse code. You did this for a few years before someone you thought was a friend...actually a female cousin of yours, turned you in to the Nazis as a spy. I am not seeing that woman in your life currently, although you may meet her later. You will just have a hit that this is who it is, and so be careful. Forgive her, but do not trust her. She is still rather like this—she turned you in for money. After your capture they tortured you, including sexual abuse. You were beaten and eventually killed by electrocution. You need to know about this because it will explain things to you that I do not know, but you do. Some of it you will understand now, some of it will come in only later.

You did not marry, nor did you have children. You appeared to be in your late twenties or early thirties when you died. I am also hearing the word or the name Serena. I do not know if that is a town, or the person who turned you in. I do not know. You need to know about this for another reason, and that is that you have had more than one lifetime as someone who worked secretly behind the scenes for the good of mankind. Pat yourself on the back. Your Guides are applauding your sacrifice, and that is the kind of applause we want. They are saying that you were sacrificing yourself on the altar of the advancement of humanity because had the Nazis taken over, well, today this would be a very different world. You were a war hero, my dear, and you were very capable of working behind the scenes to make things happen. You may be called upon to do that in some way, shape, or form again in this lifetime. Just be aware when that shows up in your life. Say yes, because you are really good at it and this time you do not have to die. This time you will not die, so fear not.

British Collaborator

This is Colonial America I am seeing, and you are playing a piccolo—those little piercing, shrill things. You are in a Colonial regiment. Gosh.

Another war lifetime! You are male and you started out as a British soldier who switched sides. You gave the Colonials valuable information about the British side, and the reason you did this was, as you observed the Americans, you realized that they were on the side of what was right. You did not have a good reason nor any right to repress them. Definitely you were not the only British soldier who defected and came over to the American side. I am seeing you right after the war marching in a parade—a little parade, but it was a big deal to you. Anyway, you were playing the piccolo, bursting with pride because you helped the Americans win their freedom from the British.

You became a citizen, married, settled down, and had three children. You owned a small dairy farm in Virginia. You lived a long and happy life, but you need to know that happened only because, as a Soul, you have the capacity to see the big picture and decide if what you are doing is the right thing and if not, putting on the brakes and actually doing the right thing. It is second nature to you.

I am also seeing—let me describe what you looked like when you were marching. You were wearing a little white wig, which is rather cute considering you wore a white wig when lecturing as the history professor in Britain. Also, you had a hobby that involved making musical instruments. It seems that you may have made that piccolo. You are pretty proud of that lifetime on the soul level and you have every right to be. One of things that they want you to know about this lifetime is that it is possible for you to pass through difficult times and come out on top, and then just have a wonderful life filled with peace. That is what you had on that dairy farm. The day that stood out the most in that life was the day where the crowds were applauding as the band played, and you were playing a piccolo that you had made yourself.

Flower Farmer

Now I see you in France in the early 1700s or 1800s, and you are a flower farmer growing many flower varieties, but especially peonies. You are a male, but you do have a lot of feminine qualities. You are one of those on the border—let us call it androgynous. You neither married nor had children. You had male lovers, but in secret. People were not talking about that in those days. Some of the lovers are a tad on the young side, but things were always consensual. You had a series of men and young boys, ages thirteen and up, working for you. You did not employ any women because you did not enjoy being around them.

What you did with the flower crops was this: some of it was cut and sold at a market just outside a small village. You would put the flowers in wooden buckets filled with water and drive them to market in a horse-drawn wagon. That was great fun for you. You loved being in your stall selling your flowers. However, what you did with the majority of your crop was distillation, making essential oils, perfumes, and hydrosols—the water left over after the distillation—which was prized as well.

You had a strong, booming business for that time period, and for that life it was good. Yet there was a part of you that felt like there might be something wrong with taking these young lovers, even though, again, it was consensual. They had a leaning in that direction anyway, and they were older teenagers. It always bothered you somewhat, but there was not anyone around saying this was wrong. You just rather sensed it was not right. You lived to be relatively old, and you died of syphilis, for which there was no cure in those days. You were in your late forties or early fifties. It was not a pleasant way to go. There were those who took care of you, yet you felt like this disease was punishment for having had lovers who were probably too young.

Your Guides want you to know that the disease was not a punishment, it was…many times disease is a way of clearing…I am hearing "karmic residue." I have not heard that phrase before: karmic residue. I am hearing that it is one way of burning off what some people refer to as "negative" karma. It is a fast, quick, easy way for the Soul to burn detritus off so that one does not have to spend several lifetimes experiencing difficult things over and over to be rid of the "negative" karma. In that sense, it did have something to do with these teenage lovers, but it was not punishment, it was a way of burning off karma for that lifetime and certain other lifetimes—just all clumped together.

So if you have strong feelings about people who today we would call pedophiles, this lifetime and illness would partially explain those feelings. Remember, though, that there is no judgment in the Akashic Records, and you have worked through that karma—what there was. These young men were willing. They came to your doorstep to get a job knowing what kind of a place it was, and there were other places to work where there were women. Yours was one of those places where there were no women and although nobody talked about it, everybody knew what that meant. These were the places for people to go who had leanings in that direction.

Aboriginal Time Travel

Next I am seeing an Aboriginal man in Australia about 200 years ago. Immediately what I am getting is that those guys knew how to open time portals, to move into time travel. A big piece of how well that worked was due to the skills of the didgeridoo player. I am seeing you with white paint in strange patterns on your body. Not only did you play the didgeridoo, but you taught others how to play so you could go into the center of that vortex and time travel as well.

They went back and forward in time and were just observers trying to keep things balanced on the planet. They tried hard not to interfere, because it was against the rules to interfere, but occasionally one of them would whisper something in a person's ear. So you can expect to hear from this guy. He is actually one of your guides. Here is how it worked:

These men would go into an altered state of consciousness brought on by dancing to the didgeridoo, time-travel and talk to other versions of themselves, other incarnations, or what they considered to be parallel realities. I think sometimes he comes to you, if you have ever seen a little, dark man with sort of matted hair almost like dreadlocks or braids—I am not sure what is going on with the hair—and beautiful white dotted patterns painted onto his skin. If you have not seen him, pay attention in your meditations or dreams, as you might see him. He has some really good information for you and some advice. This guy was really spiritually advanced, as were many of those people in Australia, those whom we call the Aboriginals. They were involved with time travel and the Dreamtime. Also their consciousness is very much connected to dolphins and whales, who are masters of the Dreamtime.

The Aboriginal man had a wife who was also quite spiritually evolved. Again, that is Earl, and she is the one who usually took over with the didgeridoo when her husband (you) wanted to journey through the time portal. So you two have been together more than once, and in different capacities.

Life Mission

Now we are going to move on to life purpose. When I read your email, it was like this loud, crashing "YES" when I got to the part about starting a spiritual center or retreat center. This will be a place where you can incorporate many things you know and want to do, including motivational speaking—as long as you remember to focus on your teaching. The point is not just to perform, but to incorporate performance as a tool for more powerful and effective teaching. Also, I am hearing that you need an instructional instrument to hand out at the end: it is often called a test. It is to help you to learn if your students comprehended what it was you were trying to teach—not to pass or fail the students. Hire somebody who knows about education, someone who has taken education classes in college, and who knows how to create such an instrument. It is actually difficult to write an effective test if one has no background in education. When you see how much your students learned, you will realize how much you taught, and change your teaching methodology if needed.

As far as the retreat center is concerned, everything will fall into place easily when you make a commitment to doing that. This does not mean you are supposed to stop running these businesses that you already have going—hire staff to run things when you have everything in place and worked out.

Again, you already know most of your initial staff for the center. This will also be a center for other teachers. It is a seed pod, a place for people to come who want to create similar centers. The first spin-off will be in Edmonton, Alberta, headed by someone else who will invite you to be on their board.

Much of your life purpose has had to do with—and you have accomplished a lot of this already—promoting cutting-edge technology, and benefitting from that effort yourself. That is not going to change. More technologies will come to you for your review so you can put them out there for people to get their hands upon. That is going to be one of your income streams. You do not need just one, but you need several different income streams. That is far more stable than only one. As far as new technology is concerned, spiritual technology will be part of the healing center.

There are two different kinds of technology. Spiritual technology is much more powerful and safer to use than machine technology. The center is going to be a place where new spiritual technologies are introduced. There will even be conferences and conventions there, energy medicine conferences, and you will host many teachers of energy medicine.

There will be more and more energy medicine modalities on the planet, and your staff will have to "test drive" them, even if it is just experiencing the modality, deciding which ones to introduce to the world because they work, and which ones to cull, or not give your stamp of approval.

Unfortunately, there will be the frauds showing up desiring fame, fortune and notoriety, but who are not genuine. Part of your task will have to do with becoming familiar—and this will happen by standing with one foot in the spiritual world and one in the technological world—with machines that can measure what is going on with the human energy field as clients are being worked upon with energy medicine. You will be using some of those machines that already exist, and ones not yet created.

You are tasked with creating a non-profit foundation. Fundraising will be your forte. And you will travel, talking to people about energy medicine, showing them the machines operating as the healers are doing sessions. Gradually people will be able to see the energy without the use of machines. The machines are "training wheels" for people as they are waking up. Thus, they get the confirmation they need. "Oh yeah, you know, as I close my eyes and I see that, that is what the machine is seeing, too. How about that? I am really seeing it." That will be nice, that will be handy and so much easier than having to go on faith, like most us have had to do.

Now, as far as your contract with Earl, he is here to support you emotionally and vice versa, but that is the only contract. Anything else you decide to do together is totally up to you. Maybe you just want to be lovers, friends with benefits, maybe you want to get married, maybe you want to go into business together—that is all up to you. The thing you agreed to do for each other that you have done in the past and in many other lifetimes is provide emotional support and a sounding board. "What do you think of this? This is what is going through my head, but what do you think?" Get and give honest feedback, because you are really good at doing that for each other.

As far as children, this is something you can do if you like, but it is not one of the things you decided was important in this lifetime—to have children or work with children. It is not to say that you cannot do it, you can, but it is not one of your life purpose or mission goals.

I am seeing you working in the future with rape victims. That is one of your life's missions or goals—to help mitigate the trauma of rape. This is not just for women; men get raped as well. I am seeing you use energy medicine to heal people and to remove energetic implants that the rapists have left in their victims. Most people do not realize they are there; they simply suffer from the ill effects.

These implants cause the trauma to continue long after the act of rape is over. I am being shown that the energetic implants are in the body, and they are right about where the second chakra intersects the pranic tube. This is something left behind which interferes with creativity, sexuality and feeling safe in the world. Additionally, energy coming from the earth through the root chakra stops at the second chakra, and due to the implant, everything above is blocked from receiving the grounding energies of the earth. I am just now seeing that for the first time; they are showing that to me. Fascinating!

To sum it up, your life purpose is to help others heal and to bring a new way of being into the earth. You are one of the midwives of a new way of healing and living and being in the new earth. For this, you will be remembered. Books will be written about your healing center, and what a difference it made in the lives of others, if you do follow through and do this work that you planned to do before you incarnated.

Lois' Notes: *Tamara wrote to me later that the reading resonated on many levels, explained a lot, and that some of the more off-the-wall things I had said which she doubted could ever happen, had happened within six months.*

Conclusion

Like anyone else, I continue to learn new things. At some point I realized I should have been telling people to lie down and close their eyes the very first time they listened to the recording of their reading. When I finally did start telling people that, many of the clients who were able to visualize emailed me stating that they could see in their mind's eye what I was about to say just before I said it. This was what had often happened when I did the readings in person or led a meditation group, so it made sense it would happen when someone first listened to a recording of their reading. It is a lovely confirmation for the client, if and when that happens.

I also learned why it was that so many of the clients I have seen usually came from the same or similar locations and time periods. I discovered this from finally reading a book on Cayce's past life readings about a year ago. According to Cayce, large groups of Souls come back into incarnation together at approximately the same time periods. This immediately resonated with my experience. I have for over twenty years seen many people who lived and often died during World War II. A lot of them were there in Germany as soldiers, citizens, spies, or those incarcerated for being Gypsies or Jews. Many were Allied soldiers or spies as well.

Additionally, I have seen many past lives in Lemuria, Atlantis, Ancient Egypt, Rome and Greece, or Native Americans many hundreds of years prior to the invasion by the white man. I have also seen past lives more recently in Europe, the UK and USA, ranging from about the 1600s to current times. There have also been many in the rest of North

America—Mexico and Canada—and South America, going fairly far back in time. While I have seen some prior lives in Asia and India, many cultures are greatly under-represented in the lifetimes I have been shown.

It is interesting to note that alive at this time are hundreds of thousands of people who were in Atlantis during its last couple of hundred years of existence. This was during the time period it was spiraling toward destruction, before it sank beneath the earth due to wrongful scientific experimentation with dark matter. I am one of those reincarnated Atlanteans who came back to make sure this kind of mass disaster does not happen again, because this is a critical time in our planet's history.

It has been suggested that groups of Souls come here to Earth together in shifts, taking time off between eras to rest or visit other planets while other groups come to Earth. Is that how it happens? This is an intriguing question.

Of course, the lifetimes I have related within the pages of this book are just a fraction of the lifetimes I have seen while doing readings for my clients for over twenty years. I have seen probably almost as many civilizations we know nothing about as I have the more recent ones that appear in our history books. Sadly, when I see these ancient lifetimes, this often means that some Souls have carried the effects of unresolved issues from past lives for a long time, if indeed there is any such thing as time.

In seeing these ancient civilizations, with such a wildly different range of artistic designs in their artifacts such as clothing, bodily adornments, furniture, architecture, homes, motorized conveyances over land, sea or air, I am endlessly fascinated. I regret every so often the long-ago burning of the ancient library at Alexandria, which could have explained so much of what I have seen, or perhaps even helped us rebuild civilization back to its former glory. I also wonder if there were illustrations in those books of the kinds of things that I have seen in these readings. Fascinated with this ancient history, occasionally I wonder if they had recorded the same or similar images as the ancient Vedic texts which have clearly illustrated UFOs, or *vimanas,* and told of violent aerial wars between them in the skies over India many thousands of years ago, even indicating the effects of nuclear radiation on the populace below.

Wondering what happened to civilization, causing us to lose all memory of these ancient times, I have come to believe that it is quite likely neither science nor our overrated conscious minds will ever fully explain everything. Simply stated, not everything can be proven empirically, and perhaps some matters we do not even need to understand logically. Some things must be experienced to be understood, and many of them cannot be articulated. I find that if I listen to my guidance and watch for synchronicity, I understand from a place beyond the intellect. I know in my gut we were once greater beings that we can imagine, that something happened, and we fell a great distance into a far more primitive existence, forgetting everything that came before. That is actually probably enough.

In doing these readings I have also come to understand that one of the greatest transgressions is violating the free will of another Sovereign Soul. If we do this, it appears that we must go through a cycle of purification, which we call karmic balancing. The way to get off the wheel of karma is by forgiving ourselves and others. Forgiveness is choosing to move on by merely letting go of what someone did to us, not allowing it to affect us any longer, no longer getting upset over the misdeed, nor retelling our story aloud or ruminating on it silently inside our heads. And whenever we forgive another person, we free up our energy for more important work.

Another seriously bad idea is to mock another, especially at their moment of death. According to Edgar Cayce's readings, that will garner one lifetime or more of being like the person mocked until we have fully learned their pain. This is often the reason some have serious disabilities.

Many times it takes a long time for the right lifetime to come along to balance that karma, too.

If you have read this book, you will have already realized that our past lives affect our personalities. Yet there are also influences which come from the body's experiences and those of its ancestors.

In between lifetimes, we can remember all our past lives as if they were parts we had played onstage. When we reincarnate, we choose to forget them so that we can learn our lessons. If we remembered everything, there would be no challenge to push against so we could grow, and therefore no point in incarnating. This forgetting is part of being on a planet that is in the third density, or has three dimensions, as some would say. My guides tell me that the word "density" is more accurate. As we evolve, we expand and become less dense, therefore occupying more densities, like fourth, then fifth, and so on.

There are some things I still do not understand. If another person does something that hurts us yet helps us balance karma, are they still accountable for what they did to us, even though they have performed a service for us? I do not know. Yet I am certain that eventually we all must reach a state of coming from the space of unconditional love all of the time. Perhaps when we all get there, this particular cycle will end, and another will begin. Or will we simply become different beings entirely?

I have been fascinated to observe in my own personal experience that facial similarities exist between people and their past reincarnations where photos are available from the earlier person. Scars from past life wounds can be carried forward in the form of birthmarks, moles, and skin anomalies from one incarnation to the next. I carry some of those marks myself, and I have been told by my Guides that the reason for this is that, within our DNA, our past lives are carried. Also, the lives and prior traumas of our ancestors are carried in our genetic code. These can affect the bodies into which we incarnate. We know that current lifetime experiences we have can affect our DNA, turning off or on certain tendencies dormant in our genes. I learned while practicing energy medicine that, if we heal the effects of trauma coming from one of our specific ancestors even though they are dead, it will shift the DNA and the subsequent life experiences of everyone descended from that ancestor, even distant cousins of whose existence we are not even aware. There are threads of light/energy coming from the DNA that connect us all laterally in current time, and even backward and forward in time.

I have seen people heal in body, mind and Soul as a result of the knowledge that comes from their past lives. As I stated in the introduction, many people have also reported being healed by just reading of other people's past lives. I believe this is because the human condition is so very universal that many of us share the same or similar issues.

On the other hand, I occasionally see people who, after following guidance to get a reading, do not actually want to hear the truth. These individuals resist, dismiss, or ignore the reading and continue on the same path, though fortunately that seems to be rare. There is nothing I can or would want to do about those folks, since we are all on our own unique path to the Light, and we each arrive in our own way. Every last one of us has the inborn, inalienable right to attain Enlightenment in our own way and at our own pace. Just as in mountain climbing, one person may rapidly and with focused determination climb the sheer, steep north face of the mountain, while another meanders slowly up the warmer south side on a gently sloping, winding footpath taking far longer. Both are equally valid approaches; one is not better than the other. After all, no two people are alike. Just take a peek at your fingerprints if you ever forget that.

Afterword

One final concept I wish to mention is this: this lifetime that you are currently living is the most significant one of all. Why? It is important because this lifetime is the one you inhabit. Being in the now moment is of utmost importance to our spiritual evolution, as well as to our ongoing mental health.

Once, when I was living in Austin in the early 1990s, I had a rather unpleasant experience with a woman obsessed with one of her past lives as a glamorous, strong, handsome, blonde WWII German fighter pilot who had died young. By the time I first met her, this prior lifetime had completely overshadowed the current one.

This woman was a professional psychic, specializing in Tarot readings, who had somehow alienated her adult children and had few friends. She was hoping to write a book about her heroic lifetime as a dashing young pilot. I suspected this was to make up for the loneliness in her current one.

I had just met her when she asked if she could regress me to see if we had known each other in a prior lifetime. Foolishly, I agreed. I say foolishly because I knew almost nothing about her. Using an odd technique to supposedly hypnotize me, she directed me back to the period of WWII. I easily went into a light trance state on my own, and indeed, I had known her, but only casually. She kept me in an altered state for a very long time, manipulating me to access information, including minor details about that lifetime of hers that she could not access on her own.

I felt violated because she had held out to me that the regression was for my benefit when clearly it was not. This was before I had ever done a past life reading for anyone but Bruce, detailed in my first book on the Akashic Records. Later I was to learn she did this with anyone who would allow her to regress them. This incident is definitely an example of how not to use past life information, as well as a comment about the abuse of ethics in psychic or spiritual readings. It is wise for us to use discrimination. At that time, I was new to this work and naïve. What I learned from the experience, besides how awful it feels to be lied to and used by a so-called healer, was how important it is to always be fully present in the lifetime that we currently inhabit.

Of course, there are extremes in either direction—those who obsess on a past life and those who say they have no need to know about past lives because the one they are living is the only one they have any interest in knowing about.

Not too long ago I had an unusual dream. In this dream, I was standing out-of-doors in the darkness of a moonless night. It was cold out, and I was standing barefoot in cold, wet grass. Before me loomed a dense, massive black cloud. It was moving toward me with the intention of consuming me, or possessing me, or overcoming me—I was not sure exactly which. Observing it for a moment I finally said, "You are not real, and you cannot harm me." It began to thin and become less dense, gradually becoming more and more transparent, until it dissipated altogether. I had no idea what that dream meant, but it would waft through my waking hours occasionally over the next week.

Then one day the following week I had the persistent urge to finally attend a firewalk hosted by someone I had known casually for over thirty years, John "Hawk" Maisel, who is a Master Firewalk Instructor. I had always intended to do this one day, and I suppose my Guides decided this was to be the day. So one Saturday night I drove down to Hawk's place in

Friendswood, Texas, to attend a firewalk. I did not know if I would walk or not; I had been to a firewalk on the Galveston beach twenty-four years earlier hosted by someone else and had not walked. I had been curious at the time, but also was simply too terrified.

This time, however, I was nudged strongly by my Guides to be there and had come a long way in not responding to the unknown with fear in that time span. I listened closely in the classroom to Hawk, who works with the devas of the fire, as he talked to us about how to approach firewalking. Hawk's deeply spiritual approach to the fire ceremony resonated with me. I would never have been in resonance with a leader who pushed a "mind over matter" approach. Before we finally went out to where the fire was being readied by his assistants, I thought that I might do this. My initial decision was to stand at the end of the runway and either be guided in the moment to walk or not—I attached no judgment to what happened. I knew that even if I did not walk, the energy of the ceremony would work with me.

It was a dark, drizzly November night and all thirty or so of us, on cue from Hawk, walked in our bare feet across the cold, wet grass of his expansive lawn to the spot near the tree line where the glowing coals waited. Hawk and the others raked, shaped and patted the coals into place. I watched all this with a very serene feeling that deepened as I looked into the coals, neither knowing nor caring if I would walk. I was in observer mode. As soon as the fire was ready, in a soft voice Hawk gently reminded us once again that firewalking was dangerous, that we could get hurt and require medical attention, and that absolutely no one was pressuring anyone to walk the coals. It was our decision alone, and he described how it would feel energetically if we were guided to go. I watched as several of the veteran firewalkers crossed the coals. I seemed to drift slowly nearer the start of the runway, simultaneously waiting my turn and wondering if I would walk at all.

All the while, as I looked at the bed of coals, I softened, feeling more and more relaxed and peaceful. Then at some point, the floating sensation pulling me toward the path of fire became irresistible. I opened my arms wide in gratitude and strode confidently across, right down the middle of the twelve-foot span of crunchy coals. Once was not enough. I did this four separate times, pausing to give others a turn. I wanted to do it again and again. I never wanted it to end. It was so joyous!

After the ceremony was over, and I was putting my socks and shoes back onto my black-soled feet so I could drive home the forty-five minutes to my condo in Houston, one of the regulars came over and sat down beside me. He announced that we were friends on various social media sites and introduced himself to me. Since he had not seen me there before, he asked where I else had done firewalking. I replied never had I done it before this night. His surprised response was that I crossed the coals like a veteran firewalker. I thought a minute and then added, "Well, I have never done firewalking before in this particular lifetime."

He replied, "Well, I think this is the only one that counts."

I smiled, looked him straight in the eyes, and emphatically, yet softly, replied in a measured tone, "Yes. This lifetime is the only one that counts...*each and every time.*"

Addendum A

The Quantum Conclusion

Reality is too complex to be trapped by a measurement, according to Dr. Deepak Chopra. In my opinion, a pervasive yet foolish notion is the trouble with empiricism: the idea that the truth of what is real can be determined by a set of rules created by humans. This misconception keeps us from living in the real world. Empiricism, the currently accepted scientific method, relies almost solely upon measurement. But reality is just not that simple, as Chopra has said. Human beings are in no position to dictate what features reality must have in order to be real. Reality is whatever it is. Our notion of how to determine what is real and true—that is what must change. It must change in order to embrace what reality is, not what we think it should be.

We now know, due to advances in quantum physics and mechanics over the last century, that our physical universe is far more complicated than was previously believed. These advances convince many that we humans are on the edge of proving that each of us has a consciousness that transcends physical form. Or, perhaps we are about to discover there is a supreme consciousness which transcends and underlies all reality, and we are part of that consciousness. Once that is firmly established and understood by a critical mass of people, everything will change. Part of that change will be that it will be finally clear to even the greatest skeptics that past lives are clearly likely within the infinite field of possibilities in which we exist.

Indeed, the odds are great that the proof of most of what we refer to as psychic phenomena will flow from our conclusions about our transcendent consciousness.

I have long held that consciousness is all there is. Consciousness creates everything out of the infinite waves of probability floating somewhere in the unmanifest field.

When I first learned about the famous "double-slit experiment" back in the 1980s, the experimenters' conclusion was that light could behave as either a particle or a wave. Which one it "decided" to be was completely dependent upon it being measured. Until it was measured or observed, it was neither a particle nor a wave, just a possibility. This decision that light was making was referred to as the "observer effect." Back then, the scientific measurement was considered the important event or deciding factor.

I am relieved to report that in the ensuing thirty years, more experiments have been done. It is now known that not only light, but electrons, behave the same way in this experiment. Electrons are bits of matter. With further experimentation it has been found that molecules and atoms behave like waves of probability as well. This means that particles of matter do not decide when, where and how they are going to show up in the physical world until they also are observed. They do not exist as anything but a probability until a consciousness interacts with them.

Observation being so important, perhaps it needs to be defined. Observation and measurement are the same thing. Measurement requires some kind of measuring device or tool. One very important distinction about the measuring device is that it includes the physicality of the human being doing the observing. The eyes, the retina on which images are registered, the optic nerve which carries that image to the brain, the physical and chemical components of the brain—all these are as much bits of the measuring instrument as any metal, glass, plastic or wooden objects that might be used for measuring purposes.

If the brain is simply an instrument, then who or what is doing the observing? It must be something outside or apart from the brain. Clearly, it has to be consciousness, since that is all that is left. In other words, when observation is broken down to its core components, all that is left is consciousness—or awareness. In the end, all there is left to do the observing, and hence the creating of reality, is consciousness.

Studies have shown that something interesting happens when we decide to take an action, like picking up a writing tool. The hand moves in the direction of the tool a fraction of a second before the changes in the brain signaling that decision have occurred. Yes, the hand moves *before* the brain thinks about picking up the tool.

The brain is therefore not where the decision is made. The brain is merely a receiver. The mind, or consciousness, is where the decision is made. Quantum physicist Nassim Haramein has said that looking for consciousness inside the brain is like looking for the announcer inside the radio.

To further support the existence of a separate consciousness, it is important to note certain facts. People who have died and been revived almost always report either standing outside of or floating above their own bodies. They can recount accurately what others at the scene were doing or saying after they died. To test this, certain hospitals even place written notes atop upper cabinets in operating rooms so that someone floating on the ceiling can read these notes and report back what was written there if asked later—assuming they return to life. And yes, some people do return to life and report what was written on top of the cabinets.

Consider that the people's brains were still inside their bodies during the time they were outside those same bodies observing themselves and their surroundings. Their consciousness was not, though. Their sense of themselves, the part that observes—the part that sees and hears—was outside the body. It therefore seems clear that we are not our bodies, nor our brains. What we are is a deathless consciousness that can leave and re-enter our bodies and still be conscious of what is going on as though the body were not necessary. It follows logically that this consciousness can enter a new body prior to the time of its birth, and leave again at death. So why could we not do that more than once? Why should we assume that this awareness of ourselves cannot or would not enter a new body several times over a long span of time if the conditions were agreeable? Why would we settle for only one lifetime? There is a mounting body of evidence supporting the belief that most of the people on the planet have held for countless thousands of generations. We reincarnate.

Addendum B
Apple Cider Vinegar Baths

This technique will release emotions from the body into the auric field. When we subsequently shower, the released emotions will be rinsed out of the aura and carried down the drain.

Fill the tub with warm water and add 2-3 cups of apple cider vinegar. Other vinegars will not work. Do not add anything else to the water or it changes the chemistry and the energetic properties, and it will not work properly.

Soak in this solution for thirty minutes, adding warm water if needed to remain comfortable. If all you have is a shower stall, sit in the tub and periodically sponge or squirt apple cider vinegar and water over your body for the thirty minutes.

After the thirty minutes are up, drain the tub fully and take a shower. If not washing your hair at that time, run your hands through the aura above and around your head and rinse your hands in the shower stream. Repeat this several times. This will clear the auric field around your head.

If you do not shower, the emotions will remain in your aura and gradually sink back down into the body again. The shower is important.

This can be used anytime you are having an especially emotional time of it, but it is not suggested you use this as an ongoing crutch to keep from dealing with issues currently causing problems in your life.

If you think you will get bored and not be able to sit still for 30 minutes, play some music and light some candles. Read a book. Turn it into "spa time."

Other Books by Lois J. Wetzel, MFA

Akashic Records: Case Studies of Past Lives

EDINA: Energy Medicine from the Stars!

Sacred Journeys and Vision Quests

To learn more about the author:
http://hotpinklotus.com
Contact: lois@hotpinklotus.com
Blog: http://akashicrecordsreadings.blogspot.com

Sign up for the newsletter online at Hot Pink Lotus to learn more from Lois Wetzel and receive notifications when she offers classes. Occasionally, she teaches others how to do Akashic Records readings the way she does them. Many of her other classes are available for self-study online and can be found on the website.

Lois is also available for intuitive consultations via telephone in the USA, or SKYPE globally. If you wish to have a Consultation or a past life reading, please see the website for instructions.

Recommended Reading

Cott, Jonathan. *Search for Omm Sety*. Grand Central Publishing, 1989.

Goldberg, Bruce. *The Search for Grace*. Llewellyn Publications, 1997.

Ramtha. *Ramtha: The White Book*. J.Z. Knight, ed. JZK Publishing, 2005.

Newton, Michael. *Journey of Souls: Case Studies of Life Between Lives*. Llewellyn Publishing, 1994.

Roberts, Jane. *The Education of Oversoul Seven*. Prentice Hall Trade, 1984.

Tucker, Jim, and Ian Stevenson. *Life Before Life: A Scientific Investigation of Children's Memories of Previous Lives*. St. Martin's Griffin, 2008.

Tucker, Jim. *Return to Life: Extraordinary Cases of Children Who Remember Past Lives*. St. Martin's Press, 2013.

Weiss, Brian. *Many Lives, Many Masters: The True Story of a Prominent Psychiatrist, His Young Patient, and the Past-Life Therapy That Changed Both Their Lives*. Fireside, 1988.

Weiss, Brian. *Miracles Happen: The Transformational Healing Power of Past-Life Memories*. HarperOne, 2013.

Wilcock, David. *The Synchronicity Key: The Hidden Intelligence Guiding the Universe and You*. Dutton Adult, 2013.

CPSIA information can be obtained
at www.ICGtesting.com
Printed in the USA
FFOW05n1618260716

9 780983 200277